# KENTUCKY'S GOVERNORS

# Kentucky's Governors

## 1792-1985

EDITED BY *Lowell H. Harrison*

THE UNIVERSITY PRESS OF KENTUCKY

Copyright © 1985 by THE UNIVERSITY PRESS OF KENTUCKY

Scholarly publisher for the Commonwealth, serving Bellarmine College, Berea College, Centre College of Kentucky, Eastern Kentucky University, The Filson Club, Georgetown College, Kentucky Historical Society, Kentucky State University, Morehead State University, Murray State University, Northern Kentucky University, Transylvania University, University of Kentucky, University of Louisville, and Western Kentucky University.

*Editorial and Sales Offices:* Lexington, Kentucky 40506-0024

LIBRARY OF CONGRESS CATALOGING IN PUBLICATION DATA
Main entry under title:

Kentucky's governors, 1792–1985.

   Bibliography: p.
   Includes index.
   1. Kentucky—Governors—Biography. 2. Kentucky
Politics and government. I. Harrison, Lowell Hayes,
1922–
F450.K48 1985     976.9′009′92     [B]     85-9228
ISBN 0 8131-1539-6

T.S.

12-3-87

# Contents

# Preface

This volume provides in convenient form a brief biographical sketch of each governor with emphasis upon the governor's administration. Each sketch has been written by a scholar with particular knowledge of the governor and the times. Dr. Thomas D. Clark, the commonwealth's best known historian, has added an essay tracing the development of the office of chief executive through the state's four constitutions. Thirty-three scholars have contributed to this cooperative work.

Despite the importance of the office, surprisingly little has been written about several governors. Full-scale biographies are available for a few of the more noted figures, such as John J. Crittenden and Simon Bolivar Buckner, whose careers transcended state boundaries, but in an appalling number of cases not even one scholarly article is available. Political history is somewhat out of favor these days, but the paucity of gubernatorial studies clearly shows the need for more research and publication in this neglected area of Kentucky history.

Three previous efforts have been made to document the lives of the state's chief executives. The late G. Glenn Clift published *Governors of Kentucky* in 1942. Now over forty years out of date, it concentrated on genealogy and devoted little attention to the governors' years in office. Robert A. Powell included the more recent governors in his *Kentucky Governors* (1976), but his brief sketches sometimes contained less information than Clift's work had. Two years later Robert Sobel and John Raimo coedited a four-volume *Biographical Directory of the Governors of the United States*. The capsule format of the entries severely limited discussion of the governors' administrations.

The contributors to this volume are well aware that because of space limitations we can do little more than briefly introduce our subjects' careers. To devote more attention to the term of office, we have kept genealogical details to a minimum. Thus, while we have tried to provide the names of parents and spouses, we have not usually included those of siblings and offspring. We hope that our contributions will be of some help to genealogists, but our volume is not directed to their special interests.

Footnotes and comprehensive bibliographies have also been omitted to conserve space, but the entries are based upon careful and sometimes prolonged research. Among the most important general sources are the *Acts* of the General Assembly and the Senate and House *Journals*, which contain the governors' legislative messages. When completed the *Guide to Kentucky Manuscripts* (1986) will provide for the first time a comprehensive survey of the manuscripts in several hundred Kentucky repositories, including the state archives. Newspapers were indispensable sources in nearly every case, although obituaries seldom provide objective evaluations of their subjects. Some old collective biographies, such as H. Levin's *Lawyers and Lawmakers of Kentucky* (1897) and two-volume *Biographical Encyclopedia of Kentucky* (1878) continue to be useful. Especially helpful for the periods they cover were E. Merton Coulter, *The Civil War and Readjustment in Kentucky* (1926), and Hambleton Tapp and James C. Klotter, *Kentucky: Decades of Discord, 1865-1900* (1977). Thomas D. Clark, *A History of Kentucky* (1960), is the standard general history of the state, but some older works remain useful. Much information about some of the governors has been published in the state's two major historical journals, *The Filson Club History Quarterly* (1926-) and the *Register of the Kentucky Historical Society* (1902-). These publications are referred to hereafter as *FCHQ* and *Register*.

The suggested readings given at the end of each sketch are not the bibliographic sources used in the research. With few exceptions, the readings cited are published works that an interested reader can locate in a library without too much difficulty. The lack of good sources for several governors points up the need for more research on their careers.

Careful readers will note considerable variation among the sketches. Guidelines were provided (and sometimes followed) for the length and general nature of the contents. The editor has tried to promote clarity and accuracy, but believes that he should not impose his own style upon contributors, who are well qualified to interpret the governors about whom they write.

Readers will also note that George W. Johnson and Richard Hawes, the governors of Confederate Kentucky, have been included, although it is obvious that neither served as the commonwealth's chief executive. These men were recognized by a large minority of Kentuckians as the heads of the provisional government that was admitted into the Confederate States of America on December 10, 1861, and it seemed appropriate to include them. They are clearly identified as Confederate.

Because of space limitations, the biographical notes on the contributors to this volume only briefly identify the scholars and recognize those who have made many contributions to the study of Kentucky's history. They have donated their knowledge and time to this project because they saw the need for such a reference work. We note with sorrow the loss of Dr. Frank H. Heck to the historical profession and Mr. Ed Ryan to journalism. Dr. Heck died in 1983 and Mr. Ryan in 1984, soon after each had completed his essay for this volume.

The fifty-two governors of Kentucky have ranged from the obscure to the nationally known. Some served during exciting and challenging times; others encountered little interference in the placid course of their terms. Some altered greatly the course of events in the commonwealth; others had little impact. Some provided able, innovative leadership; others were content to follow rather than to lead. Taken as a whole, these brief essays tell a great deal about both the governors and the history of the state. Even brief recitals of goals and accomplishments tell something about social and economic changes in Kentucky, as well as about political events.

We who have contributed to this volume owe thanks to many individuals and institutions who helped with the research. We hope that they will accept our collective thanks. Assistance provided by the Faculty Research Fund at Western Kentucky University expedited the preparation of the manuscript.

LOWELL H. HARRISON

# The Kentucky Governorship: An Overview

Historically the office of American state governor has been seen as a source of continuity in the local governing process. The governor has also served as the ceremonial head of state and has wielded widely varying amounts of political and administrative power. The states have taken different attitudes toward the amount of power they were willing to grant their chief executives in various areas of government, particularly in the legislative branches. In the rash of state-making that followed the Revolution, state constitutions were written that reflected eighteenth-century British influence and in no area more clearly than in the governorships; governors' responsibilities were styled after the old colonial governorships.

Generally all of the late eighteenth-century constitutions prescribed the qualifications, functions, and powers of the governor. Some were more precise than others. All of them undertook to differentiate the relationships of the governor to the judicial and legislative branches and vaguely to the people themselves. The first fifteen state constitutions reflected broad, general agreement on gubernatorial duties. There was, however, considerable variation in the preconceived role of the governor as a source of administrative and political powers. Most constitutions required some degree of personal maturity and prescribed an age of at least thirty for the chief executive. Certain numbers of years of residence in the state were mandatory. Modes of electing the governor ranged from selection by senates to popular vote by those eligible to elect legislators. There was no consistency in the term of the governor, which ranged from one to four years. In most cases the governor was declared ineligible to succeed himself. Some states imposed religious and property qualifications on their governors, and all required the chief executive to take an oath of office. Almost every constitution contained safeguards to thwart the governor should he be mad enough to attempt a coup and assume monarchial status.

Although the early constitutions varied considerably in their enumerations of gubernatorial rights and duties, they agreed in certain cardinal areas. To insulate him from the pressures of self-serving special interests as well as self-aggrandizement, the governor was to be paid a stipulated salary that could be neither raised nor lowered during his term of office. In most constitutions the governor had the power to call the legislature into session, to prorogue it on extraordinary occasions, and to veto legislation.

Weighing heavily on the eighteenth-century constitutional mind was the problem of assuring public safety. The states had contributed militia to the revolutionary army and had guarded their borders against invasion and occupation. Those states along the Indian frontier, such as Kentucky, were especially sensitive to the importance of maintaining local militias. All of the constitutions provided for the organization and maintenance of state military and naval forces with the governor as the commander in chief. But the governor was forbidden to lead these forces personally, except with the direct permission of the legislature.

Most governors were allotted broad appointive powers ranging from selection of under secretaries to appointments of heads of constitutionally established departments. In practice this gave the chief executive control of state and political patronage. Whether or not the framers of the constitutions had this in mind is obscured by their formal language. No doubt they did recognize this fact, because in nearly every constitution the governor was denied the privilege of succeeding himself. The constitutionalists believed that such a clause would prevent the governors from entrenching themselves in office by controlling most of the popular vote through the dispensation of public favors.

Some effort was made to write into the constitutions an element of public compassion by giving the governor the power to remit fines and grant pardons. Over the years this power was to involve Kentucky governors in many emotional appeals by families and neighbors on behalf of individuals caught in the net of criminal laws and the courts.

Finally, most early state governors were assigned the responsibility of securing written activity reports from departments and state agencies.

Of the fourteen state constitutions in existence in 1792, those of Massachusetts and Pennsylvania stated most clearly the powers of their governors. Other states were less precise, often including the powers of their chief executive within the general legislative authority, clearly implying that the executive office was to be more ceremonial than administrative. Despite the extensive debates from 1785 to 1792, Kentuckians were vague about the precise functions of their future governors. Clearly there was to be a chief executive, but no constitutionalist outlined his powers.

Whatever the contemporary views on the subject of the Kentucky governorship, their effect on the first constitution was immaterial, for there were few or no elements of originality in the final draft of the executive article. In both general texture and intent this article was lifted in toto from the second Pennsylvania constitution. The Kentucky constitutional delegates changed only a few phrases to adapt the document to local conditions.

The Kentucky governor was to serve four years and was to be elected by the electors who chose the senators rather than all of the voters. In this respect both the Kentucky and Pennsylvania constitutions reflected a fear that the eligible voters would act irresponsibly in the choice of the titular head of the state. Kentucky delegates to the second constitutional convention in August 1799 modified the executive article in accordance with governmental experiences of the first six years. The governor was required to have resided in the commonwealth for six instead of two years and was to be chosen by a direct vote of citizens entitled to vote for members of the General Assembly. Henceforth there would be a lieutenant governor, a position not provided for in 1792. This latter provision was somewhat vague about gubernatorial succession, but the intent seemed clear enough to avoid future disputes over the issue.

Understandably the prescriptions of duties and powers of the Kentucky governor were cast emphatically in the masculine gender, and so it has remained to the present. Equally emphatic is the phrase, "The supreme executive power of the Commonwealth shall be vested in a chief magistrate, who shall be styled the Governor of the Commonwealth of Kentucky." The governor was empowered to nominate, with the consent of the senate, all officers provided for in the constitution except the state treasurer, who was to be selected jointly by the two houses of the legislature. The governor was also given the power to grant pardons, to remit fines, to fill vacancies until the next meeting of the General Assembly, and to enforce all laws.

Delegates to the second convention refined the phraseology of the executive article somewhat, but made few substantive changes in either structure or intent. In addition to election by popular male suffrage, the governor was to be eligible for reelection after a lapse of seven years, was to assume his official duties on the fourth Tuesday "succeeding the day of the commencement of the general election on which he shall be chosen," and was to serve until one month after the next gubernatorial election. His powers to nominate officials, especially in new counties, were rescinded and awarded to members of the General Assembly.

In the final decade of the eighteenth century outbreaks of smallpox and fever epidemics seriously threatened the health and safety of Kentuckians. The constitutional delegates recognized the fact by giving the governor power to call the General Assembly into extraordinary session at a place other than the officially designated capital city. This power also applied in the face of threatened civil uprisings and military conflicts. A classic attempt to invoke this power in the latter circumstance occurred during a contested election in the Goebel era when the disputed governor-elect, William S. Taylor, undertook to call a meeting of the General Assembly in London, Kentucky.

The granting of pardons and the remission of fines thrust upon the governor an onerous burden of making emotional and judgmental decisions. A cursory examination of the collected gubernatorial papers in the Kentucky State Archives reveals that much of the chief executives' time was spent dealing with an endless stream of petitions from prisoners and with the pressures exerted on the prisoners' behalf by families and local politicians.

When delegates met in Frankfort in 1799 to redraft the Kentucky constitution, there is evidence that they had access to the New Hampshire constitution of 1792 and possibly the new Georgia constitution that was drafted in 1798. Both documents contained veto clauses that, in principle, were written into the new Kentucky constitution. This section was carried over into the next two constitutions, except for the current section that permits the governor to veto parts of bills and denies him the right to veto proposed amendments to the constitution or laws relating to the classification of property for tax purposes (sec. 171, Fourth Constitution).

One might argue that framers of the last three Kentucky constitutions intended to curb the powers of the governor, but in substance this is not true. The most significant curbing of his powers, and the only issue that caused any extended debate in the convention of 1849, was the question of depriving local commonwealth attorneys of their fees by the remission of criminal and penal cases.

At the constitutional convention of 1849 Archibald Dixon, the able Henderson attorney-delegate, reported for the Committee on the Executive for the State-at-Large. The committee suggested two minor editorial changes, one being that the phrase applying to election of the governor by "the citizens entitled to suffrage" be replaced by "the qualified voters of the state." Only in section 10 did the committee propose substantive revisions. Omitted were the governor's power to remit fees of the clerks, sheriffs, and Commonwealth attorneys in penal or criminal cases and the governor's authority to appoint constitutional officers. The committee proposed that future chief executives be restricted to issuing only temporary commissions to fill vacancies in the constitutional ranks until such vacancies could be filled either by the General Assembly or by popular election.

When the 1849 convention as a whole came to consider the executive article, there was remarkably little debate on the substantive powers. Nathan Gaither of Adair County suggested that the age limit be raised to forty-five, but his proposal was rejected. Proposed changes in section 10 provoked the most discussion. Thomas J. Hood, a twenty-eight-year-old Carter County lawyer, advocated that the governor be allowed to succeed himself now that the appointment of constitutional officers had been removed from his control, but this proposal was also rejected. Hood's eloquent and well-reasoned speech provoked rebuttals by such important delegates as Archibald Dixon, Garret Davis, "Kitchen Knife" Ben Hardin, and Charles A. Wickliffe. (This point has been frequently debated, and as late as 1981 the voters turned down an amendment that would permit gubernatorial succession.) The third constitution did make the governor ineligible for reelection for only four years instead of the seven previously required.

Hood also proposed a change in the governor's pardoning power that would require him to state in a separate record the conditions surrounding the granting of pardons, the book to be open at all times for public inspection. Hood argued that the power placed the governor under undue pressure. The convention, however, left the chief executive with the traditional power of granting pardons, except in cases of treason and impeachments, without formal explanations. The governor, however, was denied the power to remit fees of county officials in penal cases. Interestingly the Hood suggestion that the governor make a record of his actions in pardon cases was adopted by delegates to the Fourth Constitutional Convention in 1891.

Basically the powers of the Kentucky chief executive have remained in force since 1792, and more especially since 1849. The delegates to the Fourth Constitutional Convention in 1890-1891 did little more than make a few emendations to the executive article, none of which changed executive procedures. The most substantial addition made by the 1891 convention was in the section governing the calling of extraordinary sessions of the General Assembly. The governor must state the subjects to be considered in the special session, and no other subjects may be introduced unless the governor amends the original call.

Any practical consideration of the powers of Kentucky governorship must recognize that they extend far beyond the executive article of the constitution. During the past century and a half, and especially in the later twentieth century, it would have been impossible for state government to operate efficiently without a broadening of executive powers. Through the years the General Assembly has created myriad commissions and turned them over to the governor to exercise administrative oversight. The most important areas in which commissions have functioned are finance, taxation, highways, human resources, public utilities, recreation, environment, economics, industry and resources, and corrections. All of these commissions extend the influence of the governor into every phase of human life in the commonwealth, well beyond the limitations of executive power envisioned by delegates to the constitutional convention in 1891. Although neither the General Assembly nor the governors have ever said so openly, in order to operate a modern state government under the provisions of the archaic fourth Kentucky Constitution they have had to resort to subterfuge to meet the exigencies of the evergrowing complexities and needs of modern Kentucky society by the creation of commissions. Sometimes it seems that the constitution almost gets lost in the daily operations of the state government under the commission dispensations. Clearly, however, the essence of the supreme executive power reaches deep into the body politic of the commonwealth. Almost daily the public press has detailed the affairs of the governor's office in news stories.

For the past two centuries the Kentucky governors have been the most visible officers of the state. By constitutional mandate they have periodically summarized for the legislature and for the public the current state of state affairs. This has given them an opportunity to note their accomplishments, to make known their aspirations, and to cite the needs of the commonwealth. Often they have spoken in these messages more directly to the people than to the legislature. On occasion all of the governors have used this periodic report to transmit to the General Assembly information on specific public matters and needs. By this means strong governors have often exerted their greatest influence on the course of legislation. The broad powers of appointment give the governors great patronage strength and make them prime targets for every favor-seeker in the commonwealth.

On most occasions the governors have been central figures in party politics, often controlling the Kentucky delegations to state and national party conventions. Such control has often been the key to the success of their executive programs and policies. On many occasions governors have served ex-officio as commonwealth orators, delivering addresses on all sorts of ceremonial and dedicatory occasions and at state and local special events. They have served as the official hosts for the state, greeting and entertaining national and foreign visiting dignitaries. If the president of the United States enters the borders of the commonwealth, out of courtesy the governor is expected to be there. Once a year the Kentucky governor becomes a conspicuous national, and even international, figure when he appears on television with the winning owner and jockey, and sometimes the winning horse, at the Kentucky Derby.

From the moment Isaac Shelby became governor in 1792 until today, the governor of the commonwealth has been a primary source of political and state news. Some few have been caught up in scandal, because of either personal indiscretions or the wrongdoings of members of their administration. Often the Kentucky press has criticized the governors for maladministration of public affairs, for overindulging their patronage authority, or for other shortcomings. Even members of governors' families have been drawn into the maelstrom of public criticism.

Appraising the qualities of the fifty-one men who have served as Kentucky's chief executives before December 1983 requires extensive knowledge of the conditions of the times and the electoral mind. Perhaps no historical record can document more graphically the differences in the administrations and the personalities of the governors than the portraits of the chief executives from Isaac Shelby to John Young Brown, Jr., that line the walls of the Hall of Governors in the Old State Office Building in Frankfort.

All of the governors, with some justification, might claim that they advanced Kentucky a step closer to maturity during their administrations. Some governors initiated and stoutly supported progressive reforms and expansion of state governmental services. Others were satisfied to accept and maintain the status quo, creating as little public agitation as possible during their four years. In the rows of portraits are those of governors who in their periodic messages to the General Assembly gave ample proof that they were fully aware of the basic needs of the people. Among them were men who fought intelligently and doggedly for educational improvements, for penal reform, for internal improvements, for public welfare, and for maintenance of law and order. In moments of crisis they proved to be capable leaders. Other governors were purely political, having been elected because of their commitments to special political and personal interests rather than to the urgent needs of the citizens as a whole. Again, Kentucky newspapers over the years have been full of reports on such matters.

On occasion Kentucky governors have been elected from the party opposed to that of a majority of the legislators. In such cases the legislators have sometimes mounted assaults upon executive office by stripping or ripping away certain powers of the governor, to the injury of strict constitutional government.

In recent years the General Assembly has filled the time between its sixty-day sessions every two years by creating the Legislative Research Commission. This agency serves as both a service arm and a symbol of continuity in the legislative process. The short, biannual sessions of the legislature often handicap both the governor and the General Assembly. Governors are forced to organize their programs too quickly after their election. It has become almost mandatory that governors get their programs enacted during the first session of the assembly, because two years later they will have expended most of their patronage largess and have become lame duck governors relying solely on their powers of persuasion. No more eloquent statement can be found on this subject than that of Gov. Lawrence Wetherby in January 1953, when he told the General Assembly:

> A Kentucky governor is elected under our constitution for four years without legal opportunity, regardless of how acceptable his program has been, to put it before the public for approval or rejection. In practical application he must successfully run the legislative gauntlet during the first hurried ninety days he is in office if he is to adopt a program and have an administration worthy of history's harsh pen. The remaining general assembly two years hence is invariably plagued with vicissitudes common to "lame duck" tenures. By then the governor is on the downhill side of his term and political tension is already mounting in anticipation of the next gubernatorial contest.

In one respect the governor holds a whip hand over the assembly, because only he can call that body into extraordinary session and then only upon matters of his choice. Historically governors have been guarded in their use of this constitutional power.

At times in the past Kentucky governors have been confronted by crises of one sort or another. Isaac Shelby's second administration was interrupted by the War of 1812. In conformity with the constitutional provision the legislature adopted a resolution in August 1813 asking Shelby to assume field command of the state militia.

The succession of Gabriel Slaughter from lieutenant governor to governor after the death of George Madison caused a dispute that for the first time tested the intent and application of the succession section of the executive article; the resulting hostility had tragic results for Kentucky, as it led to the rejection of important advances in public education advocated by Slaughter. On the heels of this incident came the highly unsettling Old Court-New Court fight, which blighted at least three gubernatorial administrations. No incident, however, was more disruptive than the Civil War. During the years of this conflict the power and authority of two governors were virtually nullified. Buried in the gubernatorial papers and virtually uninvestigated by historians lies a rich lode of materials that could cast Kentucky political and social history of the later nineteenth century into a new, expanded dimension. Certainly this material promises to portray the governors of the period in a more interesting light than that heretofore accorded them.

In the last decades of the nineteenth century at least five governors faced stern challenges to enforce the law by halting the blood feuds in Appalachia, by ending outbreaks of criminality growing out of the war era, and by helping make racial adjustments after the adoption of the various postwar amendments to the United States Constitution. All of these challenges called for unflinching leadership and courage, qualities not always discernible in the Kentucky gubernatorial record. Each challenge involved unpopular political decisions. The opening of the twentieth century was seriously marred by the assassination of William Goebel, who might or might not have been found to be in line for the governorship by an honest recount of the ballots cast in the general election in November 1900. Goebel's murder was a notable watershed in the politics of governorship in Kentucky for the next two decades.

More recent governors have been called upon to deal with flood disasters, mining accidents, the Great Depression, crop failures, and labor disputes. They have been faced with urgent demands for physical and administrative changes in the state prisons and for vast improvements in state hospitals. Through the creation of the Prison Parole Board of the Department of Corrections, governors have been spared most of the ordeal of granting pardons.

In the past five or six decades every governor has been quick to point to specific accomplishments of his administration. Each has claimed a degree of success in meeting urgent demands for expanding and serving a constantly changing social structure. Each administration has been characterized in good measure by the nature of the legislation enacted, the public facilities improved and established, and the improvement in such programs as transportation and education. Every twentieth-century governor, especially those elected after 1914, has been kept constantly aware of the handicapping constitutional restrictions on his office. Much executive energy has been expended in operating a modern state government burdened with what are really mid-nineteenth century constitutional provisions.

A clear instance of near governmental disaster resulting from a long out-of-date constitutional restriction was the salary limitation imposed in the famous section 246. The court of appeals in 1948 partially moderated this provision in its "rubber dollar" decision, which permitted the establishment of relative dollar values reckoned in terms of current conditions. In 1949 the section was amended by popular vote to permit the adoption of a new and somewhat complex public salary formula.

Every modern governor has been sternly challenged to lift the commonwealth out of the national statistical doldrums, especially in the areas of education, personal income, transportation, public health, industrial development, and general social advancement. Two governors, A.B. Chandler and Wendell Ford, sponsored broad, reorganizational laws that helped modernize the state's government. Bert T. Combs and Edward Breathitt both unsuccessfully tried to break down the barrier to progressive state government by persuading the people to call a constitutional convention.

With all of its glories, burdens, powers, and frustrations the office of governor has always attracted ardent seekers after the mantle of chief executive. Candidates and their supporters have spent millions of dollars in efforts to get elected. Some men who have served once have sought reelection for second and third terms. Not all, however, have felt the urge to occupy the office again. A beloved and colorful old ex-governor once told a group of Kentucky politicians that there were two things in his life he never wanted to have again, "gonorrhea and the governorship of Kentucky."

The office of supreme executive of the Commonwealth of Kentucky is shrouded in a rich aura of prestige and dignity and is bolstered up with an inordinate amount of power, even in the face of perennial legislative declarations of independence. This intoxicating power has on many occasions extended the reach of ordinary men beyond anything they could have attained in any other position.

Kentucky's governors have in large measure reflected in their terms the will, the ambitions, and the shortcomings of the people who elected them. Often the "Chief Magistrate" has done little more than personify the general public under the conditions of the times. Doubtless many governors realized the morning after the inaugural ball that they were inadequately trained and conditioned to formulate and initiate progressive programs that would give their administrations cherished landmark status in the long draw of Kentucky history.

THOMAS D. CLARK

# ISAAC SHELBY

1750-1826

Isaac Shelby was born near Hagerstown, Maryland, on December 11, 1750, the second son of Evan and Letitia Cox Shelby. The Shelby family had come to America from Wales about 1735, living first in Pennsylvania and then in Maryland. They moved to western Virginia in 1772 and built a small store and fort near the present-day town of Bristol, Virginia-Tennessee.

Isaac Shelby gained fame on the western frontier as a young lieutenant serving in his father's regiment in Lord Dunmore's War. In 1774 the only major conflict of the war was fought at Point Pleasant where the Kanawha River joins the Ohio. Here, Shelby led a flanking movement to break the back of the Indian attack. After the fighting he remained in the Kentucky area until the outbreak of the American Revolution.

In 1777 Shelby was appointed by Patrick Henry as a commissary agent to gather supplies for the frontier outposts and the Continental Army. He also spent time in Kentucky marking and improving his initial preemption of fourteen hundred acres. But in the summer of 1780 he was called back to the settlements to lead frontier troops in the campaign against the British in the South.

On July 25, Shelby joined Gen. Charles McDowell, commander of the American troops in western North Carolina. From his base on the Broad River, Shelby led his troops against the Tories and British in the area. The Americans achieved several minor victories, but after the defeat of General Gates at Camden, Shelby and his men retreated across the mountains to their homes.

In 1781 Maj. Patrick Ferguson, commander of the British forces in the western Carolinas, decided that he could frighten the backwoodsmen into making no further forays across the mountains. Accordingly he dispatched a paroled prisoner with the warning that if the backcountry men did not desist in their opposition, he would bring an army and lay waste to the countryside.

The message only aroused the ire of Shelby. He and John Sevier began to plan a new raid against the British. Gathering volunteers from the backcountry, they crossed the mountains, arriving at a spot known as King's Mountain just inside South Carolina, where they encountered the enemy under Ferguson.

The fighting began on October 7 as the patriots made their way slowly up the sides of the "mountain." Several times the Tories and British charged with bayonets, but each time the mountain men regrouped and drove back up the hill. After three successive charges failed, the British were dislodged and gradually began to retreat. Shortly thereafter, Ferguson was fatally struck by a bullet, and resistance by the British ended.

The battle of King's Mountain was a decisive blow to the British; for Isaac Shelby, it was his moment of greatest triumph. To the men who fought on that battlefield, it was Shelby who would be known as "Old King's Mountain."

The next year Shelby decided to move to his preemption in Kentucky. He arrived on his land near the Knob Lick in Lincoln County on November 1, 1782, with his bride, Susannah Hart. Susannah was the daughter of Nathaniel Hart, one of the original partners in the Transylvania Company. Shelby became a leader in Kentucky politics because of his fame in the war. He was a participant in the conventions that preceded statehood, and he served as chairman of the committee of the whole in the first convention.

Kentucky became a state on June 1, 1792. The state constitution provided for a bicameral legislature in which the lower house would be chosen by popular vote. The people voted for their representatives and electors, who then chose the senators and the governor. On May 17, 1792, the electors met in Lexington and unanimously elected Shelby the first governor of Kentucky.

The election of Isaac Shelby was not surprising, even though there is no indication that he sought the post. The very fact that his war experiences take up many pages of his autobiography while his two terms as governor are given only one sentence indicates where his interests were concentrated. He never took the lead during the conventions and had never actually participated in the rough-and-tumble game of politics, even as a member of the Virginia and North Carolina legislatures. Shelby was a Jeffersonian Republican, although his party allegiance was not strong. He had no law experience and little formal schooling. He spoke in short, crisp sentences and lacked the personal magnetism cultivated by politicians. His main interest was in preserving property and the rights of individuals to that property. With this background, there was nothing revolutionary about the new governor's program.

The immediate needs of the new state called for setting up the machinery of government and making appointments to the various offices. Shelby's selections were well balanced and tactful. Next, his attention was directed to securing an income for the state, setting up the courts, and providing for the defense of the exposed country.

When Shelby took office, three major problems confronted Kentucky. Foremost was the defense of the state from Indian attack. The second problem was financing expeditions against the Indians. The federal government would help the state militia, but only if payment was properly authorized. The third problem was that the commercial markets in New Orleans and other locations along the Mississippi had gradually been cut off by the Spanish; the result was impending stagnation of the young state's economy.

Discontent with the federal government soon became apparent. Kentuckians recognized, behind the Indian menace, the work of Great Britain in the Northwest and of Spain in the South. Furthermore, they believed that the central government could not, or would not, do anything to protect them. Kentuckians generally felt themselves confined and opposed by the federal government, the British, the Spanish, and the Indians.

Shelby had been active in the defense of Kentucky before statehood, and security for the new state took priority with him. He realized that Kentucky's efforts to act alone had been, and would continue to be, futile. All he could do was provide militia for some of the most exposed forts in the northern and southern areas of the state. He began a campaign to pressure the Washington administration for federal assistance. The president responded early in 1792 by appointing "Mad Anthony" Wayne commander of the American forces in the Northwest with instructions to push the Indians out of the Northwest Territory.

Wayne slowly gathered troops from Kentucky and Ohio and carefully trained them, much to the consternation of the quick-to-act westerners. But the cautious approach paid off. On August 19, 1794, Wayne defeated the Indians in the decisive battle of Fallen Timbers. A short time later a peace treaty signed at Greenville provided security for the West for a time.

Governor Shelby's aid to Wayne had been cautiously given. Shelby believed in a strict interpretation of his powers under the state consti-

3

tution and had been suspicious of federal measures. However, even though he did not like some restrictions placed on the movement of settlers, he supported the terms of the treaty and enforced them as they came within his jurisdiction.

The Indian problem was just one of several interconnecting problems. Potential sources of trouble were the French struggle and the navigation of the Mississippi. Many westerners were openly sympathetic to the French Revolution, particularly after France found herself engaged in a war against both the British and the Spanish. Not the least among France's admirers was Isaac Shelby. When Citizen Edmund Genet arrived in this country in 1793 to take his post as minister, he found the situation ripe for exploitation. He included in his plans an attack against Spanish possessions in the West, using Kentucky as the base of operations.

In November 1793 Genet sent four agents into Kentucky to cooperate with André Michaux, a botanist and French agent. They succeeded in getting the aid of George Rogers Clark, the revolutionary hero. Michaux met with Shelby, but there is no evidence that the governor agreed to back the French. When Secretary of State Thomas Jefferson warned Shelby against allowing Kentuckians to participate in any French schemes, the governor responded that he did not think the French would succeed, but that if they did get such participation, he doubted his legal authority to stop Kentuckians from leaving the state. Whether in response to Shelby's letter or to other events, President Washington issued a proclamation on March 24 warning all citizens against taking up arms against a nation at peace with the United States. Shortly thereafter a change in the French government brought about the recall of Citizen Genet, and the grand scheme collapsed.

Shelby has been criticized for his reluctance to act decisively during the French intrigue, but Kentuckians had little faith in the federal government and no love for the Spanish. Shelby continued to take a limited view of his powers as governor and believed that he had no way to stop the plotting. He repeatedly asserted that the scheme was doomed from the start by the lack of money and leadership.

Shortly after the Genet incident, President Washington started negotiations with Spain for the free use of the Mississippi. On October 27, 1795, a treaty was signed giving the United States favorable terms. Ratified by the Senate the next year, the treaty meant that Kentucky's right to commerce on the Mississippi was now unquestioned.

In spite of the governor's problems, the accomplishments of his first administration were noteworthy. The state was free, at least for a time, from major Indian attacks; it was on sound financial footing; its commerce on the Mississippi was settled; courts had been established; and land claims were being processed. Shelby had handled his job with dignity and good judgment. His philosophy was that an executive must not control all power or try to govern without the help of the legislative branch. Shelby left office with the state in good condition.

For the next sixteen years Shelby remained in the background, contenting himself with improving his lands near Danville and his personal fortune. But the threat of impending war with Great Britian once again brought him into prominence. When the first calls were made for his candidacy early in 1812, the aging Shelby seems to have been genuinely reluctant to answer. As the year wore on, the imminence of war convinced him to run for office. In July Shelby publicly announced his candidacy for governor. His only announced opponent was his neighbor Gabriel Slaughter. After a campaign that centered on his military experience, Shelby won the election handily, 29,285 to 11,936.

Upon taking office, Shelby immediately plunged into the war effort. He pressured the federal government to give William Henry Harrison command of the forces in the Northwest. At his insistence the state's revised militia laws made every man between eighteen and forty-five eligible for military service, excluding ministers. Women were admonished to knit and sew for the troops.

The disastrous defeat of a detachment of Kentucky troops at the River Raisin cast a pall over the state early in 1813. It also convinced Shelby that too little planning had gone into the war effort in the West. He decided to act on his own if the opportunity arose. His chance came on July 30 when General Harrison asked for additional troops from Kentucky and requested that Shelby lead them. The governor raised some thirty-five hundred troops, twice the number requested, and led them north, joining Harrison in time for the drive against the British in Canada. On October 5, 1813, Harrison and Shelby met the forces of Gen. Isaac Proctor and the Shawnee chieftain Tecumseh at the Thames River. In the short, bloody fight that followed, Tecumseh was killed and the British troops surrendered. It was the high point of the War of 1812 in the Northwest. Shelby returned to Kentucky a hero, and Congress passed a bill authorizing the presentation of a gold medal to the governor for his services to the nation.

Shelby continued to support the war in its later stages, although its

5

conduct was still poorly planned. Kentuckians fought in the battle of New Orleans, even though they had few rifles and supplies. Other volunteers continued to man posts in the Northwest.

During these war years domestic matters received little attention from the governor, who maintained the status quo as long as possible. He mentioned domestic concerns in only a few sentences of his messages to the legislature.

In his second term as governor Shelby showed once again that he was a capable wartime leader. Kentucky, with a population of 400,000, furnished for the nation's defense forty regiments of volunteers, or over 24,000 men. Except for a few regulars, Shelby's troops made up General Harrison's entire army during the Northwest campaigns. Kentucky's attitude during the war had generally been one of enthusiastic cooperation. Shelby came into office with one purpose: to see the war effort in the West to a successful conclusion, even if the domestic program was neglected.

Upon leaving office in 1816, Shelby returned to his farm. In his last government service he joined Andrew Jackson in negotiating with the Chickasaw Indians for a tract of land between the Tennessee and Mississippi rivers in 1818. He died at his farm on July 18, 1826, and was buried in the family cemetery, located on the spot where he had pitched his tent when he first arrived at his preemption in Kentucky.

SUGGESTED READINGS: Sylvia Wrobel and George Grider, *Isaac Shelby: Kentucky's First Governor and Hero of Three Wars* (1974); Harry M. Coles, *The War of 1812* (1965); Patricia Watlington, *The Partisan Spirit: Kentucky Politics 1779-1792* (1972).

PAUL W. BEASLEY

# 1796-1804
# JAMES GARRARD
## 1749-1822

James Garrard was born in Stafford County, Virginia, on January 14, 1749, the son of Colonel William and Mary Naughty Garrard. He attended the common schools in Stafford County and studied at home, acquiring a lifelong love of books. As a young man, he worked his father's farm, and in 1769 he married his childhood sweetheart, Elizabeth Mountjoy. He served in the Virginia militia during the American Revolution, rising to the rank of colonel. In 1783 he migrated to Kentucky where he surveyed land, opened a grist mill, made whiskey, and farmed in what was to become Bourbon County. As an active Baptist minister, he founded several churches in central Kentucky. As a Virginia legislator, he helped establish Bourbon County in 1785. He served the county as surveyor, magistrate, and colonel of the militia.

Garrard's experience and reputation propelled him into the political arena. He served in five Kentucky statehood conventions and helped write the first constitution in 1792. When political parties developed, he became a Jeffersonian Republican. A complex man, he was a soldier, farmer, businessman, minister, and political leader. As a planter he opposed slavery; as a Baptist minister he advocated religious tolerance and even Unitarian ideas; as an aristocrat he favored democratic reforms; as a politician he appointed many critics and rivals to political office. Character, integrity, and magnanimity explained his success. As governor, he even pardoned a personal slave accused of poisoning food in his home.

Ironically the rise of this moral man to the executive mansion was tainted. Under the original Kentucky constitution, electors from the various districts chose the governor. In what contemporaries called "the Disputed Election" of 1796, Gen. Benjamin Logan, the frontier military hero, was the favorite candidate, while Thomas Todd, a Danville lawyer who had been secretary to all ten statehood conventions, was the intellectual giant of the campaign. Colonel Garrard was best known as a Baptist clergyman and personable Bourbon political leader. The electors failed to give a majority to any candidate. Logan with 21 votes led Garrard with 17 and Todd with 14; John Brown, a Frankfort attorney, received one vote.

The Kentucky constitution did not have a solution for this political imbroglio, but other states had held a second ballot under similar conditions, and the Kentucky electors did likewise. Garrard with his broader appeal received most of the Todd votes and won a majority. Atty. Gen. John Breckinridge questioned the validity of the second vote, while Logan protested it. Nonetheless, the secretary of state sent a copy of the certificate of election to Garrard, and Governor Shelby wrote a congratulatory note. In November 1796 the Kentucky Senate refused to reverse the election result and Garrard continued to serve as chief executive. All participants admitted the need for constitutional reform.

7

By 1800 a second constitution had been adopted that provided for the popular election of governors. General Logan, confident of a reversal of the results of 1796, immediately announced his candidacy. Todd and Garrard soon followed suit. Christopher Greenup, a prominent legislator and businessman, was the only new face in the rematch. Although the crowded field assured another close election, Garrard enjoyed the advantages of incumbency and a popular record. Surprisingly he gained support from some old Loganites. Although Greenup and Todd appealed to the same constituency as Garrard, the governor built up large margins in the Bluegrass, in Jefferson County, and in western Kentucky. Consequently he led the field with 8,390 votes. Greenup was second with 6,746, Logan dropped to third place with 3,996, and Todd ran last with 2,166.

In some ways the gubernatorial elections themselves were Garrard's greatest political challenges. Certainly for six years he achieved most of his goals as governor. He surrounded himself with men of ability, such as former Transylvania president Harry Toulmin, his secretary of state and chief political advisor. He consulted the brilliant John Breckinridge on legal questions despite their political differences, and John Edwards of Bourbon County, a former United States senator, was his closest friend and legislative leader. Following the election of 1800 he appointed his two chief rivals, Christopher Greenup and Thomas Todd, to the circuit court and the Kentucky Court of Appeals, respectively. Throughout his tenure Garrard promoted men of experience, education, and ability to the militia, courts, and other appointive offices.

James Garrard was a strong executive. He defended the power of the governor but insisted that the legislative and judicial branches maintain their independence, too. He favored an expansion of government services and was a "spender" opposed to tax reductions. He fought for an enlarged and reformed militia, supported educational institutions like Transylvania University, advocated prison reform, even education of inmates, and urged business subsidies. He frequently exercised the executive veto and had only one veto overridden in his eight years in office.

Constitutional differences led to Garrard's use of the veto and his independence from the county courts. In a famous patronage incident he refused to appoint a county magistrate as surveyor of a new county because of nonresidence. His challenges to the county courts and the legislature probably led to the reduction of executive and state powers in the 1799 constitution, as well as an increase in patronage power for the local courts.

Throughout his tenure he urged relief for the Green River farmers whose heavy debts would probably lead to loss of land. Kentucky's land problem remained unsolved by Garrard and his immediate successors. However, he advocated passage of an entitlement bill that would have upheld squatter's rights. A 1797 act relieved the squatters from paying taxes on profits they had made on the occupied land and required new owners to pay squatters for improvements.

As governor, Garrard signed enabling acts for a record twenty-six new counties. He signed several court reforms, including a bill requiring the licensing of attorneys and calling for the establishment of a court of appeals. He was especially happy with the funding and construction of a governor's mansion. Contemporaries called it "the palace," and Garrard occupied it for seven years. By the twentieth century it had been converted into a home for the lieutenant governor.

In 1798 Sen. William Garrard, the governor's son, introduced the bill calling for a second vote on the proposed constitutional convention. The governor favored another convention because of the electoral issue and his antislavery views. Although Garrard's opposition to slavery led to his defeat as a delegate and denied him an active role at the convention, delegates deliberately exempted him from the clause denying executives successive terms, thus assuring him of a unique opportunity to succeed himself and proving his popularity. Moreover, through leadership and tact Garrard effected the smoothest transition from one constitution to another in the state's history.

Garrard's most dramatic and perhaps finest hour came during the controversy over the federal Alien and Sedition Acts. He denounced the Alien Acts as oppressive, unjust, and restrictive of desirable immigration, and charged that the Sedition Act denied the freedom of speech and trial by jury for which revolutionary soldiers like himself had made such great sacrifices. While urging nullification of these hated laws, he urged the legislature to reaffirm its loyalty to the Union and to the Constitution. Although the Kentucky Resolutions clearly reflect the thinking and language of Jefferson and Breckinridge, Garrard's convictions were public record, and it was his insistence on a profession of loyalty that led to the making of such statements in both 1798 and 1799.

Another significant accomplishment of his first term was passage of a new militia reform act in 1798 that exempted jailers, tutors, printers, judges, ministers, and legislative leaders from duty. It imposed fines and penalties on "distractors" and allowed the hiring of substitutes.

The early years of his second term passed without incident. Kentuckians ignored his pleas for aid to business and development of trade with the South. By the fall of 1802 the legislature passed a controversial circuit court bill that enlarged the judiciary and permitted untrained citizen judges to preside over the courts. Garrard denounced the increased costs and questioned the wisdom of using untrained, perhaps unqualified,judges. Too, he doubted the constitutionality of the bill, which ignored the executive's power of nominating or appointing court officials. He vetoed the original bill and a second court bill because of unconstitutionality and because it permitted attorneys and judges to reside outside the districts in which they might serve. The legislature overrode his second veto of the circuit court bill, the first veto to be overridden in Kentucky history.

The greatest potential crisis of Garrard's second term arose when the closing of the port of New Orleans in November 1802 threatened his long-cherished dream of extensive trade in the Mississippi Valley. The probability of a war with Spain was immense. Garrard communicated Kentuckians' fears to the Jefferson administration and urged action. In an effort to reassure Kentuckians,the governor reported that the state militia had twenty-six thousand men and ample rifles, muskets, and powder supplies. A few months later Garrard lauded Jefferson's acquisition of the Louisiana territory as a "noble achievement."

Unfortunately Garrard's last months in office were soured by a legislative battle over the naming of a new registrar for the land office. He submitted six names to the Senate before the acrimonious conflict was resolved. The dispute left a bitter taste in the governor's mouth as he retired from the political arena. He spent his last eighteen years browsing in his extensive library, visiting friends, and enjoying a life of solitude on his Bourbon County farm. Following his death on January 19, 1822, the state erected an impressive monument in the family graveyard listing his contributions as a revolutionary soldier, sheriff, magistrate, and governor. The graveside tribute cites him for impartiality and charity. He remains one of the most honest and magnanimous executives in Kentucky history.

SUGGESTED READINGS: H.E. Everman, *Governor James Garrard* (1981); H.E. Everman, *The History of Bourbon County, 1785-1865* (1977).

H.E. EVERMAN

# CHRISTOPHER GREENUP

Christopher Greenup, owing to his knowledge of law and his varied experience in public affairs, was the best qualified of the early Kentucky governors. Born in Loudoun County, Virginia, about 1750, son of John and Elizabeth Witten Greenup, he acquired a good basic education, learned surveying, and read law. During the Revolution he served as first lieutenant in the Continental Line, 1777-1778, and later held the rank of colonel in the Virginia militia. In 1781 he settled in Lincoln County, one of the three divisions of trans-Appalachian Virginia, where he engaged in extensively surveying and land speculation. Commissioned as an attorney at law, he was admitted to practice in the county court in 1782, and in March 1783, after Virginia had created the district of Kentucky, he became a member of the bar of the district court, which sat at Harrodsburg before moving to Danville. From 1785 until the admission of Kentucky to the Union, he was clerk of the district court.

Meanwhile, Greenup's interests expanded into other areas. In 1783 he became a trustee of Transylvania Seminary, purchased two lots in Lexington, and was named clerk of the trustees of that town. Two years later he was chosen to represent Fayette County in the Virginia House of Burgesses. He was appointed a justice in Mercer County after its creation in 1785, and he participated in the founding of the Danville Political Club (1786), in two conventions (1785 and 1788) preceding the separation of Kentucky from Virginia, in the establishment of the towns of Danville and Warwick (1787), and in a group organized by Danville to promote manufactures (1789). During a brief return to Virginia in 1787 he was married on July 9 to Mary Catherine Pope, daughter of Nathaniel and Lucy Fox Pope.

Greenup moved to Frankfort in 1792, the year Kentucky became a state. As a member of the dominant Jeffersonian Republicans he was an elector of the first governor and members of the first Senate. He himself was appointed a judge of the new court of oyer and terminer, a position that he resigned immediately. He was then elected one of Kentucky's first two representatives in Congress, where he served from 1792 to 1797. Mercer County sent him to the state House of Representatives in 1798, and from 1799 to 1802 he was clerk of the state Senate. He ran second to James Garrard in the gubernatorial race of 1800. In 1802 he accepted appointment as a circuit court judge. On June 5, 1804, he resigned the judgeship and announced his candidacy for governor. Elected without opposition in early August, he took the oath of office on September 5 and delivered his first address to the General Assembly on November 6, 1804.

Greenup came to the governorship at a time when the future of the state seemed bright. The Louisiana Purchase had eliminated Spanish control of commerce on the lower Mississippi River. It had also opened a vast territory to the west and in Kentucky had increased patriotic fervor for the Union and, with some notable exceptions, increased attachment to the Jeffersonian Republicans. Moreover, the new governor said, "there seems to exist a love of order, a prevailing respect for the constituted authorities, and a growing disposition to support and aid them in the due execution of their respective functions."

Relations between governor and the General Assembly were generally harmonious throughout Greenup's term of office, although legislative response to his recommendations was rarely as thoroughgoing as he desired. He was prompt in discharging the duties of chief executive and careful in selecting appointees for office. He did not hesitate to use the veto, usually with the result that acts he disapproved of were modified in accordance with his objections. On only two occasions were serious efforts made to override his veto: in December 1805 when the legislature attempted to repeal part of the act incorporating the Kentucky Insurance Company, and in 1808 when it voted to rescind an annuity granted in 1806 to the venerable ex-Judge George Muter. In both cases the governor's will prevailed.

In his first annual message Greenup directed attention to problems of greatest concern to him: "the Judiciary establishment, and those laws which direct the mode of proceeding in criminal as well as civil cases." He urged "that the power of the judges be well defined, and their salaries competent." Next in importance was the "system of Revenue laws," which had impoverished the treasury and reduced the "value of state paper during the last three years." He also urged examination of the laws governing the militia, recommended revision of the act "authorizing the executive to proclaim a reward for the apprehension of criminals," and suggested the enactment of laws stating conditions under which proprietors of lands forfeited for nonpayment of taxes might be reinstated.

Both the House and Senate professed agreement on the need for action and began considering each matter. Only with regard to the apprehension of criminals and to forfeited lands, however, did they take action. So cautious were they in grinding out piecemeal legislation on the other issues that Greenup returned year after year with further recommendations concerning the judiciary, revenue, and the militia. Additional matters that engaged the attention of governor and the General Assembly in the remainder of his term were the penitentiary, which was established in 1798, conflicting land titles, and two corporations, the Ohio Canal Company (chartered in 1804) and the Bank of Kentucky (created in 1806), in both of which the state subscribed shares. To his credit, Greenup broke new ground in his last annual address by urging, without result, that the state grant aid to education.

The ordinarily quiet course of events during Greenup's administration was disturbed in 1806 by revelations of earlier intrigues connected with the so-called "Spanish Conspiracy" and by the culmination of Aaron Burr's activities in the West. The sensational revelations published by a newly established, Federalist-connected newspaper in Frankfort not only caused acute embarrassment to several prominent Kentuckians but also led to a legislative investigation, at which Greenup was called to testify and which precipitated the resignation of a judge of the court of appeals. When the editors of the paper leveled charges against the governor himself, he wielded a vigorous pen in successful defense of his conduct.

The visits of Burr to Kentucky evoked no concern among state officials until President Jefferson's proclamation of November 27, 1806, was published locally and an official communication was received on December 19 from the federal district attorney bearing alarming news of the passage of "certain vessels of mr. [sic] Burr's flotilla" down the Ohio on a mysterious and treasonable mission. With legislative approval the governor stationed small units of the militia at strategic points along the river. By that time the danger, if any, was over, and he was able to report to the next General Assembly on December 30, 1807, that "the machinations of some designing characters which lately threatened the peace and tranquility of the Union" had "been happily counteracted and suppressed without the effusion of human blood. . . ."

As Greenup's administration drew to a close, one cloud loomed on the horizon—infringement of American rights on the seas by warring European nations. Although Greenup referred to "a foreign power, who has never ceased to manifest her hostility towards us," and suggested that the legislature "make a public expression of the sentiments of the citizens of this state" and adopt measures to answer any call by the federal government, there was little that Kentuckians could do except hold meetings, pass resolutions, and fan their hostility toward England.

In retirement Greenup played a minor role in politics and, as health permitted, remained active in business. He died at his home in Frankfort, April 27, 1818, more than a decade after the death of his wife in October 1807 and was buried in the state cemetery. His will, drawn up in 1817, divided his estate, including lands in Kentucky, Virginia, and Ohio, among his two sons and four daughters. It also confirmed the emancipation of one slave and freed another, presumably the only one he owned at the time. Reflecting on Greenup's "career of public service," one eulogist declared, "He has been the most useful man in Kentucky."

SUGGESTED READINGS: Orlando Brown, "The Governors of Kentucky [1792-1825]," *Register* 49(April 1951): 102-106; William E. Connelley and E. Merton Coulter, *History of Kentucky*, vols. 1, 2, edited by Charles Kerr (1922).

JAMES F. HOPKINS

1808-1812
# CHARLES SCOTT
1739-1813

Charles Scott was born in about April 1739 in what is now Powhatan County, Virginia. Orphaned in 1755 by the death of his father, Samuel, a farmer and a member of the House of Burgesses, Scott enlisted in Washington's Virginia regiment in October 1755. During the French and Indian War, Scott was stationed at various frontier posts and won praise for his scouting missions, which were to form the basis of his reputation as a woodsman. He rose from private to captain when assigned to Col. William Byrd's expedition against the Cherokees in 1760.

In February 1762 Scott married Frances Sweeney. They were to have eight children: Eliza (Elizabeth), Merritt, Samuel, Daniel, Charles, Martha, Mary (Polly), and Nancy (a twin is believed to have died in infancy).

Before the Revolution, Scott, with the help of slaves owned by his wife, farmed and ran a mill on his 666-acre tract along Muddy Creek and the James River. In the spring of 1775 Scott raised a company of volunteers and during the summer was regarded by the Virginia Convention as commander in chief of the Virginia forces. Until the British governor, Lord Dunmore, departed in August 1776, Scott was constantly in the field; he had a major role in the battle of Great Bridge, December 9, 1775. On February 13, 1776, Congress elected Scott lieutenant colonel of the Second Virginia Regiment and in that summer made him colonel of the Fifth Regiment. Then in Adam Stephen's brigade, Scott joined Washington's army in November 1776 as it retreated through New Jersey. He fought in both battles of Trenton, December 26, 1776, and January 2, 1777. While the main American force was encamped at Morristown, Scott led light infantry raids against British detachments, chiefly foraging parties. His major engagement was the battle of Drake's Farm on February 1. In April 1777 Scott was promoted to brigadier general. His brigade fought at Germantown, Brandywine, and Monmouth, where his controversial retreat was a factor in giving the field to the British. During late summer and fall 1778 Scott commanded Washington's light infantry and served as Washington's chief of intelligence.

In May 1779 Scott led Virginia militia in preparing a defense against the brief Mathew-Collier invasion of lower Tidewater Virginia. Scott remained in Virginia collecting troops for the Southern army, and then joined General Lincoln's army at Charleston on March 30, 1780. After the capitulation of the Americans on May 12, Scott was held prisoner of war at Haddrell's Point across from Charleston. He was paroled in March 1781 and exchanged for Lord Rawdon in July 1782.

Scott visited Kentucky in 1785 and after selling his Virginia farm, brought his family to Kentucky in 1787, settling on the Kentucky River nine miles southwest of present-day Versailles, where he built a two-story log cabin, a stockade, and a tobacco inspection warehouse. Scott dreamed of founding a town called Petersburg on his property and having it become the state capital. Marauding Indians from across the Ohio plagued Scott and other early Kentucky settlers for years. Scott's son Samuel was killed and scalped across the Kentucky River in full view of his father. His son Merritt met the same fate while serving in General Harmar's expedition in 1790.

Scott served one term in the Virginia House of Delegates, 1789-

1790, and from 1796 to 1808 he was a presidential elector. Scott led the Kentucky Mounted Volunteers on several Indian expeditions. On the first expedition along the Scioto River in April 1790 he only tracked Indians. A campaign along the Wabash River in May and June 1791 yielded only women and children hostages. The volunteers under Scott joined Anthony Wayne's regular army in October and November 1793 and again in the summer of 1794, when Scott commanded the Kentucky troops at the battle of Fallen Timbers on August 20, 1794.

Scott's wife died in October 1804. In 1807 Scott married Judith Cary Bell Gist, widow of Col. Nathaniel Gist, and moved to the Gist plantation, Canewood, which straddled the Bourbon County line in northwestern Clark County.

Over the years Scott was increasingly venerated as a hero of both the Revolutionary War and the Indian wars. Capitalizing on this esteem and on his standing as a recognized leader of veterans' interests in Kentucky, Scott ran for governor in 1808. He had long been a Jeffersonian Republican, the dominant party in Kentucky at that time; few state leaders were admitted Federalists. Jesse Bledsoe, professor of law at Transylvania University, successfully promoted Scott's candidacy and managed his campaign. Scott won with 22,050 votes; John Allen, a young lawyer, received 8,430 votes; and Green Clay, a wealthy landowner and speculator, received 5,516 votes.

Bledsoe, as secretary of state, appears to have been the driving force behind Scott's administration, although Scott firmly made the decisions. An injury from falling on the icy steps of the governor's mansion during the first winter of his administration left Scott on crutches the rest of his life. Bledsoe usually delivered the governor's messages to the legislature.

Scott, as governor, had a strong sense of representing the people and upholding the public interest. He lectured the legislature on propriety and constitutional principles. Once, when the legislature rejected a nomination, Scott refused to submit another. Most touching was Scott's lengthy veto of an act that deprived George Muter of a pension that had been promised him by the legislature. Muter, aged and infirm, had been persuaded to step down as chief judge of the court of appeals. The veto was overridden.

Scott eloquently expressed the state's war sentiment, after first attempting to cool it down by reminding the people that England and France were both culprits in violating American rights. Scott was not a war hawk in the sense that Henry Clay was, but he did emphasize the need to uphold the national honor. When the federal government called for militia on the eve of the War of 1812, Scott effectively appealed for volunteers. He was influential in promoting the career of William Henry Harrison. Shortly before leaving office, Scott appointed Harrison brevet major general of the Kentucky militia, thus giving Harrison instead of Gen. James Winchester command of the state's militia.

Scott urged the legislature to increase taxes enough to prevent the state's borrowing, but to keep in mind that "a just and sound policy had ever dictated that the burthen of taxes should be made to bear as lightly as possible on the shoulders of the poor, by exempting articles of the first necessity." Scott advocated various militia reforms, including conversion of the militia into a youth army. He persistently called for legislation to encourage self-sufficiency and market expansion for Kentucky produce and manufacturers. He advocated higher pay for public officials and harsher penalties for repeat criminal offenders. Scott frequently extolled the Union and warned against the dangers of disunion. Although the legislature gave scant attention to Scott's reform proposals, it passed upon his recommendation a replevy law that stayed execution on debts for one year if debtors gave bond and security.

Scott retired to Canewood where he died on October 22, 1813. In 1854 his remains were moved from Canewood to Frankfort Cemetery.

The honors of war and state sought Scott rather than the reverse. He had a strong sense of duty and sincere modesty in military and public life. Two personal faults singled out by his contemporaries were tippling too much in his later years and the use of profanity—the latter trait being made much of in anecdotes, mostly apocryphal, attributed to him. Scott won affection from soldiers and citizens alike.

SUGGESTED READINGS: Orlando Brown, "The Governors of Kentucky (1792-1855)," *Register* 49(April 1951), 93–112; William E. Connelley and E. Merton Coulter, *History of Kentucky*, edited by Charles Kerr (1922), 5 vols.

HARRY M. WARD

1816

# GEORGE MADISON

1763-1816

George Madison, the first Kentucky governor to die in office, was born in Rockingham County, Virginia, in June 1763 to John and Agatha Strother Madison. He was a brother of James Madison, who later became president of the College of William and Mary and the Episcopal bishop of Virginia, and a second cousin of James Madison, future president of the United States. Little is known of his early life other than he began a long and honorable military career by joining the Virginia militia as a youth during the Revolutionary War. While still a young man, he migrated west. His brother Gabriel was residing near Harrodsburg in Lincoln County, Virginia, at least as early as 1783. Land entries in this county, from which Mercer County was formed in 1785, were recorded for both Gabriel and George in 1784 and 1786.

As a militia officer, the future governor distinguished himself and was twice wounded fighting against the Indians in the Northwest Territory in 1791 and 1792. On March 7, 1796, almost four years after Kentucky became a state, Gov. Isaac Shelby appointed Madison auditor of public accounts, a position that as a Jeffersonian Republican he held for the next twenty years. He was listed as a property holder in Frankfort in 1797. He became a trustee of the Kentucky Seminary founded in Franklin County in 1800, sat on the grand jury that refused to indict Aaron Burr on December 5, 1806, and was appointed a director of the Bank of Kentucky, chartered in 1806. At the outbreak of the War of 1812 he again took up arms. As a major of Kentucky volunteers he fought bravely at the battle of Frenchtown, January 18, 1813, and was made a prisoner of war four days later. His captors marched him and his men to Malden, the British base in Canada located on the lower Detroit River, and then transferred him to Quebec, where he was held until 1814.

Back in Kentucky on September 6, 1814, he attended a public dinner in his honor where he received a hero's welcome. Failing health led him to give up the office of auditor of public accounts, but yielding to popular demand, he announced his candidacy for governor in 1816. The only other entry in the race, James Johnson, withdrew in his favor, leaving Madison to be elected without opposition. A visit to Blue Lick Springs shortly after the election failed to arrest the progress of his disease, and too weak to return to Frankfort, he took the oath of office before a justice of the peace in Bourbon County on August 5, 1816. His only official act as governor was to appoint Isaac Shelby's son-in-law, Charles S. Todd, secretary of state.

Governor Madison died October 14, 1816, at Paris, in Bourbon County. He was buried in Frankfort. His wife, Jane Smith Madison, a native of Botetourt County, Virginia, had died in 1811. They were survived by five children.

SUGGESTED READINGS: Orlando Brown, "The Governors of Kentucky [1792-1824]," *Register* 49(July 1951), 202–212; Eli Smith, *A Funeral Sermon on the Death of Governor Madison, Delivered before the Legislature of Kentucky and the Citizens of Frankfort* (1817).

JAMES F. HOPKINS

1816-1820
# GABRIEL SLAUGHTER
1767-1830

Gabriel Slaughter, a Democratic Republican, was elected lieutenant governor in August 1816. He assumed the duties of chief executive following the death of George Madison and completed Madison's term. Slaughter was never accorded, and probably did not expect, the title governor, and throughout his administration was called lieutenant governor or acting governor.

He was born in Culpeper County, Virginia, to Robert and Susannah Harrison Slaughter, December 12, 1767. That he acquired at least a respectable education and more than a common store of knowledge is suggested by the language and content of his messages to the legislature. As a young man, he was married twice—first to a cousin, Sarah Slaughter, around 1796, and then to Sarah Hord on March 9, 1797. Both women were from Caroline County.

The date of Slaughter's removal to Kentucky is uncertain. Gen. Robert B. McAfee recalled that as a schoolboy in 1792 he had boarded in Slaughter's home in Mercer County, and the future acting governor had certainly settled in by 1795, when he compiled a list of taxable property in part of Mercer County, including his own six slaves, six horses, and fourteen cattle. In that same year he was appointed a justice of the peace. The voters sent him to the state House of Representatives, 1797-1800, and to the Senate, 1801-1808. As an active member of the militia, he became a major in 1802 and a colonel in 1803. His election to the office of lieutenant governor in 1808 by a decisive margin over three opponents encouraged him to announce for the governorship four years later.

Fate was against him in this instance, for with the outbreak of the War of 1812 popular demand brought ex-Gov. Isaac Shelby into the race. Slaughter stubbornly continued his own campaign, thereby arousing the ire of Bluegrass politicians, who doubtless remembered his votes in the Senate seven years earlier for a proposal to take banking privileges away from the Lexington-based Kentucky Insurance Company. One Lexingtonian now warned a friend that "The d.n creature *Slaughter* is so industrious that all Shelbys friends will have to be on the alert." The Old Soldier won handily, however, and when Shelby called for volunteers for the New Orleans campaign against the British, Slaughter raised and commanded a regiment that rendered distinguished service in the battle of January 8, 1815. After the war, Slaughter announced for the office of lieutenant governor and again was elected in 1816.

On October 19, five days after Madison's death, Slaughter "entered upon the duties of Governor" and produced evidence "of his having taken the Oath prescribed by the Constitution of the State as Lieutenant Governor and acting Governor of the Commonwealth." Immediately Shelby's son-in-law, Charles S. Todd, secretary of state by appointment from Madison, courteously offered to step aside if Slaughter preferred another appointee. To the chagrin of Todd and his friends, the offer was accepted as a resignation, and Slaughter filled the vacancy with John Pope, former United States senator, now highly unpopular for his federalism and his opposition to the recent war. Republican newspapers reacted with outrage and continuing abuse of the acting governor and his appointee.

In his first address to the General Assembly, which met in early December and whose members resolved to wear "crape on the left arm during the present session" in memory of the late "beloved Chief Magistrate," Slaughter eulogized Madison, while avowing a determination not to shrink from duty, requesting the co-operation of the legislators, and abjuring party spirit. His conciliatory approach failed to disarm the opposition, which proposed in the lower house on January 27, 1817, the election of "a governor to fill the vacancy occasioned by the death of" Madison. When this measure was defeated, a determined effort was made in August to stir voters to elect legislators willing to act against Slaughter and Pope.

So successful was that campaign, which "agitated the State as it had never been moved before," that one of its proponents crowed: "I believe it has forever silenced the Demon of discord. here the Federalist are completely silenced." Early in the ensuing session the victors in the House of Representatives pushed through a bill providing for the election of not only a governor, but also a lieutenant governor. This brazen move was too much for members of the Senate, who defeated the bill and brought to an end endeavors of that kind. Later in the session Slaughter and Pope were censured by the legislature for failing to require the proper security and oath of office from the state treasurer.

Although his appointments were examined closely and often rejected, his recommendations were largely ignored, and his vetoes were usually overridden, Slaughter submitted to the General Assembly each year an able evaluation of the state of the commonwealth and offered suggestions that often reflected enlightened views. Throughout he urged public support for education as a necessity in a republic and as a means of destroying "that factious and odious distinction between the rich and the poor," suggested possibilities for financing public education, and in 1817 proposed a system of district schools, free to the poor, in all "settled parts of the state." The response to these pleas was a series of acts, passed over his veto, authorizing lotteries for the aid of certain individual schools. He was equally persistent and unsuccessful in calling for the repair and enlargement or replacement of the overcrowded and increasingly dilapidated penitentiary and in suggesting a program of moral and vocational instruction and financial reward for the rehabilitation of selected prisoners. He also favored legislation to improve navigable streams and to construct and maintain roads. In December 1817, he advocated creation of a state library at Frankfort.

Neither the acting governor nor the legislature foresaw the impending collapse of the economy. In December 1817 Slaughter painted a rosy picture of conditions, but on January 26, 1818, the legislature, disturbed by a scarcity of money, chartered forty-six independent banks whose notes soon flooded the state and were virtually worthless. Refusal of the Bank of the United States to pay a state tax levied on its branches in Lexington and Louisville in 1817 led Slaughter to question the power of Congress to locate such branches within a state without its consent. Taking a strong states' rights stand, he challenged the legislature to repeal the tax or enforce it.

By the time the next legislature assembled, Kentuckians knew full well that the Panic of 1819 was upon them. Slaughter promised "cordial cooperation" should legislators "devise any constitutional expedient, which while the rights of the creditors are duly regarded, will afford to the debtors exemption from individual sacrifices," and fulminated against the infringement of state sovereignty by Congress in creating the Bank of the United States and by the United States Supreme Court in denying "to the states the power of taxing it." Believing "that the existence of the bank . . . is incompatible with Republican civil liberty," he suggested collaboration among the states in a constitutional amendment to vindicate their rights.

The General Assembly, in turn, overrode his veto of a measure to postpone sales under execution of court decrees for sixty days, and then with his concurrence abolished damages allowed on protested bills of exchange and repealed the legislation establishing independent banks. Furthermore it established regulations on sales of property under execution that allowed the defendant to replevy for one or two years, depending on whether the plaintiff agreed to accept notes of the Bank of Kentucky in payment. In consequence, during the last months of the Slaughter administration Kentucky was propelled into the relief controversy, which was to have repercussions beyond state boundaries.

After leaving the governor's office, Slaughter was not yet ready to abandon politics. He was defeated in a race for the state Senate in 1821, but won a seat in the House of Representatives over four opponents two years later. Upon completion of his service there, he retired to his farm in Mercer County. Fittingly, in view of his interest in education and prominence as a lay leader in the Baptist church, he was appointed in 1829 to the first board of trustees of Georgetown College.

He died September 19, 1830, survived by his third wife, who before their marriage in 1811 had been Elizabeth Thomson Rodes, widow of Waller Rodes of Scott County, Kentucky. Elizabeth lived until 1843. Slaughter was the father of five children, at least one of whom died before he did.

SUGGESTED READINGS: Orval W. Baylor, *John Pope, Kentuckian* (1943); Orlando Brown, "The Governors of Kentucky [1792-1824]," *Register* 49(July

1951), 212-224; John Frederick Dorman, "Gabriel Slaughter, 1767-1830, Governor of Kentucky, 1816-1820," *FCHQ* 40(October 1966), 338–356; Edsel T. Godbey, *The Governors of Kentucky and Education, 1780-1852*, in College of Education, University of Kentucky, *Bulletin of the Bureau of School Service* 32(June 1960).

JAMES F. HOPKINS

1820-1824
# JOHN ADAIR
1757-1840

John Adair, a politician in the Jeffersonian Republican tradition, served as governor of Kentucky from June 1, 1820, to June 1, 1824. He was born to Baron William and Mary Moore Adair in the Chester District of South Carolina on January 9, 1757, and went to school in Charlotte, North Carolina. In 1784 he married Katherine Palmer; they had twelve children, including ten daughters. After serving in the American Revolution, Adair moved to Kentucky in 1787. He settled in Mercer County and quickly became active in state politics. He served in both the 1792 and 1799 Kentucky constitutional conventions and for many years in the Kentucky House of Representatives, beginning in 1793. He was twice (1802, 1803) Speaker of that body. In 1805 he moved to the United States Senate where he filled the seat vacated by John Breckinridge, who had resigned. Adair remained in that post for a year before he himself resigned, having unsuccessfully sought a full term as senator in his own right.

In 1805 Adair, who owned a substantial amount of land near Harrodsburg, Kentucky, purchased a tract of land in Louisiana. In December 1806 he traveled south to inspect his holdings. When he arrived in New Orleans, he was arrested on orders from Gen. James Wilkinson and charged with conspiring with Aaron Burr to separate the Southwest from the United States. Adair shortly thereafter initiated a countersuit in federal court, and after a period of several years, the court found in his favor. In addition to an apology (Wilkinson actually had no evidence implicating Adair), he won $2,500 in damages.

During the period between his political activities in the late 1700s and early 1800s and his involvement in the War of 1812, Adair spent much of his time on his farm near Harrodsburg. When the War of 1812 broke out, former Gov. Isaac Shelby asked Adair to serve as his aide. Adair agreed and acquitted himself well in the Canadian campaign. In addition he served as commander of the Kentucky rifle brigade under Andrew Jackson, 1814-1815.

After the war, Adair farmed and involved himself in Kentucky politics. In response to the great boom and period of land speculation that followed the war, the newly created Second Bank of the United States imposed a strict credit policy, an action that had particularly negative effects on states like Kentucky. As the speculative bubble burst, the Panic of 1819 hit the nation and a severe depression followed. Adair was adamant that the state government provide some measure of relief for hard-hit Kentucky debtors.

In 1820 Adair won the hotly contested governor's race with 20,493 votes to William Logan's 19,947, Joseph Desha's 12,418, and Anthony Butler's 9,567 votes. All of the candidates were Democratic Republicans. It was an extraordinarily close election by any standard, and Adair found himself governor at a very tempestuous time in the nation's and the state's history.

Adair's first message to the state legislature on October 17, 1820, emphasized the need for better state funding of education, improved navigation of the Ohio River, and a better penitentiary system. "Our penitentiary institution," he told the legislature, "will require your early attention." The themes he expressed in his first message would be pronounced again and again in subsequent years. He would continue to urge reform of the penitentiary system, although hard "reform" it might seem to twentieth-century minds: solitary confinement and hard labor. But he also called upon the legislature to appropriate funds for "aid of moral instruction" to all prisoners, most of whom were illiterate. The themes of educational progress and prison and insane asylum reform came up in his administration consistently. It was debtor relief, however, that dominated political concern in this phase of state history.

Clearly first on Adair's agenda was relief for the beleaguered landowners who were bordering on bankruptcy. "It will be admitted by all that the people of this state feel . . . a severe and universal pressure in their monied transactions. To relieve them in some measure, I trust, is the wish of all."

In response to the people's plea for relief, the Kentucky legislature responded with various measures. Perhaps the most important and extremely controversial act was the creation of the Bank of the Commonwealth. This bank was to be a people's bank, a bank that in its first two years of existence would issue nearly three million dollars in paper currency and lend out nearly the same amount. If any creditor refused to accept these inflationary bills, the law barred him "from pressing his claim in court for two years." One of the most articulate and active opponents of Adair and his program was Robert Wickliffe, who called this bank "an association of bankrupts to borrow money." In November 1820 Adair signed into law the bill creating the Bank of the Commonwealth.

The bank bill was only one of many relief bills that Adair approved. A number of these measures were declared unconstitutional by the state Court of Appeals, which found in favor of the creditor class. The court's findings were based primarily on the contract clause of the United States Constitution which forbade states from issuing laws "impairing the obligations of contracts." The governor, upset by the court's action, used his 1823 message to attack all those who opposed relief as "ignorant or designing men." For the remainder of his term Adair supported relief and concerned himself with what to do about the court that was clearly frustrating the desires of a majority of Kentucky's citizens. There was some thought of direct removal of the members of the court, but it was clear that no two-thirds majority of both houses of the state legislature could be raised. Likewise, a constitutional convention was deemed impossible. Therefore everything would hinge on the 1824 state elections—if the relief party could gain a two-thirds majority in both houses, the offending and conservative judges could be removed.

Adair could not succeed himself, and after leaving office, he spent much of his time on his farm. He did serve one undistinguished term in the United States House of Representatives, 1831-1833. He died on May 19, 1840, at the age of eighty-three and was buried in Frankfort.

SUGGESTED READINGS: Arndt M. Stickles, *The Critical Court Struggle in Kentucky, 1819-1829* (1929); Steven A. Channing, *Kentucky: A Bicentennial History* (1977).

CHARLES J. BUSSEY

# JOSEPH DESHA
1768-1842

Joseph Desha was born on December 9, 1768, to Robert and Eleanor Wheeler Desha. When he was thirteen, he moved with his family from Monroe County, Pennsylvania, to Fayette County, Kentucky. Three years later the Desha family moved to Tennessee. Young Desha lived near Nashville until 1792 when he moved back to Kentucky with his wife of three years, Margaret Bledsoe. Desha settled in Mason County in the state he would call home for the last fifty years of his life.

Desha's military background included service under Gens. Anthony Wayne and William H. Harrison in the 1794 Indian war. Later, as an ardent supporter of the War of 1812, Desha would serve again under General Harrison. Desha's key interests, however, were agriculture and politics, and he was active in both. A Jeffersonian Republican, Desha served in the Kentucky House of Representatives in 1797 and again in 1799–1802; he was in the Kentucky Senate, 1802-1807, and moved from that post to the United States House where he served six consecutive terms, 1807-1819. Desha's congressional career was undistinguished. In 1820 he ran for governor in Kentucky and lost to John Adair. Four years later Desha came back as the prorelief candidate and trounced Christopher Tompkins 38,378 to 22,499. Tompkins represented the conservative, antirelief party. A third candidate, William Russell, picked up an insignificant 3,900 votes.

Desha's tenure as governor came at a time when the commonwealth was in turmoil. The key public issue that had crowded out all other issues for the past four years was relief for debtors. These people were the victims of the Panic of 1819 and the subsequent depression. John Adair, Desha's predecessor, had likewise championed the cause of relief. During his administration, the legislature had created a new Bank of the Commonwealth, which was specifically designed to aid debtors. In the same session the legislature had passed numerous other relief measures, many of which the Kentucky Court of Appeals had struck down as unconstitutional. The closing months of Adair's term had seen the governor and the legislature frustrated in their attempts to do something about the court's blocking of relief measures.

The election of 1824 posed a referendum on the issue, and the people of Kentucky spoke in favor of relief. Not only did Desha win the governor's race, but it appeared that the prorelief forces had captured a two-thirds majority of both houses of the legislature and could thus remove the antirelief judges of the so-called Old Court.

The new legislature met in November and the Old Court members (John Boyle, William Owsley, and Benjamin Mills) were summoned to Frankfort for questioning. They appeared as called and were courageous in answering questions, but they refused to be cowed and talked about the situation in Kentucky as "another Shay's rebellion." One judge went so far as to say that "no country was ever legislated out of debt nor will ever be." Perhaps because of their courage, the state legislature narrowly failed to vote the two-thirds majority needed to remove them.

In December there was mad activity among partisans on both sides of the issue, culminating in a wild legislative session on Christmas Eve 1824. The prorelief Desha forces successfully backed passage of a court reorganization bill that abolished the Old Court and created a New Court. The governor himself was illegally on the floor of the chamber that evening lobbying for the bill. He "displayed intense excitement," and he quickly signed the bill into law.

The next year Kentucky was the focus of the nation. The Old Court refused to give up its post or its records. The New Court, composed of William Taylor Barry, James Haggin, John Trimbel, and Benjamin Patton, all appointed by Governor Desha, was sitting. In February 1825, F.P. Blair, a young journalist and New Court clerk, forcibly entered the office of the Old Court clerk, Achilles Sneed, and removed all of the court's records.

At this stage, little else was going on in the commonwealth. The Old Court began to operate politically, and in the fall of 1825 their conservative group won control of the House. They trotted out former governor Isaac Shelby, who called the Bank of the Commonwealth and other relief measures "the child of folly and inexperience." The Old Court faction continued its political thrust and in 1826 won control of the Senate. Shortly thereafter the newly constituted legislature passed a bill abolishing the New Court and repealing the court reorganization bill. Desha, of course, vetoed it. In his veto message Desha found "nothing of that spirit of forbearance which is necessary to conciliate the exasperated feelings of party contention, and lead to union and harmony." The legislature quickly overrode his veto, the bill became law on December 30, 1826, and for the first time in years the state began to calm down.

There were several important issues involved in the Old Court-

New Court controversy, some of which have not yet been resolved. Does the court system have the right to frustrate the will of the majority? In 1824 the majority favored relief for debtors. In recent years the focus has been on such topics as busing to achieve racial balance. One important result of the court controversy, however, was the rise to prominence of F.P. Blair and Amos Kendall, two of Governor Desha's close associates. Both would soon leave Kentucky for Washington, where they would play key roles in Andrew Jackson's presidencies.

Two other issues were prominent during Desha's tenure. In 1818 Horace Holley, a New England Unitarian, had assumed the presidency of Transylvania University in Lexington. While he attracted a marvelous faculty and enhanced the national reputation of the school, Holley's religious convictions infuriated orthodox Christians. Consequently they tried to get rid of him by labeling him an infidel, an immoral and coarse man, a drinker, and a gambler. Holley withstood all pressure until 1826 when Governor Desha, in his annual message, came out against Holley. That was the beginning of the end, and with state funds drying up, Holley left his post in 1827.

The other issue of prominence during Desha's term was a matter that should have been settled in the beginning at the local level. Before it was over, though, it became a cause célèbre. On November 2, 1824, Governor Desha's son Isaac brutally murdered a Mississippian named Francis Baker who was visiting Kentucky. Local juries twice found the young man guilty of murder and sentenced him to hang. These verdicts were handed down despite the high-powered legal counsel the governor provided for his son. One defense attorney, for example, was William Barry, the man the governor had just appointed to head the New Court. Finally, in 1827 Governor Desha used his constitutional power to pardon his son.

After Desha left office, he retired from public life and went to his Harrison County farm where he remained until he died on October 12, 1842.

SUGGESTED READINGS: Arndt M. Stickles, *The Critical Court Struggle in Kentucky, 1819-1829* (1929); Steven A. Channing, *Kentucky: A Bicentennial History* (1977).

CHARLES J. BUSSEY

# THOMAS METCALFE

Thomas Metcalfe, Kentucky's tenth governor, was born in Fauquier County, Virginia, March 20, 1780, one of five children of Sarah Dent Chinn and John Metcalfe, a Revolutionary veteran. The family moved to Fayette County, Kentucky, about 1804, later settling permanently in Nicholas County. Following a skimpy education in the common schools, young Thomas became a skilled stonemason, picking up his lifelong nickname of "Stonehammer." His marriage to Nancy Mason, a daughter of Burgess and Jane Lee Mason, in about 1806 produced four children.

Metcalfe's public life began with service in the lower house of the state legislature from 1812 to 1816. During this time he entered the War of 1812 as a captain of volunteers, leading his company at the battle of Fort Meigs. In 1819 Metcalfe was elected to Congress, serving in the House until 1828. While in Washington he built a reputation as a friend of the common man and promoter of western democracy. He opposed banks, argued that a two-thirds vote of the federal Supreme Court should be necessary to declare a state law unconstitutional, and fought unsuccessfully for credit extension to purchasers of public lands. His 1821 proposal to grant preemption rights to squatters anticipated the Preemption Act of 1841 by twenty years, yet he had history against him when he opposed restrictions upon slavery in the Louisiana Purchase. He favored internal improvements and protective tariffs, a position that soon allied him with Henry Clay and his American system. This alliance was strengthened in 1825 when Metcalfe followed Clay in voting for John Quincy Adams for president. When John J. Crittenden withdrew his name as a Kentucky gubernatorial candidate in late 1827, the Adams-Clay forces turned to Metcalfe.

In December 1827 Thomas Metcalfe became the first Kentucky gubernatorial candidate nominated by party convention rather than the discredited caucus system. His running mate on the National Republican ticket, Joseph Underwood, was given the same unanimous convention vote. In January 1828 the Democratic convention in

Frankfort nominated William T. Barry for governor and John Breathitt for lieutenant governor.

Metcalfe and Barry had much in common, but the contrasts between them were promoted heavily by their campaign managers. Unlike Barry, Metcalfe had much less than a college education, and he had literally pounded out his living as a stonemason. He was a candidate Jacksonians might cross party lines to vote for, thus his presentation as a hard-working man of the people. Moreover he had missed direct involvement in the court struggle with all of its latent hatreds— this in contrast to Barry, who had been chief justice of the New Court as well as John Adair's lieutenant governor. For these reasons, it was to be the paradox of the election that Old Stonehammer instead of Barry would ride to victory on the ample coattails of the Democrat Old Hickory Jackson!

The elections of 1828 in Kentucky, whether state, local, or national, were conducted with a fervor for political manipulations seldom matched in the state's history. Great political heat had developed as an aftermath of the state banking and court struggle and the "tainted" Adams presidential victory of 1824. The Adams-Clay forces hoped first to elect a governor, then win control of the legislature, and finally send one of their men to Washington as a senator. They managed only to elect a governor and that by the narrowest of margins.

The results of the 1828 election were far from decisive for either candidate, but they did destroy the assumption that Clay and Adams were unbeatable in Kentucky. Metcalfe won by 38,930 votes to 38,231 for Barry. An awkward consequence of the close vote came in John Breathitt's defeat of Underwood by a margin of 1,087 votes, thus saddling Metcalfe with a Democratic lieutenant governor.

Metcalfe's administration began an era during which governors of Whig sentiment sat in Frankfort for all but two years from 1828 to 1851; yet during these years the state was usually under the shadow of Democratic administrations in Washington. Any understanding of Metcalfe's administration must acknowledge that he, and most of his Whig successors, labored under a double political burden, for domestic and national politics became closely interwoven after the termination of the relief struggle and the rise of political parties. In short, Metcalfe and his program were squarely in the path of the political tornado generated by the struggle for supremacy between the forces of Henry Clay and Andrew Jackson. This, as much as Metcalfe's admitted penchant for internal improvements, explains the extent to which roads, canals, and railways dominated his administrative agenda.

In his 1828 address to the General Assembly Metcalfe held that internal improvements are "most essential to the welfare of the state," whether this might be work on a Louisville canal around Falls of the Ohio, a railroad between Lexington and the Ohio River, or a new turn-pike between Maysville and Lexington. Most Kentucky legislators, re-gardless of party, agreed with Metcalfe, going on to incorporate the Lexington and Ohio Railroad and subscribing thousands of dollars of stock in the Green River Navigation Company, the Shelbyville and Louisville Road, and fatefully the Maysville Road. Aid for the Mays-ville-Lexington Road was soon forthcoming from Congress, which passed a bill authorizing $150,000 for the completion of this sixty-mile link in the interstate road connecting Zanesville, Ohio, with Nashville, Tennessee. Jackson vetoed the bill on May 27, 1830, citing constitutional reasons, but he probably also had a political object: to strike at the Clay party and the American system.

Kentuckians of all political persuasions were stunned and infuri-ated by Jackson's veto. Obviously the states had to build their own roads, so Metcalfe in his message of 1830 highly recommended "this great highway to the favorable consideration and patronage of the leg-islature." The fact that Forest Retreat, his Nicholas County estate, lay along the road may have added to his enthusiasm. In any event, the Maysville Road, now U.S. Route 68, was built in great part by state patronage.

Metcalfe and state politicians of both parties had been damaged by the Clay-Jackson fight over internal improvements, but they were also losing allies in several sister Southern states over their stance on the 1828 Tariff of Abominations. A large majority of the General As-sembly of 1829-1830 issued a resolution supporting the tariff "to en-courage and protect the manufactures of the United States. . . ." Ken-tucky legislators also would not sanction South Carolina's threat of nullification, agreeing instead with Governor Metcalfe's opinion that "such obstruction if acquiesced in by the General Government, would amount to virtual dissolution of the Union—if resisted by Civil War. These were the principles upon which Kentucky and her parent state acted at the memorable period of 1798 [the Kentucky and Virginia Resolutions], and I do but act upon the same principle." Metcalfe was one of the first governors to nudge Kentucky toward the border state stance she would hold during the Civil War.

Governor Metcalfe's concern for common schools was genuine, but his efforts in behalf of education left much to be desired. The General Assembly passed three resolutions concerning education in 1829, Metcalfe's first full year in office. These called for a report on common schools, a listing of all school-aged children, and instructions to Kentucky's Congressmen to try for a federal land appropriation to help finance the state's schools. Only the first resolution produced any results: a report that showed that only one-third of the state's children were in any kind of school. The report, prepared by the Rev. Alva Wood and Benjamin Peers, and its recommendation for remedial legislation were ignored by Metcalfe and the legislature. The governor did sign an "Act for . . . the Establishment of Uniform Schools" in 1830, but this superb bill had been amended to make county participation nonobligatory, thus weakening it beyond repair. This excellent act showed that Metcalfe and the legislators knew what it took to have fine schools but that they lacked the courage to stand on that knowledge or break with the past. The Metcalfe administration's handling of education was its greatest failure and certainly the one that had the most lasting impact on the populace.

Metcalfe must be ranked as one of the better governors of his era. He denounced nullification as well as Jackson's spoils system, and his recommendations usually became law, among them prison reform, simplification of the judicial system, abolition of the branches of the Bank of Commonwealth, protection of the occupying claimants of Kentucky lands, and patronage for the American Colonization Society.

Metcalfe later served as a state senator, 1834–1838, and in 1839 he was a member of the Whig National Convention. The next year he was elected president of the state Board of Internal Improvements; he retained that position until 1848. Then he was appointed and subsequently elected to the United States Senate, serving from June 23, 1848, to March 3, 1849. While there, he denounced secession and declared that Kentucky would always uphold the Union. Shortly after this, he retired to Forest Retreat, his Nicholas County farm. He died there of cholera on August 18, 1855, and was buried in the family graveyard.

SUGGESTED READINGS: Leonard Curry, "Election Year—Kentucky, 1828," *Register* 55(July 1957), 196–212; Edsel Godbey, *The Governors of Kentucky and Education, 1780-1852* (1960).

FRANK F. MATHIAS

# JOHN BREATHITT

John Breathitt was the only Jacksonian Democrat elected during the state's Whig era, 1828-1850, and the second governor to die in office.

Breathitt was born on September 9, 1786, near New London, Virginia, the eldest son of William and Elizabeth Whitsett Breathitt. William, who had earlier emigrated from Scotland, moved his family from Virginia to Kentucky early in the nineteenth century, settling at Russellville in Logan County. The few schools in this backwoods area afforded but the scantiest education, but young John taught himself surveying and soon acquired enough capital to sustain himself while reading law under Judge Caleb Wallace. He was admitted to the bar in 1810, quickly developing a lucrative practice and an interest in politics. In 1811 he was first elected to the state House of Representatives from Logan County, where he served until 1815. Two of his brothers were also rising rapidly, one in law, the other in politics. James Breathitt was destined to serve many years as commonwealth attorney, while George became Pres. Andrew Jackson's private secretary.

Breathitt was married twice, and although he was only forty-seven when he died, he survived both wives. He first married Caroline Whitaker of Logan County in 1812, and then after her death, Susan M. Harris, a daughter of Richard Harris of Chesterfield County, Virginia. His first wife bore him a son and a daughter, his second wife a daughter.

Breathitt took a giant step toward the governor's chair when he, a Democrat, beat the Clay-Adams candidate, Joseph Underwood, by 1,087 votes in the 1828 race for lieutenant governor. This saddled Gov. Thomas Metcalfe, the Clay-Adams victor, with a Democratic lieutenant governor. Fate perhaps dictated that Breathitt would face the same problem when he became governor.

In December 1831 Kentucky's National Republicans and Democrats met in conventions at Frankfort to nominate candidates for the 1832 governor's race. The Democrats nominated Breathitt as their candidate. Benjamin Taylor, a near nonentity, was chosen as Breathitt's running mate, probably with an eye toward using his home county of Fayette to balance Breathitt's influence in the Green River country.

33

The Clay-Adams National Republicans countered with Richard A. Buckner of Green County for governor and James T. Morehead of Warren County as his running mate. A religious fanatic with a strong aversion toward the Sunday mails, Buckner failed to command even the support of several of his party's newspapers during the campaign. Morehead, however, proved himself a strong campaigner and should have been placed at the head of the ticket.

There was no state or local issue of significance in the gubernatorial race; all eyes were turned toward the presidential election of November, in which Kentucky's Henry Clay would try to settle past grievances with Andrew Jackson. The gubernatorial race was awaited as an indicator of trends to be expected in November.

The election was closer than either side had expected. Breathitt won by only 1,242 votes, receiving 40,715 votes to Buckner's 39,473. Interestingly the Jackson Purchase counties gave Breathitt 1,856 votes to Buckner's 276; thus his majority here was 338 votes larger than the 1,242 vote majority given him throughout the state. The honors for illegal voting in the election went to Oldham County, which cast 162.9 percent of its potential vote two to one in favor of Breathitt over Buckner.

The results of the election were similar, although in a reversed way, to those of the 1828 election. Breathitt was elected as a Democratic governor, but Morehead, a Clay man, was chosen lieutenant governor. Unlike the 1828 election, the Clay forces carried the state legislature, thus giving them control over the election of the next United States senator.

Jackson carried the nation in November. He had hardly started his second term in office before being faced with South Carolina's nullification ordinance holding the tariff acts of 1828 and 1832 to be without effect in that state. Governor Breathitt reacted almost as emphatically as the president. In doing so, he received the support of Clay and Jackson men alike. His message denouncing the actions of South Carolina was soon translated into a set of resolutions condemning that state's course as one leading to disunion and civil war. The resolutions were passed on February 2, 1833. Breathitt's vigorous leadership in this matter gave early support to the growing sense of union in Kentucky, thereby turning the state away from the path that ended at Appomattox. More important, Kentucky's actions during this crisis were keenly watched in other states, for the Kentucky Resolutions of 1798 and 1799 set the precedents for John C. Calhoun's theories on nullification. Breathitt's opposition meant that in a union of states the majority must rule and that squabbles over tariffs were not really comparable to the tyranny of alien and sedition laws of earlier years. This may have been Breathitt's most lasting contribution as governor.

A compromise tariff and a cooling of tempers permitted Kentucky and the nation to forget nullification for a while and turn to another issue. Jackson was soon carrying out the threat implied in his earlier veto of the bill to recharter the Second Bank of the United States. The bank would be destroyed by shifting federal deposits to state banks. Moreover, his plan to let each state dispose of its public lands to finance internal improvements further incited National Republican wrath, especially in Kentucky where public land had been sold years ago. The Clay-Adams legislature prepared a set of resolutions condemning the land policy and the proposed destruction of the only sound banking institutions in the state. On January 23, 1833, Breathitt returned the documents unsigned. He objected to attacks on the land policy because Kentucky had used a similar policy throughout her history, and "that which was good policy in our own state cannot be the less so, if practiced by the general government." Jackson himself might have given Breathitt's objection to opposition pleas to save the bank, for the governor asserted that its destruction was the only way to rid the nation of foreign financial power.

A few weeks later Breathitt was rebuffed for his opposition to National Republican desires. His party hoped for the creation of several state banks to receive a share of the federal deposits being distributed by the Jackson administration, and his annual message to the General Assembly advocated their establishment. A bill was introduced to this end, but it was cut down by National Republican opposition to one bank, the Louisville Bank of Kentucky. Its future, and that of state banks in general, seemed uncertain until the elections of 1833 returned to the legislature men who favored state banking. The subsequent creation of sound state banks did much to end the political strife that had hung like a curse over state financial institutions for two decades.

Shortly after Governor Breathitt took office, the Lexington and Ohio Railroad project raised a state-level constitutional issue that probably took as its source the federal issue developed by Jackson over the Maysville Road veto two years earlier. Kentucky's first railroad, the Lexington and Ohio, had been chartered on January 27, 1830. It was capitalized at $1 million, with the right of directors to increase it to $2 million. Subscription books had been opened a week later, and well over $200,000 was subscribed the first day. The enthusiasm that prevailed as actual work on the railroad started in October 1831 waned sharply when the project failed to attract a steady stream of needed investors. Late in 1832 the Board of Internal Improvements held that a state construction loan of $300,000 would not violate constitutional restrictions upon the use of public monies, for the state would receive company bonds in return for its investment. Dissenters on the board, however, declared that "to pledge . . . the state for the redemption of a loan . . . to a company of individuals, would establish . . . a ruinous precedent."

Governor Breathitt devoted most of his December 1832 address to the General Assembly to the question of internal improvements, and he included strong support for completing the Lexington and Ohio Railroad. The majority of the legislators evidently agreed with him, for on February 2, 1833, the railroad was rechartered and authorized to borrow $300,000 in construction costs. After receiving a full mortgage on all railroad property, a state loan of $150,000 was approved. Fortunately neither Breathitt nor the legislators could foretell that this railroad would not be completed to Louisville until 1851 and then only under a threat from Cincinnati to build a competing line.

By February 1833 Governor Breathitt was a very sick man. Vigorous opponents in the General Assembly, infuriated at Jackson's high-handedness, were on the verge of renaming themselves Whigs. The governor could do little with them. He had done even less with the always pressing problems of common schools, paying little more than lip service to education in spite of the formation of two promising groups aimed at gaining state support for the schools. Whatever he may or may not have done in this and other matters of state will never be known, for he died of tuberculosis on February 21, 1834. His short term of office is memorable mostly for his stalwart defense of the Union, for on other issues he and his administration were hopelessly entangled in conflict with the powerful opposition majority.

Governor Breathitt is buried in Maple Grove Cemetery at Russellville. The state erected a monument for him, and later a county was named in his honor.

SUGGESTED READINGS: Frank F. Mathias, "The Turbulent Years of Kentucky Politics" (Ph.D. dissertation, University of Kentucky, 1966); John Breathitt, "Commencement of a Journal from Kentucky to the State of Pennsylvania," *Register* 52(January 1954), 5-24.

FRANK F. MATHIAS

# JAMES TURNER MOREHEAD

James Turner Morehead became governor following Gov. John Breathitt's death in office on February 21, 1834. Morehead, a Whig, had served as lieutenant governor under Breathitt, a Democrat, since their election on a split ticket in August 1832. Morehead served until June 1836, the end of the gubernatorial term.

James Turner Morehead was born on May 24, 1797, near Shepherdsville, Bullitt County, Kentucky, a son of Armistead and Lucy Latham Morehead. He became the state's first native-born son to rise to the governorship. Armistead's father, Charles Morehead II, of Fauquier County, Virginia, was the grandfather of both James Morehead and Charles S. Morehead (governor, 1855-1859) as well as the great-grandfather of Simon Bolivar Buckner (governor, 1887-1891). James was also a second cousin of John Motley Morehead, elected governor of North Carolina in 1840.

Soon after Morehead's birth the family moved to Russellville where James later began his education. He attended Transylvania University, 1813-1815, then studied law under Judge H.P. Broadnax and John J. Crittenden. He was admitted to the bar in 1818 and soon won a reputation as an able lawyer after opening a practice in Bowling Green. On May 1, 1823, he married Susan A. Roberts of Logan County.

Morehead gradually became involved in public affairs during the riotous 1820s. Although he favored the proposed bankruptcy laws at this time, he could not sanction the New Court established by the relief party and became instead a known supporter of the Old Court. His rise to political prominence was rapid after the settlement of the court controversy. He was elected to the lower house of the state legislature in 1828, serving until 1831. In that year he became chairman of the committee on internal improvements, reporting the bill for a state subscription to the Maysville-Lexington Road. During the same year he served as a member of the National Republican convention at Baltimore that nominated Henry Clay for the presidency.

Morehead's rise to the governor's office began with his nomination as candidate for lieutenant governor at the state National Republican convention in Frankfort, December 1831. Richard A. Buckner headed the ticket, but Morehead won by a larger margin than anyone in the race. Indeed, of the four men involved, he was the only one to carry his home county, in this case Warren. Morehead defeated Benjamin Taylor by a margin of 2,582 votes, led both tickets, and with the defeat of his running mate wound up National Republican lieutenant governor alongside Gov. John Breathitt, the victorious Democrat.

Governor Breathitt's death from tuberculosis on February 21, 1834, came as a sharp blow to Democratic hopes, for Lieutenant Governor Morehead, a Clay man, was sworn into office the next day. James Guthrie, a leading Democrat, was elected president of the Senate, filling the vacancy caused by Morehead's assumption of duties. Morehead showed a conciliatory attitude by retaining Lewis Saunders as secretary of state. A Democratic editor believed that Morehead's attitude "augurs well in favor of an impartial administration of the Executive Department."

Conciliatory gestures on the part of the Whigs (the new name for the National Republicans) ended with the returns from the elections of August 1834. When the General Assembly convened for the 1834–1835 session, it counted a five-man Whig majority in the senate and a vast forty-nine man majority in the house. In spite of Democratic cries of irregularity James Guthrie was ousted as president of the Senate, and James Clark, who would soon campaign as the Whig gubernatorial candidate, was elected in his place. But Morehead and the Whigs would not let Guthrie off easily. He was soundly thrashed by John J. Crittenden a few weeks later when the legislature voted 94-40 against him in selecting a United States senator. In short, Morehead came to power about the time Whig victories in state elections began to be taken for granted.

It was the fate of James Morehead to come to power in the middle of a gubernatorial term; thus he had no call to continue the political plans of his Democratic predecessor or time to develop many ideas or issues of his own. It is true that he had power in the legislature, but any governor of this era was little more than the executor of the will of that body; the office offered few leadership opportunities. Moreover, state revenues came to little more than $400,000 annually, and in their use the governor's hands were tied to the point that patronage was inconsequential. These things must be kept in mind in any assessment of Morehead as governor or any other governor of the era.

Morehead could hardly go wrong politically in backing internal improvements, that most popular of all causes in antebellum Kentucky.

He successfully urged the legislature to launch surveys and lay plans for the improvement of navigation in Kentucky's rivers. He was the first ex officio president of Kentucky's permanent Board of Internal Improvements, later becoming board president by appointment of the next governor. Unfortunately the Morehead administration's fine plans for rivers were never executed owing to the Panic of 1837. But at least the Lexington and Ohio Railroad was completed to the bluffs above Frankfort during his administration in 1835.

Morehead paid only lip service to the genuine needs of education, but in this he was typical of most governors of his era. Nevertheless, two groups that became active during this gubernatorial term soon had a decided effect on education in the state. Late in 1833 the Kentucky Association of Professional Teachers united in Lexington as the first teachers' organization in the state. In February 1834 the Kentucky Common School Society was formed, and it soon had the support of the teachers' group. Efforts were quickly under way to gain public and political recognition of the need for, and an acceptance of, a common school system. Although the 1830–1837 era produced little legislation other than the severely weakened 1830 school law, public and political attention was gradually being awakened, and legislation to produce a uniform system of education would soon follow. Morehead deserves some credit for giving his blessing to this development.

Morehead agreed with others of his political persuasion that the old title of National Republican no longer described a faction opposed to the new principles and policies of the Jackson forces. Jackson's celebrated "removal of the deposits" of the Bank of the United States late in 1833 generated the political heat needed to bring about a re-dedication and a new name for all opposing forces. The name Whig was used by Morehead and the anti-Jacksonites as perfectly fitting for their opposition to the usurpation of King Andrew. Whig first appeared as the party name in the Lexington *Intelligencer* on April 25, 1834. An appeal was made for all freedom-loving Kentuckians to enter the ranks of this new party. The first great Whig convention was called for July 4, 1834, at Frankfort. Some five thousand people from forty-five counties sent delegates to the event hosted by Governor Morehead.

Morehead must be ranked as an adequate caretaker governor. He did nothing to hinder education, presided over the birth of the Whig party, and gave his energy to the politically safe path of advancing internal improvements. He also favored judicial reform and denounced the abolitionists, two courses that would not hurt him or his party in Kentucky. Although Morehead was an eligible incumbent, factionalism within the party made him temporarily unavailable to Whig leaders; thus he was not nominated to run in 1836.

Morehead served again in the state House in 1837-1838. A slavery advocate, he joined John Speed Smith as a commissioner in an 1839-1840 trip to Ohio's General Assembly to arrange for the return of fugitive slaves. In 1841 he and his faction overcame the manipulation of Robert "Old Duke" Wickliffe's group, thus winning Morehead appointment as United States senator. He served from February 20, 1841, to March 3, 1847. Ever the supporter of his colleague Henry Clay, Morehead was prominent in his defense of the federal bank bill. He was against the annexation of Texas, yet when war came, he joined other Whig senators in voting it support. He wrote and published some items of merit, particularly *An Address in Commemoration of the First Settlement of Kentucky* (1840) and *Practice in Civil Actions and Proceedings at Law* (1846). James T. Morehead spent his last years practicing law in Covington, where he died on December 28, 1854. He was buried in the state cemetery in Frankfort.

SUGGESTED READINGS: Willard Rouse Jillson, "Early Political Papers of Governor James Turner Morehead," *Register* 22(September 1924), 272-300, and 23(January 1925), 36-61.

FRANK F. MATHIAS

1836-1839
# JAMES CLARK
1779-1839

James Clark, the son of Robert and Susannah Clark, was born in Bedford County, Virginia, near the Peaks of Otter on January 16, 1779. He was brought to Kentucky as a child by his parents who settled in Clark County on a farm near the Kentucky River. He was educated under the tutorship of James Blythe who afterward served as a professor at Transylvania University. Clark returned to Virginia and studied law under his brother, Christopher Clark. After completing his studies, he made an extended trip into the West for the purpose of finding a suitable place to practice his profession, but finally came back to

Winchester in Clark County to take up practice. Admitted to the bar in 1797, Clark soon had an outstanding reputation and an extensive practice. He took a special interest in politics, and in 1807 and 1808 he was elected to the lower house of the General Assembly. His brother Robert had paved the way for him by representing Clark County in the legislature for several years. Clark's first marriage was to Susan Forsythe in 1809. After her death he married Margaret Buckner Thornton in 1839.

On March 29, 1810, he was appointed a judge of the Kentucky Court of Appeals and served on the bench for two years. In 1813 he was elected to the lower house of Congress and was reelected in 1815. An examination of the *Debates and Proceedings* of Congress reveals that his two terms were served without distinction and his service was terminated in 1816 by his resignation. In 1817 he was appointed judge of the circuit court of Kentucky. While serving in this position in 1822, Clark rendered his historic decision in the case of *Williams v. Blair*, declaring the stay law for the benefit of debtors to be unconstitutional. The stay law had been passed by the legislature to give relief to the debtors from the Panic of 1819. Debtors were relieved of bankruptcy proceedings by a moratorium on the debt they owed. Clark cited the clause in the federal Constitution that stated that no government should have the right to make a law "impairing the obligation of contracts" and added that the states in accepting the Constitution had agreed to that provision. Judge Clark declared in closing: "The opinion I have expressed on this subject . . . is different from that entertained by some," but he felt it was his duty to "interpret the laws and constitution as he understood them." Clark's ruling was in harmony with the recent ruling of the United States Supreme Court in the case of *Dartmouth College v. Woodward* (1819).

His opinion caused such dissatisfaction that the legislature, convened in extra session, passed a resolution of condemnation and summoned Judge Clark to appear before the house to answer the charge. On May 27, 1822, he answered the charge in writing and ably defended his decision. Clark argued that in pronouncing a law void that is incompatible with the Constitution, the judiciary does not assume superiority over the legislature. "It merely affirms the paramount obligation of the fundamental rule. It announced only that the will of the people, as expressed in their constitution, is above the will of any of the servants of the people." After the legislature discussed the matter for a day the question of removing Clark was taken; the result was 59 for removal, 35 against. As there was not a constitutional two-thirds for removal, the resolution lost. In October 1823 the decision in *Williams v. Blair* was sustained by the state supreme court. The General Assembly abolished the Court of Appeals and legislated a new court to take its place, thus initiating the struggle between the Old Court and the New Court forces that went on for several years.

In 1825 Clark was again elected to Congress to fill a vacancy left by Henry Clay, who accepted a position in John Quincy Adams's cabinet. Clark was reelected twice and served in the House of Representatives until 1831, but he was not an active member. He rarely spoke and apparently lacked influence in the body. In 1832 he was elected to the upper house of the Kentucky legislature where he served as chairman of the committee on internal improvements at a time when Kentucky was growing and undergoing a transition in transportation. He was chosen speaker of the senate in 1835.

As a political ally and friend of Clay, he was a bitter political opponent of Andrew Jackson and was active in organizing the Whig party in Kentucky.

In 1836 Clark was elected governor of Kentucky on the Whig ticket by a vote of 38,587 to 30,491 for Matthew Flournoy, the Democratic candidate. Clark's 1837 message to the legislature proposed a constructive and far-sighted program. He stressed the importance of keeping public finances on a sound footing. Since the auditor had to deal with the sinking fund for internal improvements as well as state finances, he suggested that the auditor's office be upgraded and strengthened. Clark expressed concern about fugitive slaves and requested the legislature to amend the criminal code to deal with the rising volume of crime. Clark's strongest appeal was made in the interest of education. He admonished the lawmakers to express their patriotic feelings by immediately establishing a public school system in every county.

The General Assembly responded by passing an act that established the first common schools in the state. The act provided for a state board of education, a state superintendent of public instruction, and commissioners of schools in each county. The legislature failed to revise the criminal code or to strengthen the auditor's office. Concern was shown for the security of slave property by the passage of a law to prohibit stagecoach owners from permitting slaves to use their coaches to escape to freedom. Another law enlarged the reward for apprehending fugitive slaves in transit.

At the opening of the second session of the General Assembly in December 1838 the governor again turned to financial matters. He proposed that the commissioners of the sinking fund for internal improvements be given more flexibility in investing funds and paying interest. A law was passed by the General Assembly granting this flexibility and adding a second auditor to the auditor's office. Clark called for a law giving the governor power to prevent the propagation of abolitionist views in the state. Abolitionist propaganda was aimed at inflaming the mind of the slave, Clark insisted, not converting the slaveholder. The legislature, however, refused to restrict freedom of speech; it only passed a resolution enabling the governor to deal with citizens who might be guilty of enticing slaves away from their masters.

Clark discharged his duties as the chief executive of Kentucky with dignity and honor until his death on August 27, 1839. He was buried in Winchester. Clark was a man of culture, refinement, and conservative philosophy, but he was courageous and completely independent. Clark's status as an administrator was equaled by his standing as a jurist. As a judge he was known for his logical thinking and for literary skill that he revealed in his judiciary decisions.

SUGGESTED READINGS: Jennie C. Morton, "Governor James Clark," *Register* 2(September 1904), 9-12; Arndt M. Stickles, *The Critical Court Struggle in Kentucky, 1819-1829* (1929).

VICTOR B. HOWARD

1839-1840
# CHARLES ANDERSON WICKLIFFE
1788-1869

Charles A. Wickliffe was the second of five successive Whigs to hold the governorship between 1836 and 1850. Though he dressed conservatively, Wickliffe was so politically independent that the partisan press often called him a "trimmer," a nautical term meaning one who adjusts with the winds. In a day when political loyalty ranked close to godliness, Wickliffe nevertheless enjoyed a prominent place among his contemporaries.

The future governor's parents, Charles and Lydia Hardin Wickliffe, came from Virginia four years before Charles was born in a log cabin some six miles from Springfield on June 8, 1788. Wickliffe's father, "with small means and a large family," could provide little education for his children, but he brought them up "in habits of industry and economy." Charles studied law in Bardstown under his cousin, Martin D. Hardin, and in 1809 was admitted to the bar.

Wickliffe developed a speaking style characterized by cool-headed logic and satire. Another cousin, Ben Hardin, criticized his speeches for their lack of feeling, suggesting that he could never excite public opinion because of his penchant for "throwing snow-balls." Nevertheless, when Hardin left Bardstown to serve in the United States Congress, young Wickliffe took over his position as commonwealth attorney. He soon attracted statewide attention by enthusiastically supporting the War of 1812 as a member of the state House of Representatives (1812-1814) and participating as a general's aide at the battle of the Thames.

Wickliffe depended on his brother, Robert J. Wickliffe, to advise him. Robert was amassing an immense fortune in Lexington, including some two hundred slaves, which eventually made him the leading slaveholder in the state.

In 1813 Wickliffe married Margaret Cripps, a lively, sociable young woman. They contracted with John Rogers, the builder of St. Joseph's Pro-Cathedral, to build Wickland in Bardstown. This "home of three governors" remained in the family for over one hundred years, housing Wickliffe's son, Robert, who became governor of Louisiana, his grandson, J.C.W. Beckham, governor of Kentucky from 1900 to 1907, as well as Govenor Wickliffe himself.

After several terms in the lower house of the Kentucky legislature (1812, 1813, 1820, 1821), Wickliffe served in the United States House of Representatives (1823-1833). In 1825, when the presidential election went to the House of Representatives, Wickliffe ignored Clay's advice and voted for Jackson, the choice of the Kentucky legislature.

Wickliffe began to realize that Clay's party was an uneasy lodging place for independent politicians like himself. When he became chairman of the House Committee on Public Lands, he attacked Clay's surplus revenue distribution plan as unfair to the younger states. Then Clay's willingness to limit slavery, as evidenced in the Missouri Compromise, conflicted with his strict constitutional interpretation of property protection. He wrote Clay, complaining about his slowness in attacking the fugitive slave problem, but Clay did not answer, perhaps punishing Wickliffe for insubordination.

But if Wickliffe often disagreed with Clay's policies, he had even more trouble supporting the Jacksonians. During the bank war he wrote his brother in despair about Jackson's attacks on the national bank. He publicly urged Kentuckians to strengthen the Clay party in Kentucky as "the nucleus around which the rest may yet rally and save the Government." Now it was the Jackson party that attacked him for his inconsistency. In 1833, perhaps knowing he could not be reelected, he left Congress to take care of his domestic and business affairs.

In 1836 the Whigs chose Wickliffe to run for lieutenant governor along with gubernatorial candidate James Clark. In Whig-dominated Kentucky the two were easily elected. Clark's majority was 8,096, while Wickliffe's was only 3,338, suggesting that some loyal Clay supporters had not forgiven him his Jackson vote. As lieutenant governor, Wickliffe automatically served as president of the Kentucky Senate. Historian Lewis Collins was impressed with his "commanding person, dignified manners, and prompt decision" in that office.

Wickliffe was fifty-one years old in 1839 when Governor Clark became ill and died in office. He became governor on September 5, 1839, just one year before the term ended.

Kentucky, like the rest of the nation, was suffering from the Panic of 1837, and Wickliffe wrote a financial advisor that "Never have I seen more gloom or heard greater complaints exchanged of the tightness of the times." Wanting to avoid a repetition of the financial crisis of the 1820s, he promised that "Kentucky will preserve her public faith untarnished." Since the state's largest financial burden was for river improvements, he called a meeting to find $200,000 immediately to finance the sale of internal improvement bonds.

In his annual message to the General Assembly on December 3, 1839, Governor Wickliffe announced that the banks had again suspended specie payment because some $2 million in coin had recently left the state. He complained that for ten years state expenses had exceeded revenue, and he urged the assembly to take responsibility for raising taxes. The deficit for the past year alone was $42,000; surely Kentuckians could afford more than the ten cents they were paying on every one hundred dollars worth of property? The governor did support increased expenditures in three areas, however—river improvements, the protection of state archives, and education, especially for teachers and farmers. He reminded the legislators that most of the state's revenue came from the farmers; therefore part of the money should be spent to support an agricultural "society" to teach not only practical farming methods but also moral and intellectual matters. The

General Assembly, however, refused to do more than borrow money to keep current expenses paid.

Governor Wickliffe patiently handled the endless requests for patronage, military commissions, pardons, tax rebates, and divorces that plagued the antebellum governors. Before leaving office, he announced proudly that Kentucky "now enjoys a confidence and a tax credit of which she may justly boast" because the interest due to holders of state securities had been paid. It must have been disappointing to him, however, that when Robert P. Letcher took over as governor in September 1840, the banks had not yet resumed specie payments.

Even before leaving office Wickliffe worked to elect Whigs to Congress. When Vice-President John Tyler became president after William Henry Harrison's death, Wickliffe was repaid for his efforts by being named postmaster general (1841-1845). President Tyler had shared a room with Wickliffe when they were both congressmen, and they agreed on many issues. The appointment was not popular with the Clay Whigs who were frustrated by Tyler's political independence. They were incensed when Wickliffe played a major role in pushing through the annexation of Texas after the issue helped defeat Clay's 1844 presidential bid. To make matters worse, Democratic President James K. Polk sent Wickliffe on a secret mission to Texas, where he remained until that nation passed an order of annexation. It was obvious that the Kentuckian had left the Whig party.

A delegate to Kentucky's constitutional convention of 1849, Wickliffe was attacked for his political inconsistency. In his reply he boasted that in his half-century of public life he had seen political dynasties come and go and had survived the excitement. He apologized for "throwing too much of my own affairs" before the convention, but obviously he enjoyed doing it, speaking for nearly an hour.

Before the Civil War Wickliffe was a member of the Washington and border state peace conferences, and in 1861 he was a successful Union candidate for the United States House of Representatives. He was thrown from his carriage in 1862 and permanently crippled, but he remained politically active. The Peace Democrats ran him for governor in 1863, but because military authorities considered his campaign subversive, he was soundly defeated by regular Democrat Thomas Bramlette, 68,422 votes to 17,503.

Just before his death at age eighty-one, he made a two-hour speech before the Court of Appeals that impressed those who heard it with his vitality. Then in the summer of 1869 he became ill while visiting a daughter in Baltimore and died on October 31. He was buried at Bardstown. Within a century, Wickliffe's brand of political independence would become more commonplace, but when Wickliffe practiced it, it took real courage to support one's beliefs instead of one's political party.

SUGGESTED READINGS: Jennie Morton, "Governor Charles A. Wickliffe," *Register* 2(September 1904), 17-21; Lucius Little, *Ben Hardin: His Times and Contemporaries* (1887).

HELEN BARTTER CROCKER

1840-1844
# ROBERT PERKINS LETCHER
1788-1861

Robert Perkins Letcher was a consummate politician, actively involved in the public affairs of his state and nation for nearly half a century. Born in Goochland County, Virginia, February 10, 1788, he was seventh of the twelve children of Stephen Giles and Betsey Perkins Letcher. His parents brought their family to Kentucky about 1800 and soon settled in Garrard County. There the senior Letcher opened a brickyard. Young Robert worked without enthusiasm in the brickyard and took the initiative in gaining admission to the highly regarded school of Joshua Fry near Danville. He studied law and began practice in Garrard County. Following the early death of his first wife, Susan Oden Epps, he married Charlotte Robertson, sister of George Robertson, a future chief justice of Kentucky. Charlotte survived her husband. No children were born to either marriage.

Letcher represented Garrard County in the Kentucky House of Representatives during the sessions beginning in 1813, 1814, 1815, and 1817. From 1823 to 1833 he represented in Congress a thinly settled, rugged district that extended from Garrard County near the center of the state to Harlan and Whitley counties on its southeastern border. When the General Assembly redistricted the state in February 1833, Garrard County was included in the Fifth District with Anderson, Mercer, Lincoln, and Jessamine counties. Here Letcher contended with Thomas P. Moore of Harrodsburg, a Jacksonian Democrat who had represented the same district, except for Garrard County, from 1823 to 1829 and had recently returned after serving four years as United States minister to New Grenada. The outcome was a disputed election that the United States House of Representatives tardily settled by ordering a new election. Letcher won by 258 votes and took his seat for the rest of the session ending March 1835.

When it became clear in 1824-1825 that the choice of a president would devolve upon the House of Representatives, Letcher, an admirer and intimate of Henry Clay, served as an intermediary between Clay and John Quincy Adams in the delicate conversations that preceded the House vote. On that vote the pro-Clay delegations from Kentucky, Ohio, and Missouri made possible Adams's election and Clay's appointment as secretary of state.

During Adams's term as president, Letcher took a proadministration stance; during Jackson's administration he was a member of the opposition. In accordance with Clay's internal improvements policy, he pushed for the Maysville Road bill, vetoed by Jackson in 1830. In 1833 he introduced Clay's tariff compromise in the House of Representatives.

At the elections of 1836, 1837, and 1838, Garrard County again returned Letcher to the Kentucky House of Representatives. In each of these years he sought the speakership of the House. In 1836 another future governor, John L. Helm, speaker the previous term, defeated him narrowly. In 1837 he ran against Helm and ex-Gov. James T. Morehead. After nine ballots Helm withdrew, whereupon the House chose Letcher 50-48 over Morehead. In 1838 he was reelected without opposition.

A state convention held at Harrodsburg in August 1839, nearly a year before the election, chose Letcher as the Whig nominee for governor by 48-26 over Judge William Owsley after two other contenders withdrew.

"Black Bob" Letcher, then fifty-one years of age, was not a handsome man. A lover of rich food and drink, he had a heavy body, short legs, short arms, and a very short neck. But he was a gregarious man with a gift for friendship. In 1831 ex-Pres. John Quincy Adams had described him as "a man of moderate talents, good temper, playful wit, and shrewd sagacity." Understanding that Letcher would not return to Congress, Adams added: "He will be a loss to the House, for . . . often in the heat of angry and fierce debate he throws in a joke, which turns it all to good humor." He also had a gift for electioneering, already demonstrated in thirteen successful campaigns. In some of his campaigns he enlivened his stump-speaking and distracted his opponents' listeners by playing his fiddle, responding to the crowd's call for any popular tune in his repertoire.

48

Letcher's Democratic opponent for the governorship, Judge Richard French of Winchester, was no match for him in their debates in several central Kentucky counties. When the votes were recorded, Letcher had a majority of 15,720 in a total poll of 95,020. His party gained a comfortable majority in both houses of the General Assembly, which was to meet in December.

The new governor, inaugurated September 2, 1840, assumed office in the midst of a major economic depression. As a good Clay Whig, he blamed the economic stringency on the federal government's failure to renew the charter of the Bank of the United States. Letcher insisted that Kentucky's credit must be maintained at a time when other states were repudiating their obligations. Supported throughout his term by Whig majorities in both houses of the General Assembly, he halted the state's outlays for the building of turnpikes and of locks and dams on the Green, Kentucky, and Licking rivers.

The governor resisted the passage of any major legislation for the relief of debtors, but he approved some minor palliatives. In 1842 the legislature made modest additions to the items of personal property exempted from foreclosure. The next year it eliminated the summer terms of circuit courts, thus delaying some foreclosures. It also passed legislation to facilitate a moderate expansion of credit by the existing state banks. Letcher had already intervened personally with officers of the banks to encourage them to extend new small loans.

In spite of the depression Letcher was able to report a small and increasing surplus in the state treasury each full year of his term. In June 1842 the state banks, which like banks all over the country had suspended specie payment on their notes in 1839, resumed specie payment. When Letcher left office, a friendly newspaper reported that Kentucky bonds, worth about eighty cents on the dollar when he took office, had been above par for more than a year. The worst of the economic stress was over.

Throughout his term Letcher gave much of his attention to national politics, partly because of its perceived effect on Kentucky's economy. But of overriding importance to him were the preparations for Henry Clay's presidential candidacy in 1844. When Clay was defeated, Letcher took the loss harder than the Old Prince himself.

On his retirement Letcher continued to live and practice law in Frankfort. He was a jovial member of an intimate circle of political and personal friends that included John J. Crittenden and Orlando Brown.

In 1847 the ex-governor was a stubborn contender with two fellow

Whigs and a Democrat for a seat in the United States Senate. After the twenty-eighth ballot, his friends withdrew his name; the General Assembly then gave the coveted place to Whig Congressman Joseph R. Underwood of Bowling Green, whose section had long been neglected in the distribution of honors.

Letcher zealously supported Gen. Zachary Taylor as the Whig nominee for president in 1848. Crittenden, who had reluctantly left the Senate to accept his party's nomination for governor, felt obliged to decline Taylor's invitation to become secretary of state. Instead, he proposed that Letcher be made postmaster general; he believed that Letcher's political counsel would be helpful to the president, who was completely inexperienced in civilian politics.

Taylor declined to make that appointment but recognized Letcher's services by naming him minister to Mexico. In February 1850 the ex-governor assumed his duties in Mexico City. He was neither happy nor successful in his Mexican mission. His primary duty was to negotiate a treaty to safeguard the interests of American citizens who had bought a concession to construct a line of transit across the Isthmus of Tehuantepec. He signed such a treaty and then on instructions from a new secretary of state hammered out a second agreement that was somewhat more favorable to the concessionaires. In April 1852 the Mexican legislature rejected the treaty. In August the Kentuckian returned home.

The following spring, Letcher was drafted to recover for the Whigs the congressional seat won by John C. Breckinridge in 1851. Letcher, twice the age of the young incumbent, had grown corpulent and short of breath. Nevertheless he gamely entered a grueling campaign that lasted more than three months. It involved an almost daily series of joint debates that took the candidates to every corner of the seven-county district. Though abundantly supplied with funds, Black Bob was now no match for his magnetic, articulate opponent. Still he carried the rich Whig strongholds, Fayette, Woodford, and Bourbon counties. Breckinridge, who ran up huge majorities in the traditionally Democratic counties, Scott and Owen, had an overall majority of 526 in a poll of 12,538 votes.

That was Letcher's last try for public office. Like Crittenden and most Kentucky Whigs, he supported the Know-Nothing or American candidates for state office in 1855. He spoke for ex-President Fillmore in Pennsylvania and New York as well as Kentucky during the presidential canvass of 1856. Still a confidant and counselor of Senator

Crittenden, he encouraged him to take a firm stand against the Lecompton Constitution for Kansas in 1857-1858. In 1860 he stood
with Crittenden in support of the Constitutional Union nominee for
president, John Bell. By election day his health had failed badly; on
January 24, 1861, he died at his Frankfort home. He was buried in
Frankfort.

SUGGESTED READINGS: Will D. Gilliam, Jr., "Robert Perkins Letcher, Whig
Governor of Kentucky," *FCHQ* 24(January 1950), 6-27; Mrs. Chapman
Coleman, ed. *The Life of John J. Crittenden, with Selections from His Correspon-
dence and Speeches* (1871), 2 vols.

FRANK H. HECK

1844-1848
# WILLIAM OWSLEY
1782-1862

William Owsley was born in Virginia on March 24, 1782. The next
year his parents, William and Catherine Bolin Owsley, trekked to Kentucky and settled near Crab Orchard in Lincoln County. Owsley grew
to a tall six feet, two inches, and was of slender build. He became a
schoolteacher, a deputy surveyor, and a deputy sheriff. One of his students, Elizabeth Gill, six years his junior, became his wife in 1803.
Owsley was encouraged by Judge John Boyle to study law and in 1809
was elected to the lower house of the legislature.

He was appointed to the Court of Appeals in 1810 but was
squeezed out when the number of justices was reduced. In 1811 he
again served in the Kentucky House, and two years later Gov. Isaac
Shelby reappointed him to the Court of Appeals. Owsley held this
position until 1828. The Court of Appeals became the focal point of
controversy as the governor and legislature attempted to give Kentuckians relief from the effects of the Panic of 1819. Various laws were
passed that would enable hard-pressed debtors to postpone payment.
Such measures were wildly popular but in the view of the judges illegal. John Alexander McClung, who wrote the "Outline History" for
Collins's *Historical Sketches of Kentucky*, declared that "in simplicity
and purity of character, in profound legal knowledge, and in Roman-
like firmness of purpose, the *old court* of appeals of Kentucky have

seldom been surpassed." Attempts to remove them failed but an act replacing them with a new court passed. The two courts, the old and the new, existed side by side. Finally, in part because the hard times that had brought on the relief legislation had passed and the economy had mended, support for the New Court slipped and Old Court partisans won a signal victory in 1826.

After resigning from the court in 1828, Owsley carried on an extensive legal practice. In 1831 he was again elected to the House and from 1832 to 1834 he served as a state senator. James T. Morehead appointed Owsley secretary of state in 1834, an office he held until 1836.

Later, Owsley moved to Frankfort to concentrate his legal efforts on appeals. He was called upon by the Whig party to run for governor in 1844 against Gen. William O. Butler, a War of 1812 hero who was described as "by far the most . . . formidable candidate the democratic party had ever run in the state." The campaign for governor was almost lost in the canvass for president—Henry Clay vs. James K. Polk. Democrats argued that it was time to oust the Whigs who had had a stranglehold on the state executive office. The race was tight with Owsley winning 59,680 to 55,056, a majority substantially less than that of his predecessor or successor.

Owsley's reserved manner contrasted sharply with that of his predecessor, Robert Perkins Letcher. Owsley has been characterized as a "born jurist" and a "stern and unbending" man. A fiscal conservative and loyal Whig, he told his first General Assembly that such issues as the tariff and currency would have been better handled if Henry Clay had been elected president. He considered his chief accomplishment the fact that "for the first time since the State embarked in works of internal improvements, the debt of the State was decreased. . . ." Though the sum was inconsequential, only several thousand dollars, Whigs quickly "admire[d] the business air" of the Owsley administration. Owsley consistently encouraged the legislature to fund public education: "Nothing but money will do it, and it is left to the appropriate department—the legislature—to determine on the expediency or inexpediency of raising it." Legislators voted only a small tax, and Owsley's major achievement in education was the appointment in 1847 of Robert J. Breckinridge as superintendent of public instruction, the man generally recognized as the chief architect of public schooling in antebellum Kentucky. The state penitentiary, which had been severely damaged by fire before Owsley's inauguration, required more funds for its rebuilding and improvement than he wanted to spend.

National events, chiefly the Mexican War and the antislavery issue, had impact on the Owsley administration. Though considering the war "deeply to be deplored," the governor responded with alacrity to requests for troops, writing to the secretary of war that "Kentuckians are no laggards in a cause like this." Indeed, the call for 2,400 state volunteers brought forth 13,700 men. The slavery issue was raised not only by the Mexican War but also by Cassius M. Clay's *True American* newspaper that was suppressed in Lexington. Owsley became personally involved in the antislavery issue when he pardoned Delia A. Webster (of Vermont) who had been convicted of helping slaves escape to Ohio. He sent troops into Clay County to prevent the rescue of a Dr. Baker who had been sentenced to die.

Owsley and Ben Hardin, a man who hungered after a United States Senate seat, became bitter enemies. Hardin believed that by supporting Owsley he would be consulted in matters of patronage. Owsley appointed Hardin as his secretary of state, but Hardin became increasingly frustrated at having little say in appointments. On September 1, 1846, Owsley removed Hardin and appointed George B. Kinkead in his place. Hardin resisted the move, the Kentucky Senate voted thirty to eight that no vacancy existed, and the Court of Appeals upheld Hardin. His position vindicated, Hardin resigned.

Owsley's reputation was tarnished by Ben Hardin's eloquent accusations of nepotism.

> I now tell Governor Owsley, beware how you portion your children and your connections with the offices that belong to the people. They will not tamely submit; . . . We, gentlemen, who are for a [constitutional] convention, ought to rouse up, when we look at the extravagant claims and pretentions of Governor Owsley, and when we see public offices taken from more deserving men and given in marriage portions to the governor's daughter, grandson, and others of the connection.

The push for a new constitution was, according to some, brought on in part by the "acts or omissions" of the governor. Not only was there a desire to make Kentucky safer for slavery, but also there was a movement for the abolition of life tenure terms for judicial offices.

It was during Owsley's tenure that the body thought to be that of

53

Daniel Boone was reinterred in Frankfort. In a related development, the governor and the legislature were unwilling to purchase Chester Harding's portrait of Daniel Boone, the only one done from life.

Owsley told his last General Assembly that the approaching end of his term "excites in my breast no emotions of regret." He believed that he had carried out his duties "honestly, independently and faithfully." As to an evaluation of his administration, "More than justice I neither expect nor desire."

After leaving office, Owsley returned to private life in Boyle County. At the age of eighty, two months after the battle of Perryville, Owsley died on December 9, 1862, a forgotten man. Owsley County *was* named for William Oswley, but *before* he ran for governor.

SUGGESTED READINGS: Lucius P. Little, *Ben Hardin: His Times and Contemporaries* (1887); Jennie Chinn Morton, "William Owsley," *Register* 3(January 1905), 21–29.

STUART SEELY SPRAGUE

1848-1850
# JOHN JORDAN CRITTENDEN
1787-1863

John Jordan Crittenden was born September 10, 1787, in Woodford County, Kentucky, a few miles from Versailles, one of four sons of John and Judith Harris Crittenden. Crittenden was of Welsh descent on his father's side and of French Huguenot descent on his mother's side. In 1803 John J. Crittenden was sent to Pisgah Academy, Woodford County, to prepare for college. He continued his education at Washington College (later Washington and Lee) and completed his studies at the College of William and Mary where he graduated in 1807. Crittenden studied law in the office of George M. Bibb, a renowned jurist.

Since central Kentucky was well supplied with excellent lawyers, Crittenden began his practice in Russellville, Logan County, in the recently developed Green River country of western Kentucky. In 1809 Pres. James Madison named Ninian Edwards governor of the Illinois Territory, and Edwards appointed Crittenden attorney for the territory and aide-de-damp. In 1802 Gov. Charles Scott gave Crittenden a similar aide-de-camp position in the First Kentucky Militia. During the

War of 1812, Crittenden became aide-de-camp to Gov. Isaac Shelby and was present at the battle of the Thames, receiving from the governor a special commendation for his faithfulness in carrying out orders.

During the same period Crittenden's professional and political career advanced. His thorough knowledge of law and his oratory gained him a host of clients, and his oratory also attracted him to public service.

In 1811 Crittenden was elected to the legislature from Logan County, the first of six successive terms. When a vacancy in the United States Senate developed in 1817, the Kentucky legislature elected him to the seat from which he resigned in March 1819. Although he was the youngest member in the body, Crittenden took an active part in the affairs of the Senate, assuming immediately his lifelong role as champion of the unrepresented and the downtrodden. He introduced an amendment to provide for the reimbursement and indemnification of individuals fined under the Sedition Act of 1798.

To attract more legal business and to be at the center of political activity, Crittenden moved in 1819 to Frankfort where the federal district court and the state supreme court met. In 1825 he ran for the state legislature as a representative of Franklin County and lost, but he won the seat in a special election in 1829 and served three terms before retiring.

From 1819 to 1835, Crittenden devoted himself chiefly to his law practice. He was primarily engaged in defending the accused, and he usually won his case. He was in great demand as a defender in murder trials. In 1854 his closing speech to the jury in the murder trial of Matt F. Ward was so effective that the jury declared Ward not guilty. The verdict caused such a protest that a public meeting passed resolutions calling for Crittenden's resignation from the United States Senate.

In the presidential election of 1824, Crittenden supported Henry Clay, his candidate for the next quarter of a century. But when Clay had been eliminated and the election went to the House of Representatives, Crittenden switched to Jackson. After John Q. Adams became president, however, Crittenden supported the administration.

In 1834 Crittenden became secretary of state of Kentucky under Gov. James T. Morehead, but the next year he was again elected to the United States Senate. There he opposed Jackson's Indian and banking policies as well as Martin Van Buren's financial measures. Reelected to the Senate in 1840, he resigned in 1841 to become attorney general

55

under William Henry Harrison. However, he resigned this post after John Tyler succeeded to the presidency.

Kentucky again sent Crittenden to the Senate in 1842 to fill an unexpired term, and he was elected to a full term beginning in 1843. In 1847 Crittenden supported Zachary Taylor for the presidency on the Whig ticket instead of Clay. Crittenden resigned from the Senate in 1848 to run for governor, partly because he believed it would help Taylor carry Kentucky. He campaigned extensively in the state for both himself and Taylor. At Versailles, in one of his best efforts, Crittenden answered his Democratic opponent, Lazarus W. Powell, who charged that the Whig party was without principles or platform. Crittenden portrayed Taylor as a man whose life had been guided by principles of justice, courage, truth, and patriotism. Crittenden was elected governor over Powell by a vote of 66,860 to 57,397.

In his message to the legislature, Crittenden earnestly urged the General Assembly to call a constitutional convention because the people of the state had expressed their will on the matter. Since the people had approved a two-cent increase in taxes on each hundred dollars worth of property for the state's common school system, he called on the legislature to "let no effort be considered too great—no patience too exhausting, and no means too expensive" to cultivate the young minds of the youth of the state. Crittenden also asked the legislature to appropriate money for a comprehensive geological survey, and he called attention to the need to rebuild the penitentiary, which had been destroyed by fire. Finally, he urged the General Assembly to establish a sinking fund "for the payment of the interest and for the gradual extinction" of the public debt.

The Crittenden administration's most significant accomplishment came in the field of public education. As Speaker of the House in 1830, Crittenden had helped secure the passage of a bill authorizing local taxes for common schools. Robert J. Breckinridge, appointed state superintendent of schools the year before Crittenden took office, laid the groundwork for a public school system, and Crittenden strongly supported his efforts.

The General Assembly responded to the urgency of Crittenden's message by passing a common school law on February 26, 1849, that set up guidelines for the state superintendent of schools, school commissioners, sheriffs, and county clerks in administering the common schools. The legislature authorized the levy of a 2 percent property tax for a public school fund and provided that the proceeds from tolls on the Kentucky, Green, and Barren rivers be set aside for education. During Crittenden's administration the common school system was given a sound financial foundation.

In July 1850 Crittenden resigned as governor to accept the position of attorney general in the cabinet of Pres. Millard Fillmore. At the end of Fillmore's term, Crittenden returned to Kentucky to resume his law practice, but in 1854 he was elected for the fourth time to the United States Senate.

After the Whig party ceased to exist, he supported the Know-Nothing party in the 1850s. In 1860 Crittenden allied himself with the Constitutional Unionist party. When Lincoln was elected and the Union began to divide, the senator advanced the Crittenden Proposition on January 16, 1861. He sought to restore the Union by constitutional amendments that would extend the Missouri Compromise line to the Pacific and prohibit Congress from abolishing slavery in the District of Columbia or interfering with the interstate slave trade. These proposals, like others he made, were not accepted.

Crittenden returned to Kentucky to help keep his state in the Union. In May 1861 he presided over a border state convention that sought to mediate between the hostile parties, but the war had already begun. In June he was elected to the United States House of Representatives, and in July he secured the passage of the famed Crittenden Resolution that declared the war was not being fought for the purpose of interfering with the established institutions of the states.

In 1811 Crittenden had married Sally O. Lee, a daughter of John Lee of Woodford County. She died in 1824, and after two years of mourning he married Mrs. Maria K. Todd. In 1853 the twice-widowed statesman wed Mrs. Elizabeth Ashley. Crittenden died July 26, 1863, while he was preparing to run for reelection. He was buried at Frankfort.

Inscribed on Crittenden's tomb are these words: "For fifty years he devoted himself with inflexible integrity, consummate wisdom, and patriotic zeal, to the course and service of his native state, and of his whole country." This inscription correctly sums up his life and character.

SUGGESTED READINGS: Albert D. Kirwan, *John J. Crittenden: The Struggle for the Union* (1962); Mrs. Chapman Coleman, ed., *The Life of John J. Crittenden, with Selections from His Correspondence and Speeches* (1871), 2 vols.; Allen E. Ragan, "John J. Crittenden, 1787-1863," *FCHQ* 18(January 1944), 3-28.

VICTOR B. HOWARD

# JOHN LARUE HELM

1802-1867

John Larue Helm served two brief terms as governor of Kentucky. Elected lieutenant governor in 1848, Helm became chief executive for a mere thirteen months in 1850 when Gov. John J. Crittenden resigned to serve in the cabinet of Pres. Millard Fillmore. Then seventeen years later (1867) Helm was elected governor but died just five days after assuming office.

John L. Helm was born in Hardin County, Kentucky, near Elizabethtown, on July 4, 1802. Helm's father, George, was a prominent local farmer and politician, and his mother, Rebecca Larue, was a member of the pioneer family for which neighboring Larue County was named. After a common school education, Helm prepared to be a lawyer by studying in the offices of well-known Elizabethtown attorneys like Samuel Haycraft and Duff Green. He was admitted to the bar in 1823, and a year later was named Meade County attorney. Helm married Lucinda B. Hardin in 1830, and the couple had six daughters and five sons. One son, Ben Hardin, served as a brigadier general in the Confederate army and was killed at the battle of Chickamauga.

As an attorney and local politician, John Helm was an early and forceful advocate of railroad development, especially a north-south line through his native county. As lieutenant governor, he worked with the state legislature to secure a favorable charter for the Louisville and Nashville Railroad and four years later (1854) became the company's second president. As L&N president, he was an effective salesman of stock subscriptions along the proposed main route. Helm resigned the railroad presidency in 1860 soon after the line was completed between Louisville and Nashville.

John L. Helm became a state leader in the emerging Whig party when he was still in his twenties. From 1826 to 1849 he served in the Kentucky legislature with hardly a break, first in the House, then in the Senate; in several sessions he was selected House speaker. Years later, on the eve of the Civil War, Helm chaired a statewide meeting that advocated neutrality for Kentucky, and for the duration of the conflict he was an outspoken critic of the Lincoln administration. In 1865 Helm was returned to the state Senate, serving as chairman of the committee on federal relations, where he pushed for removal of legal proscriptions against former Confederates.

Helm first served as governor from July 31, 1850, to September 2, 1851, following Crittenden's resignation. As governor, he was a fiscal conservative who strongly opposed a legislative plan, which was later passed over his veto, to cover deficits in the state school fund by transfers from the sinking fund. As a legislator the governor had earlier backed the sinking fund as an effective instrument for orderly debt retirement. Helm warned that merger of the two funds would weaken the commonwealth's commitment to pay off its debts, as well as deny Kentuckians direct control over funds for public education through referendum.

The governor was quick, however, to commit the powers of the state to stimulate economic growth. In addition to his support for railroad building, he called for a state-sponsored survey of mineral reserves and a census of the commonwealth's agricultural and manufacturing resources. In addition, he advocated improved salaries for judges to help insure an independent judiciary, election reforms to curb widespread voting irregularities and violence at the polls, and legislation against carrying a concealed deadly weapon. Helm succeeded in getting voting reforms, but his other proposals appear to have fallen on deaf ears.

In 1867 Helm ran for governor on the Democratic ticket and defeated Sidney M. Barnes, the Republican candidate, by 90,255 votes to 33,939. Union Conservative William B. Kinkead had 13,167 votes. Helm became ill during the campaign, and the oath of office was administered at his bedside on September 3, 1867. Helm's newly appointed secretary of state read the gravely ill governor's inaugural statement at the Hardin County courthouse. In that address Helm called for an end to Civil War bitterness and promised to remove all political disabilities from former Confederates. He also charged that a radical Congress was meddling in the affairs of the states. The governor promised state protection for blacks, but strongly denounced proposals for black suffrage. Governor Helm died on September 8, 1867, just five days after his inauguration, and was buried on the family farm near Elizabethtown.

SUGGESTED READINGS: Jennie C. Morton, "Sketch of Governor John L. Helm," *Register* 3(September 1905), 11–14; General Assembly of Kentucky, *Biographical Sketch of the Honorable John L. Helm, Late Governor of Kentucky* (1868).

TOM OWEN

# LAZARUS WHITEHEAD POWELL

1812-1867

Kentucky statesmen generally favored the public school system, but few leaders supported the schools with the enthusiasm and decisiveness of Lazarus Powell. Born on October 6, 1812, in Henderson County, Powell utilized education to rise from the tobacco patches of his father's farm to the governor's mansion. Lazarus and Ann McMahon Powell, his parents, had only rudimentary learning, but they encouraged their son by financing his early training at a local school and then under a tutor in Henderson. Ambitious and studious, Lazarus was an outstanding student at St. Joseph's College in Bardstown. After graduation, he studied law with John Rowan and at Transylvania University.

Admitted to the bar in 1835, Powell returned to Henderson and practiced law with Archibald Dixon for four years. In 1837 he married Harriet Ann Jennings, who bore him three sons before her death in the ninth year of marriage. Powell was a Democrat in Whig country—most of the men in his college class were ardent Whigs, the Whig party dominated state politics, and even his law partner was Whig. It was an upset when he won his first campaign for the Kentucky House of Representatives in 1836. However, a Whig defeated him for reelection in 1838, and in 1848 as Democratic nominee for governor he lost to John J. Crittenden, 65,860 votes to 57,397.

When the Democrats nominated Powell for governor in 1851, the political balance was shifting. The Whigs had opposed the popular constitution of 1850 and were beginning to decline. The Whig nominee was Powell's friend and former law partner, Archibald Dixon, and when they canvassed the state, they stayed at the same taverns, dined together, and spoke from the same platforms. Powell persuaded his audiences with well-reasoned arguments and Dixon inspired them with the fiery rhetoric that made him the dean of criminal lawyers in western Kentucky. Powell won by 850 votes (54,613 to 53,763), the first Democrat elected governor since 1832, but the Whigs maintained control of the General Assembly.

Powell relieved periodic attacks of chronic rheumatism by hosting dinner parties and walking on crutches, but he refused to allow illness to deter him from sometimes leading and sometimes blocking the Whig assemblymen. He agreed that Kentucky should participate in the national transportation revolution, and since the state constitution prohibited additional state indebtedness, the administration vigorously encouraged private investment. After the 1853-1854 legislative session, a reporter observed: "The number of charters for turnpike and railroad companies that have been granted or amended is amazing." From 1850 to 1855 the railroad track in operation increased from 78 to 242 miles.

Transportation developments increased the demand for capital, but on that issue Powell clashed head-on with the Whigs. In spite of his contention that the existing state banks were sufficient, the assembly approved charters for several new banks, which would have greatly increased the bank notes in circulation. Vetoing the charter of the Planters and Manufacturers Bank of Kentucky in 1854, Powell condemned speculation and cautioned that excessive banking would cause inflation and threaten the state with economic depression. With this veto and others he succeeded in limiting the growth of bank capital.

Feeling their power slipping away, the Whigs determined in 1854 to continue their domination of the Kentucky delegation in the United States House of Representatives. Redistricting on the basis of the 1850 census, the legislature practiced obvious gerrymandering. The governor vetoed their plan, pointing out that the striking "want of geographic symmetry" violated the principle of equal representation and gave the Whigs dominance in eight of ten districts. The Whig plan passed over his veto and placed the Democratic party at a disadvantage in the House for the rest of the decade.

Governor Powell pointed out that Kentucky lagged behind two-thirds of the states in conducting a geological survey. In his 1853-1854 message, he empahsized that soil research would enable farmers to enrich the soil, increase production, and contribute to prosperity. "You owe it to science," he told the legislators, "to the progressive spirit of the age in which we live, to the mining, manufacturing, agricultural and other industrial interests of the state to cause this work to be commenced without delay." The Assembly approved and in selecting a state geologist Powell made his outstanding appointment. David Dale Owen, son of Robert Owen, founder of the socialistic community in New Harmony, Indiana, was the leading geologist in the Midwest. Experienced, dedicated, and sagacious, he was a rare scientist who appreciated the necessity of impressing the legislature to gain state appropriations. Owen employed Transylvania professor Robert Peter as chemist. The governor took great interest in the work and by the end of his term the survey was advancing steadily.

When Powell was elected, Robert J. Breckinridge, superintendent of public instruction since 1847, had made excellent progress in establishing a public school system. Powell stressed public education's contribution to democracy: "The surest guaranty we can have for the continuance and perpetuity of our free institutions, is the education of our children." Under Gov. John Helm, Breckinridge had secured legislative approval for using the sinking fund (for discharging the state debt) to pay the back interest on school bonds. When the act was passed over his veto, the former governor had refused to administer it. In contrast, Powell paid the amount due ($67,013) and predicted correctly that a precedent had been established. Later, he signed a bill placing before the voters in 1855 a proposed school tax increase from two cents to five cents per one hundred dollars of taxable property. It passed by a landslide—82,765 for 25,239 against—and Powell had made a significant contribution to the development of one of the two strong state school systems in the antebellum South. North Carolina was the other.

In 1858 Powell was elected to the United States Senate, but before Congress met, Pres. James Buchanan appointed him one of two commissioners to settle the difficulties with the Mormons in Utah. In the Senate, Powell upheld the union and worked vigorously for compromise. During the Civil War he condemned the government's policy of military interference in elections and political arrests. Considering him overly critical, the Kentucky General Assembly requested his resignation, and fellow Kentucky Senator Garret Davis tried in vain to have him expelled. At the end of his term in 1865 he returned to the practice of law in Henderson. In 1867 he was a contender for the United States Senate, but Garret Davis was elected. By the time of his death in Henderson on July 3, 1867, Powell's criticisms of the Lincoln administration for it violations of civil rights seemed justified, and the legislature erected a monument at his grave in Henderson and published a biographical tribute.

SUGGESTED READINGS: John D. Wright, "Robert Peter and the First Kentucky Geological Survey," *Register* 52(July 1954), 201–212; Turner W. Allen, "The Turnpike System in Kentucky: A Review of State Road Policy in the Nineteenth Century," *FCHQ* 28(July 1954), 239-259; Willard R. Jillson,

"Governoir Powell's Recommendation to the Legislature Relative to the Establishment of the First Kentucky Geological Survey," *Register* 25(May 1927), 187-189.

JAMES A. RAMAGE

1855-1859
# CHARLES SLAUGHTER MOREHEAD
1802-1868

Charles Slaughter Morehead was born on July 7, 1802, in Nelson County, the son of Charles and Margaret Slaughter Morehead. After graduating from Transylvania University with baccalaureate and law degrees, he practiced law in Christian County and then in Franklin County. In 1823 Morehead married Amanda Leavy, daughter of William Leavy of Lexington, and after her death, he married her sister, Margaret, in 1831. Charles and Margaret appreciated fine music and theater, and they delighted in receptions, dances, and parties. When he was governor, Frankfort society was illuminated with unusual gaiety. He was elected to the Kentucky House of Representatives in 1828-1829, and he served as state attorney general, 1830-1835. With Mason Brown, he published the two-volume *Digest of the Statute Laws of Kentucky* (1834). Back in the lower house, 1838-1842 and 1844, he served as speaker, 1840-1841 and 1844. As a Whig, he represented his district in the United States House of Representatives, 1847-1851.

After the Whig party died in the 1850s, Morehead, along with most Kentucky Whigs, joined the American party, claiming that it was more "union" than the Democratic party. Even though Kentucky had only a small minority of foreign-born and Roman Catholic residents concentrated in Louisville, the intolerant oratory of the campaign of 1855 appealed to the voters. In an election marred by bloody riots in Louisville, Morehead won by 69,816 votes to 65,413 for his Democratic opponent, Beverly L. Clarke, and the Americans carried both houses of the legislature. But at his inauguration Morehead proclaimed "perfect equality" for naturalized citizens.

Kentucky's public school system was growing so rapidly there was a desperate shortage of qualified teachers. Morehead responded by renewing a proposal for the establishment of state-supported teacher education at Transylvania University. In lobbying for the bill incorporating the plan, Superintendent of Public Instruction John D. Matthews appealed to sectional tension by warning that Yankee teachers were infiltrating the system and corrupting the pure Southern minds of Kentucky children. The bill passed in 1856, reorganizing Transylvania as a state school with a teachers' college. The legislature had not only provided teacher education, it had also acquired a state university to be funded with state taxes that theretofore had been regarded as revenue for the public schoiols. Kentucky was only the ninth state to fund a teachers' college, and seventy-five students soon enrolled in the program.

Two years later, when the legislature met again, great opposition to the teacher program had developed. To forestall an attack, Governor Morehead pointed out that Transylvania had no present connection with any religion and that it was above religious and political strife. He asserted that teacher training was indispensable to the public school system and that its continued support was the most vital issue of the day. But the House by 69-22 and the Senate by 20-12 withdrew funding. Opponents of the project rallied around the argument that it was illegal to use public school money for higher education.

The geological survey initiated under Governor Powell was completed and published under Morehead. Financed by private investment, road and railroad construction continued, increasing railroad mileage from 242 miles in 1855 to 568 miles in 1860. Morehead signed two new bank charters, but beginning with the charter for the Bank of Harrodsburg, he vetoed several bank bills, and others died in the General Assembly. At Thanksgiving 1857 the governor was grateful for prosperity, but reflecting on the recession of that year, he complained that commerce was in distress. In December he reported that paupers were on the increase—over $21,000 had been expended from state funds for their relief.

In 1854 the General Assembly had terminated the militia system by scheduling muster once every six years. The legislators considered the militia out of date and useless, but the governor was uncomfortable without an organization for emergencies. When the legislature refused to reorganize the militia, Morehead began furnishing arms to volunteer companies. Upon the governor's recommendation the legislature chartered the Kentucky State Agricultural Society in 1856 and appropriated funds for an annual state fair to encourage production of quality farm products.

Continuing the humanitarian reforms of the 1840s, Morehead inaugurated changes in the state prison. From 1855 to 1856 the prison population in the penitentiary in Frankfort increased from 183 to 237, and as there were only 126 cells, the statutory requirement of solitary confinement at night was impossible to administer. The prison hospital was inadequate, and the agreement with the warden was a complicated partnership that defrauded the state. Through the cooperation of the legislature, Morehead enlarged the prison to 252 cells, "dry and airy, with an iron bedstead and good bed and comfortable bedding in each." He segregated women on the upper floor, and he dreamed of the day when young offenders could be separated from hardened criminals and convicts could be rehabilitated. The legislature approved a new leasing system wherein the warden paid a fixed amount for authority to administer the prison and to receive income from convict labor.

After his term, Morehead practiced law in Louisville for two years. He attended the Washington Peace Conference in February 1861, and the Border State Convention in May 1861. His neutrality leaned toward the South, and his condemnations of the Lincoln administration led to his arrest in September 1861 and his imprisonment for four months in the North. Released in January 1862, he fled to Canada, Europe, and Mexico. After the war he lived on his plantation in Greenville, Mississippi, where he died on December 21, 1868. He was buried in the state cemetery in Frankfort.

SUGGESTED READINGS: John D. Wright, *Transylvania: Tutor to the West* (1975); Wallace B. Turner, "The Know-Nothing Movement in Kentucky," *FCHQ* 28(July 1954), 266–283; E. Merton Coulter, "The Downfall of the Whig Party in Kentucky," *Register* 23(May 1925), 162-174.

JAMES A. RAMAGE

1859-1862
# BERIAH MAGOFFIN
1815-1885

Beriah Magoffin, Kentucky's gubernatorial casualty of the Civil War, was born in Harrodsburg on April 18, 1815. His father, Beriah Magoffin, Sr., had come to the United States from Ireland; his mother, Jane McAfee Magoffin, was from one of Kentucky's pioneer families. After studying in local schools, Beriah graduated from Centre College in 1835 and from the Transylvania University law course in 1838. He began a legal practice in Jackson, Mississippi, but soon returned to

Harrodsburg in 1839. On April 21, 1840, he married Anna Nelson Shelby, a granddaughter of Isaac Shelby. They had ten children who survived infancy.

In 1840 Whig Governor Letcher appointed Magoffin police judge in Harrodsburg, despite his strong Democratic affiliation. As a consequence of his party regularity, Magoffin was a candidate for presidential elector in 1844-1856 (he was successful only in 1856), and he was a delegate to Democratic national conventions in 1848, 1856, 1860, and 1872. Elected to the Kentucky Senate in 1850, he refused nomination to the United States House of Representatives the next year. A candidate for lieutenant governor in 1855, he lost to a Know-Nothing. Nominated for governor in 1859, Magoffin defeated Joshua Bell, 76,187 to 67,283, and took office in September. His administration was dominated by the sectional crisis and the Civil War.

Magoffin's views were revealed in several letters to other governors and to editors. He accepted slavery, and he was convinced that Southern rights had been violated in the territories and in regard to fugitive slaves. While he believed in the right of secession, he hoped to prevent it through collective action. Magoffin contended that a conference of slave states could formulate demands that the North would accept as an alternative to dissolution of the Union. If those conditions were not met, he predicted that Kentucky would join the other slave states with a special convention making the decision to leave the Union.

In January 1861 Magoffin was still trying to organize a conference of border states, but his hopes of preventing secession were fading. He sought a state convention to determine Kentucky's course of action, but the Unionist majority in the legislature, fearing that secessionists might gain control, refused to call the convention. On April 15 Magoffin curtly rejected Lincoln's call for volunteers, but a week later he also rejected a Confederate call for an infantry regiment. Well aware of the state's divided sentiments, the governor participated actively in the formulation of Kentucky's policy of neutrality, which he proclaimed on May 20, 1861. But Unionist suspicion of him was so strong that his powers were steadily eroded.

Magoffin declared that his purpose was "to abide by the will of the majority of the people of the State" and to stand by the constitutions of Kentucky and of the United States as expounded by their respective supreme courts. The will of the people was clarified by summer elections in 1861. After June 20, Unionists held nine of Kentucky's ten Congressional seats, and after August 5, Unionists had majorities of

76-24 and 27-11 in the Kentucky House and Senate. The governor's veto power was thus nullified, and his position became increasingly difficult.

Magoffin's protests over violations of the state's neutrality were ignored, and in early September 1861, when opposing forces moved into the state, the legislature told him to demand the withdrawal of only the Confederate troops. When his veto was promptly overridden, Magoffin obediently issued the proclamation. His detractors were puzzled by the governor's refusal to join the exodus of pro-Confederates from the state and baffled by his denunciation of the sovereignty convention that met in Russellville in November to create a state government that was admitted into the Confederate States of America on December 10. Magoffin condemned "in unqualified terms" the actions of the "self-constituted" convention, for it did not represent the wishes of a majority of the state's citizens.

Despite such proof of his belief in majority rule, Magoffin's position continued to deteriorate. His numerous vetoes could only delay the work of the "resolution legislature," and many of his constitutional powers were taken away from him. Wartime needs led to the calling of several special sessions of the legislature, and each session saw the governor's power diminished. He and the legislative majority could agree upon such innocuous measures as a bill to allow common schools that had been disrupted in 1861 to complete their term in 1862, but they disagreed on other actions. Magoffin bitterly opposed a bill passed over his veto in March 1862 that forfeited state citizenship for anyone who was in civil or military Confederate service or who gave voluntary aid to the rebels. The 20-5 and 55-26 margins of the override were typical of such votes. Magoffin was increasingly irked by the military rule of Brig. Gen. Jerry T. Boyle who in Magoffin's opinion consistently violated the civil rights of states' righters who were not secessionists. On July 28, 1862, when the governor issued a call for another legislative session to begin on August 14, he complained, "I am without a soldier or a dollar to protect the lives, property and liberties of the people, or to enforce the laws."

The legislative majority, its suspicions of Magoffin unallayed, refused to cooperate, and the new session seemed destined to repeat the warfare of previous meetings. But delicate discussions had been underway, and on August 16 Magoffin indicated a willingness to resign if his successor, although a Unionist, was "a conservative, just man . . . conciliatory and impartial toward all law-abiding citizens." He might

67

have resigned earlier, the beleaguered executive explained, but ". . . I should have been regarded as either tacitly admitting the truth of the charges against me, or as quailing before the threats of my enemies." No formal charges had been filed, and he had not quailed. But Lt. Gov. Linn Boyd had died in 1859, and Speaker of the Senate John F. Fisk, next in line of succession, was not acceptable to Magoffin. As a result of the negotiations, on August 16 Fisk resigned as Speaker, James F. Robinson was elected Speaker, and Magoffin announced that he would resign as of ten o'clock on the morning of August 18. On that historic Monday, Robinson was sworn in as governor and Fisk was immediately reelected Speaker.

Beriah Magoffin returned to his farm and his lucrative legal practice at Harrodsburg. Astute real estate investments in Chicago made him wealthy. He remained interested in politics, and he served one postwar term, 1867-1869, in the Kentucky House. Magoffin urged Kentucky to accept the results of the war, ratify the Thirteenth Amendment, and grant civil rights to the blacks. He died at home on February 28, 1885, and was buried in the Harrodsburg cemetery.

SUGGESTED READINGS: E.M. Coulter, *The Civil War and Readjustment in Kentucky* (1926); Michael T. Dues, "Governor Beriah Magoffin of Kentucky," *FCHQ* 40(January 1966), 22–28; Lowell H. Harrison, "Governor Magoffin and the Secession Crisis," *Register* 72(April 1974), 91-110.

LOWELL H. HARRISON

1861-1862 CONFEDERATE

# GEORGE W. JOHNSON
1811-1862

George W. Johnson, the first governor of Confederate Kentucky, was born near Georgetown in Scott County on May 27, 1811. His parents, Maj. William Johnson and Betsy Payne Johnson, were of Virginia heritage, and his paternal grandparents were among Kentucky's early pioneers. George was educated at local schools and at Transylvania University where he received the A.B. degree in 1829, the LL.B. in 1832, and the M.A. in 1833. In 1833 he married Ann Viley, daughter of Capt. Willa Viley, a wealthy farmer and horse breeder. They had ten children, seven of whom lived to adulthood. After briefly practicing law in Georgetown, Johnson decided that he preferred farming, and the young couple moved to a farm adjacent to Captain Viley's holding. The farm prospered, and Johnson later acquired a thousand-acre cotton plantation in Arkansas. He was renowned in both states for his genial hospitality.

Johnson was not politically ambitious, but he accepted election to the state House of Representatives in 1838, 1839, and 1840, and in 1852 and 1860 he was a Democratic candidate for presidential elector. By the mid-1850s he was convinced that the Old Union was being destroyed by such radical groups as the abolitionists and the Republicans. A wealthy slaveholder himself, Johnson saw slavery as a state issue, not as a national concern. He supported John C. Breckinridge for president in 1860, but Johnson did not see the election of Lincoln as grounds for secession since the Republicans would not control Congress or the Supreme Court. As secession progressed, Johnson argued that if Kentucky joined the Confederacy the forces would be so equal in strength as to preclude recourse to war.

Johnson played an active role in Kentucky politics in 1861, and he went to Richmond to secure Jefferson Davis's promise that the Confederacy would respect Kentucky's neutrality. When that tortured status ended in early September, Johnson was so closely identified with the Southern cause that he fled the state to avoid arrest. Soon afterward he joined Gen. Simon Bolivar Buckner in Bowling Green as a volunteer aide. His age and a crippled arm appeared to preclude active military service.

George Johnson and other Kentucky Confederates deluded themselves into believing that the Unionist government in Frankfort did not represent the wishes of a majority of the state's citizens. Unwilling to accept their embarrassing status, they held a meeting in Russellville on October 29-30. Johnson introduced the key resolutions and chaired the committee that formulated the report. Citing the inherent revolutionary power of a free people, it called for a sovereignty convention to meet in Russellville on November 18 for the purpose of "severing forever our connection with the Federal Government, and to adopt such measures, either by the adoption of a provisional government or otherwise, as in their judgment will give full and ample protection to the citizens in their persons and property, and secure to them the blessings of constitutional government." Johnson was on the Committee of Ten that made arrangements for the convention.

George Johnson directed the work of the sovereignty convention that denied the legitimacy of the Frankfort government and declared Kentucky "a free and independent State." The provisional government that was established consisted of a governor and a ten-man council, one from each congressional district. Other officers were to be appointed, and Bowling Green was selected as the temporary capital of Kentucky. The convention voted unanimously for Johnson as governor. One of his first acts was to request admission to the Confederate States of America; this was granted on December 10, 1861.

Isolated from his beloved family, during the late fall and winter Governor Johnson labored under impossible conditions to create a viable government. His jurisdiction extended only as far as Confederate troops advanced, and Unionist sentiment was strong within the Confederate sector. Johnson attempted to raise troops, but with much of the state under federal control he was not able to reach Kentucky's assigned quota. He was even less successful in raising revenue and securing weapons, and his government had to depend upon Confederate largess for most of its support. Johnson appointed numerous local officials to replace Unionists, but their impact was minimal, for the Confederate occupation of southern Kentucky ended in mid-February 1862. Johnson liked and respected Gen. Albert Sidney Johnston and worked closely with him in the unsuccessful effort to establish the Confederate presence in southern Kentucky.

When General Johnston abandoned Bowling Green and his southern Kentucky line, Governor Johnson and the council joined the retreat across Tennessee. A journalist reported the capital of Kentucky as "now being located in a Sibley tent" near Johnston's headquarters. When Johnston attacked the Union army at Shiloh on April 6, 1862, George Johnson served as a volunteer aide to Gen. John C. Breckinridge and Col. Robert P. Trabue. After his horse was killed under him, the Governor fought on foot with Company E of the Fourth Kentucky Infantry. That evening he insisted on being sworn in as a private.

On Monday afternoon, April 7, Johnson was hit by bullets in the right thigh and abdomen. He lay unattended on the battlefield until the next day when he was recognized by Union Gen. Alexander McDowell McCook, a fellow Mason. Despite every possible attention, Johnson died aboard a hospital ship on April 8. Unionist friends had his body sent home, and he was buried at Georgetown.

SUGGESTED READINGS: Lowell H. Harrison, "George W. Johnson and Richard Hawes: The Governors of Confederate Kentucky," *Register* 79(Winter 1981), 3-39; "Letters of George W. Johnson," *Register* 40(October 1942), 337-52.

LOWELL H. HARRISON

# RICHARD HAWES

1797-1877

When George Johnson died, the council of the Confederate Provisional Government elected Richard Hawes as his successor. The son of Richard and Clara Walker Hawes, Richard was born in Caroline County, Virginia, on February 6, 1797. The family moved to Kentucky in late 1810, but Richard may have attended the academic department at Transylvania University even earlier. The youth attended Samuel Wilson's school in Jessamine County and may have taken some law courses at Transylvania, but he became an attorney in 1818 after reading law with Charles Humphreys and Robert Wickliffe. In that same year he married Hetty Morrison Nicholas, youngest daughter of the late George Nicholas. They had two children; neither survived Hawes.

In 1824 Hawes moved from Lexington to Winchester where he practiced law and was part owner of a rope walk and bagging factory. In 1843 he moved to Paris where he enjoyed modest prosperity. Henry Clay was his idol, and Hawes was an active Whig. He was elected to the state House of Representatives in 1828, 1829, and 1836, and from 1837 to 1841 he represented Clay's famed Ashland district in Congress. When the Whig party dissolved in the 1850s, Hawes became a Democrat. He supported James Buchanan for president in 1856 and John C. Breckinridge for that position in 1860.

Hawes had an active role in the confused events of 1861 that preceded Kentucky's entrance into the Civil War. He was one of three Southern Rights members of the six-man committee that recommended state neutrality. By late July he advocated recognition of the Confederacy and an equitable division of the nation's assets and liabilities, although he still hoped for reunion.

Hawes fled the state in September to avoid certain arrest. Despite his age and lack of military experience, he secured a commission as major and an appointment as brigade commissary in Gen. Humphrey Marshall's command in eastern Kentucky. Because of this assignment Hawes was not involved in the formation of the Provisional Government, and he declined appointment as state auditor. As commissary, he performed adequately under difficult circumstances, but he sometimes upset his superiors by sending military suggestions directly to

71

Richmond authorities. General Marshall expressed no regrets when on January 27, 1862, he recommended acceptance of Hawes's resignation.

However, the difficulty in finding a successor and Hawes's illness with typhoid fever delayed his departure. It was probably during his convalescence that he learned of his election as Johnson's successor. Hawes joined the exiled government during the late spring of 1862 as it resided with the Kentucky troops in the Army of Tennessee. A Confederate invasion of Kentucky was under consideration, and on August 27 the council requested Hawes to go to Richmond to urge that action upon President Davis. He was also to arrange for the use of any funds that might be appropriated upon Kentucky's behalf. The governor predicted that his government would soon exercise control over most of the state, but Davis was noncommittal in his responses.

Delayed by this trip, Hawes and the other members of the state government did not leave Chattanooga until September 18, well behind the armies of Braxton Bragg and E. Kirby Smith. When Hawes caught up with Bragg in Kentucky, he found the general eager to install the Provisional Government in Frankfort so the Confederate conscription act could be put into effect. Hawes was installed on October 4, 1862, in an elaborate ceremony. Accepting at face value Bragg's statements about holding the state, the governor expounded upon the ways in which he would bring Kentucky fully into the Confederacy.

But federal troops were already advancing in force, and the members of the Provisional Government were soon reported to have left Frankfort "in dignified haste." When the Confederate armies withdrew from the state after the indecisive battle of Perryville, the Provisional Government left the state for the second and last time.

In exile for the rest of the war, Hawes and the other members of his administration spent most of their time with the Army of Tennessee, although the governor made several trips to Richmond in futile efforts to secure another military advance into the Bluegrass state. They tried to fulfill the functions of their offices, but Hawes admitted that he was "almost powerless." He was dealt a severe blow in 1864 when Davis ruled that the $1 million secretly appropriated in August 1861 to assist Kentucky in maintaining her neutrality could not be used once Kentucky was admitted into the Confederacy. Hawes made frequent suggestions concerning military affairs and personnel, but there is no evidence that his recommendations were effective in determining military policy.

Governor Hawes attracted considerable attention when he publicly chastised Bragg for saying that "cowardly Kentuckians" who had refused to join his army had been largely responsible for his 1862 failure to hold the state. Admitting that some wealthy Kentuckians "loved their estates more than their liberties," Hawes held Bragg responsible for the debacle. Bragg should have defeated Don Carlos Buell before Buell ever reached Louisville; Bragg should have concentrated his entire army at Perryville; Bragg should have fought again after Perryville; Bragg should not have abandoned Kentucky where he did. Hawes reflected the opinions of ranking Kentucky officers who could not be as free as the governor in criticizing the general they hated.

When the Confederacy collapsed in the spring of 1865 and the exiled Provisional Government quietly expired, Richard Hawes returned to Paris and resumed his legal career. In 1866 he was elected county judge of Bourbon County; he was reelected without campaigning in 1870 and 1874. In January 1869 he declared void the apprenticeship contracts used by the Freedmen's Bureau on the grounds that the act applied only to states that had been in rebellion. In 1866 Hawes also became master commissioner of the circuit and common pleas courts, a position he held until his death on May 25, 1877, at his Paris home. He continued to take an active interest in local and state Democratic politics until his death, and as late as 1871 he was mentioned as a possible candidate for governor.

SUGGESTED READINGS: Lowell H. Harrison, "George W. Johnson and Richard Hawes: The Governors of Confederate Kentucky," *Register* 79(Winter 1981), 3-39. A number of his wartime letters are in *The War of the Rebellion: A Compilation of the Official Records of the Union and Confederate Armies* (128 vols., 1880-1901), especially Series I, vols. 4, 7, 16, 20, 33, and 52.

LOWELL H. HARRISON

1862-1863
# JAMES F. ROBINSON
1800-1882

Few Kentucky governors entered office under as delicate and precarious conditions as did James F. Robinson. By the summer of 1862 when he assumed the reins of government in Frankfort, Kentuckians already had cast their lot with the Union, not the Confederacy. But pro-

Southern sentiment remained strong as swarms of Kentuckians headed southward to enlist in the Confederate army. Kentucky was a state under siege, externally and internally. It writhed in pain over the causes of the Brothers' War. The right to own slaves, the superiority of the Caucasian over the Negro, a belief in state sovereignty—most white Kentuckians adhered to these principles no less than citizens in neighboring states that joined the Confederacy. The Commonwealth was pulled apart by loyalties North and South. Families were divided over the question. But cool heads prevailed in Kentucky. In the tradition of Henry Clay and John J. Crittenden, its leaders opted for the status of a loyal border state. The Unionist legislature elected in 1861 took steps—loyalty oaths, fines, penalties—to discourage support of the Confederacy. It overrode the vetoes of Gov. Beriah Magoffin, the openly pro-Southern governor elected in 1859 on the Democratic ticket. By the summer of 1862 Kentuckians identified Magoffin with all the woes of their troubled state.

Magoffin was blamed, for example, for Confederate infiltration on the one hand and for the abuses of the state's Union defenders on the other. Stripped of his control over the state militia and silenced by his political opponents, Magoffin decided to step down, but only if his hand-picked successor, Senator James F. Robinson, could replace him. With the lieutenant governorship vacant (Linn Boyd had died in office), Speaker of the Senate John F. Fisk was heir to the governorship. But Magoffin rejected Fisk, favoring a candidate who "would be a conservative, just man, of high position and character, and [one whose] policy would be conciliatory and impartial toward all law-abiding citizens." All agreed that the sixty-one-year-old Robinson, a Scott County native, fit the bill. But for Robinson to be next in line of succession, Fisk would have to resign as speaker and Robinson be elected to replace him. On August 16, 1862, this circuitous political strategy went into effect. Fisk resigned, Robinson was inserted in his place, and Magoffin agreed to step down effective August 18. In resigning, Magoffin hoped that his successor would "be more successful than I have been in protecting all classes . . . in their rights under the constitution and laws."

Governor Robinson's broad appeal stemmed from his reputation as a moderate conservative. Born on October 4, 1800, the son of Jonathan and Jane Black Robinson, he attended Forest Hill Academy and graduated from Transylvania University in 1818. After reading law, Robinson entered the Kentucky bar and became a respected and successful lawyer-farmer in Georgetown. In 1851, declaring himself a Whig and supporter of the principles of Henry Clay, Robinson ran unopposed for the Kentucky Senate seat representing Scott and Fayette counties. He served only one term. During the secession crisis, Robinson favored the Crittenden Compromise, opposed war, and urged Kentuckians to remain calm. Yet he realized that the state could not remain neutral in an internecine struggle. In 1861 Robinson recaptured his senate seat, this time as a Democrat, in a close contest with James B. Beck. He served briefly (September 3-5, 1861) as speaker and was reelected to that post on August 16, 1862. Two days later Robinson was sworn in as Magoffin's successor and completed his term of office.

Robinson inherited seemingly insurmountable difficulties as governor. By late summer 1862 the Commonwealth remained divided in loyalties and was subjected to invasion not only by Union and Confederate troops, but by roaming bands of guerrillas as well. Federal troops wreaked havoc on the state's civil affairs. Military arrests, confiscation of property, and interference with Kentucky's slave population outraged many. As if these uncertainties were not grave enough, just weeks after Robinson took office, the state was invaded by Confederate forces as well as bands of irregulars whose "outrages . . . are a disgrace to the age and to civilized warfare." Throughout his brief administration, Robinson struggled to protect Kentuckians who resided in counties bordering Confederate Virginia and Tennessee.

To defend her citizens more effectively, Robinson explained, Kentucky needed to increase her sources of revenue. The dislocation brought on by war disrupted the collecting of tax monies by sheriffs. With the added revenues that he requested, Robinson hoped to revive the moribund Kentucky militia. Governor Robinson also expressed concern over the ruinous effect the war had upon education within the Commonwealth. He urged the legislature to investigate the condition of schools within the state, especially in the war-ravaged districts. The governor also implored legislators to take advantage of the Lincoln administration's offer to donate public land for an agricultural and mechanical college.

Maintaining harmonious federal/state relations proved to be Robinson's foremost challenge as governor. He noted with pride that by January 1, 1863, his state already had sent fifty-one regiments— 44,000 soldiers—to the United States army. This was a remarkable accomplishment, he explained, because Kentuckians remained "to a considerable extent divided in reference to the rebellion." These troops fought bravely, from Mill Springs to Shiloh, recalled Robinson. But despite Kentucky's loyalty, the governor lamented the shabby treatment accorded her by the federal government and her sister loyal states.

Specifically, Governor Robinson objected to the attitude of federal officials that Kentucky was disloyal. This led them repeatedly, he charged, to violate the civil and property rights of Kentuckians. He condemned implementation of martial law and the suspension of the writ of habeas corpus. Farms were destroyed, provisions seized, forage collected, and commodities impounded. Such "oppressive and inexcusable" actions, Robinson said, underscored the philosophy of Lincoln's administration: ". . . that *military necessity* is not to be measured by *Constitutional* limits, but must be the judge of the extent of its powers." "If military necessity is not to be measured by Constitutional limits," warned Robinson, "we are no longer a free people."

Robinson complained most bitterly against the army's policy of protecting runaway slaves and the Emancipation Proclamation. Slaves, he insisted, were private property protected by state laws. By luring blacks away from Kentucky's farms, the army was both violating state statutes and inviting servile insurrection. Robinson described the Negro as "the creature of superstitious ignorance and savage cruelty" who, under Kentucky masters, is "gradually emerging from his low estate to one of comprehension of the true principles of the Christian religion and human civilization." Emancipation, according to Robinson, would result either in the reversion of the blacks to savagery or to their annihilation by whites. He charged that Lincoln had "lent too facile an ear to the schemes of abolition partisan leaders, who have . . . blinded his better judgment, alarmed his fears." The governor urged Kentucky to resist all emancipation schemes, to hold fast, "not abate one jot or tittle of her opposition to Secession or to Abolition."

The Emancipation Proclamation, of course, never took effect in Kentucky. But the outrage it engendered within the state was an accurate measure of Kentuckians' fears of federal interference in racial and political matters. By late 1863 another volatile question, the recruitment of black troops in Kentucky, dominated state politics. In the August 1863 gubernatorial race Robinson supported his successor, Union Democrat Thomas E. Bramlette. According to historian William B. Hesseltine, Robinson's move to disfranchise Kentucky's Southern sympathizers smoothed Bramlette's victory. The issues that plagued Robinson during his thirteen months as governor, especially the nature of federal/state relations, would dominate Bramlette's administration. On final evaluation, Robinson was far less outspoken against the federal government than was his successor. A transitional figure between Magoffin and Bramlette, Robinson advanced the Union cause during one of Kentucky's most crucial hours. Once the state firmly supported the Union war effort, Robinson began to raise constitutional questions that became more heated and controversial under Bramlette.

After leaving Frankfort in September 1863, Robinson abandoned politics. He grew increasingly wary of Lincoln, and supported Mc-Clellan in the 1864 presidential campaign. He retired to Cardome, a three-hundred-acre farm in Scott County. Governor Robinson continued to practice law, served as president of the Farmers' Bank of Georgetown, and chaired the Georgetown College Board of Trustees. He died October 31, 1882, and was buried at Georgetown.

SUGGESTED READINGS: "Notes Concerning the Life and Death of Governor James F. Robinson," *Register* 5(January 1907), 14-22; Lowell H. Harrison, *The Civil War in Kentucky* (1975); "Message of Governor James F. Robinson to the Senate and House of Representatives, January 8, 1863," *Journal of the House of Representatives of the Commonwealth*, 1861-1863, 2 vols. (Frankfort, 1861, 1863), 2, 1111-1127.

JOHN DAVID SMITH

1863-1867
# THOMAS ELLIOTT BRAMLETTE
1817-1875

Thomas Elliott Bramlette was born on January 3, 1817, in Cumberland (now Clinton) County, Kentucky, the son of Col. Ambrose S. and Sarah Bramlette. He received a common school education. Characterized as able, industrious, and honest, he began the study of law, was admitted to the bar in 1837, and soon developed a prosperous practice. In September 1837 he married Sallie Travis, by whom he had two children, Thomas and Corinne. Following his wife's death in 1872, he married Mrs. Mary E. Graham Adams in 1874. Emulating his father, he was elected to the legislature in 1841, but after only one term returned to his legal practice. In 1848 John J. Crittenden named Bramlette commonwealth attorney. Resigning in 1850, he moved his law practice to Columbia, where in 1856 he was elected judge of the Sixth Judicial District. Judge Bramlette's decisions were rarely reversed in the Court of Appeals.

With the outbreak of the Civil War, Bramlette declared for the Union. Receiving a commission as a colonel in the Union army, he resigned his judgeship to raise the Third Kentucky Volunteer Infantry. However, in 1862 President Lincoln appointed him United States district attorney for Kentucky, and he moved to Louisville. In 1863 Bramlette was commissioned a major general and, while organizing his division, was nominated by the Union Democrats for governor. He was elected over his regular Democrat opponent, Charles A. Wickliffe by 68,422 to 17,503. At his inauguration on September 1, 1863, Bramlette declared his intention to "affiliate with the loyal men North and South whose object and policy is to PRESERVE the UNION *and the* CONSTITUTION. . . ." Addressing the legislature in December, the governor declared that the state had fulfilled its quota for the Union army and that Kentucky stood "ready to give yet more, even to the last dollar, if needed, to defend our government." Bramlette also expressed his concern over the increased violence in the state caused by bands of guerrillas and bushwackers. On January 4, 1864, Bramlette issued a proclamation declaring that Rebel sympathizers would be held responsible for all guerrilla raids. If a loyal citizen were seized, five Rebel sympathizers would be arrested as hostages for the safety and return of the loyal citizen. At his insistence the legislature passed a stringent law that provided that anyone aiding or abetting guerrillas could be imprisoned and fined up to one thousand dollars.

Kentuckians had taken exception to the Emancipation Proclamation, but when Gen. Jeremiah T. Boyle ordered the recruitment of Negro soldiers, Kentuckians became irate. To avoid a confrontation, Bramlette went to Washington where he secured a pledge that Negroes would not be recruited unless Kentucky failed to meet her quota. But hardly had the governor returned before Boyle's successor, Gen. Stephen Burbridge, ordered the enlistment of all ablebodied Negroes. Bramlette was furious: "If you require a soldier we offer you a Kentuckian. Will nothing but a negro satisfy?" Although his formal proclamation called for Kentuckians to remain calm and to offer no resistance, Bramlette continued his opposition.

Meanwhile the legislature attempted to elect Bramlette to Congress, but he declined. When the Kentucky delegation to the National

78

Democratic Convention was instructed to vote for Gen. George B. McClellan for president and Bramlette for vice-president he again asked that his name be withdrawn. However, Bramlette actively supported McClellan throughout the campaign.

On July 5, 1864, President Lincoln suspended the writ of habeas corpus in Kentucky. An angry governor protested, declaring that innocent people would suffer as a result of it. Further antagonism toward the federal government resulted when General Burbridge interfered in the election of the appellate judge, banished President of the Senate Richard T. Jacob from the state, and used federal troops to "neutralize" the polls during the presidential election of 1864. As a result of this hostility toward the federal government, McClellan carried the state.

As the legislature reconvened in January 1865, Bramlette again condemned the recruitment of Negroes, the violation of state law by General Burbridge, and the "arrest, imprisonment, and banishment of loyal citizens without a hearing." He urged greater support for schools as well as the asylum for the insane, and the ratification of the Thirteenth Amendment. Stating that he considered slavery to be "irrevocably doomed," Bramlette urged the General Assembly to ratify the amendment but also to insist upon compensation for lost property. However, the legislature ignored his plea. After authorizing the building of turnpikes and allowing the school districts to levy special taxes, the legislature responded to his request to establish an agricultural and mechanical college in Kentucky.

Hardly had the legislature adjourned when news arrived of President Lincoln's assassination and the elevation of Andrew Johnson to the presidency. Governor Bramlette proclaimed a day of fasting, humiliation, and prayer. The reconvened legislature passed resolutions on the death of Lincoln and requested the new president to end martial law and to withdraw all Negro troops from the state.

Although General Burbridge had been replaced by Gen. John M. Palmer, conflicts between state and federal authorities continued, particularly when Palmer attempted to break the institution of slavery by "spiriting" Negroes out of the state. As the August election approached, Bramlette issued a proclamation to all election officers declaring that every "white male citizen" twenty-one years of age and two years a resident could vote, provided that he had not expatriated himself. The Democrats won an outstanding victory: They gained control of both houses, captured five of the nine congressional seats, and elected the state treasurer. To mollify Kentucky, President Johnson in the fall of 1865 declared an end to martial law and restored the writ of habeas corpus.

As the legislature gathered in December 1865, Bramlette in a special message announced that he would grant a general pardon to all indicted in the courts for treason or acts of war within Kentucky against the United States. The legislature validated his action on January 13, 1866. In the interim, the Thirteenth Amendment was ratified, and because of atrocities committed against freedmen in the state, Gen. Oliver O. Howard announced the extension of the Freedmen's Bureau to Kentucky. A furious governor declared that the bureau "should be firmly met and resisted in every legal form." The legislature passed seven acts conferring certain civil rights upon Negroes, relieving them of their legal disabilities as slaves, subjecting them to the same punishments as whites, and authorizing schools for their education. Not only did the governor oppose the Fourteenth Amendment, claiming that it destroyed the "just balance of power between the state and the National Government," he objected strenuously to the Fifteenth Amendment as well. The legislators rejected both amendments and in response to the Fifteenth Amendment insisted that Kentuckians were "unalterably opposed to negro suffrage."

In his last address to the legislature, Bramlette noted the unusual prosperity of the state. A change in the labor system had occurred, courts were now open, and in general Kentuckians were law-abiding citizens. The governor then urged the legislature to amend the criminal code to make punishments fit the degree of criminality, to establish a House of Correction for youth to prevent them from becoming hardened criminals, to make provision for asylums for Negroes, to revise the laws in reference to blacks "to remove . . . unreasoning fanaticism," to encourage the immigration of "a superior class of laborers," to open up the mineral resources of eastern Kentucky, and to build turnpikes through bond issues. He was particularly pleased to report that the Agricultural and Mechanical College had been established at Lexington.

At the inauguration of Gov. John L. Helm at Elizabethtown, Bramlette gave an overview of his governorship, noting that when he had taken office, civil war had ravaged Kentucky, but now the state was prosperous, the percentage of crime had declined, and the state's debt had been reduced by over $5.8 million. He closed his address by urging Kentuckians to abandon their sectional hatred, for "a common fate, for weal or woe, unites us in a common destiny."

Upon retirement, Bramlette returned to Louisville where he re-established his law practice. He became a patron of many charitable organizations, especially of the Louisville Public Library. However, after a brief illness, he died on January 12, 1875.

Thomas E. Bramlette was a masterful politician who was not above resorting to election manipulation if necessary. Regardless, Bramlette provided strong leadership during a time when the state was divided in its sympathies between the North and the South. While he was a strong Union man, he was not a sycophant. Throughout his governor-ship Bramlette continued to oppose what he called "federal usurpa-tion" of the rights of the states, not merely for Kentucky, but for the Southern states as well. He attempted to resolve the labor problem by encouraging immigration into the state. He sought to stimulate eastern Kentucky by opening up its rich mineral resources. While he was anx-ious to restore harmony to Kentucky by relieving former Confederates of their disabilities, his reasons were partially political, for he hoped to attract them into the Democratic party. By pardoning all individuals within Kentucky who had been indicted for treason or acts of war against the United States, he released many unsavory characters who would be a source of violence in the coming decade. Perhaps his great-est accomplishment was his sponsorship of the Agricultural and Me-chanical College that was established in Lexington.

SUGGESTED READINGS: "Governor Thomas E. Bramlette," *Register* 5 (January 1907), 27-28; E. Merton Coulter, *The Civil War and Readjustment in Kentucky* (1926).

ROSS A. WEBB

1867-1871
# JOHN WHITE STEVENSON
1812-1886

John White Stevenson was born at Richmond, Virginia, on May 4, 1812, the only child of Andrew and Mary White Stevenson. Mary Stevenson died giving birth to John, while his father, Andrew, rose to prominence as a United States congressman during the son's child-hood. The elder Stevenson later served as minister to Great Britain under Martin Van Buren. John Stevenson was educated by private tu-tors in Richmond and Washington, D.C., and in 1832 was graduated from the University of Virginia. After reading law under a cousin, the young attorney moved to Vicksburg, Mississippi, and in 1841 to Covington, Kentucky. Two years later, he married Sibella Winston of nearby Newport. They had five children, Sally C., Mary W., Judith W., Samuel W., and John W. Stevenson.

In Kentucky, Stevenson quickly became involved in Democratic politics. In 1845 he was elected to the first of two successive terms in the Kentucky House of Representatives, and he was a delegate to the 1849 state constitutional convention. In 1848, 1852, and 1856, Stevenson was a delegate to the Democratic national party convention. Just before the Civil War (1857-1861), he was elected to two terms in the United States House of Representatives where he argued for Kansas statehood under the Lecompton Constitution and for the Crittenden plan for preserving the Union. He was defeated for reelection in 1860. In the 1860 presidential race Stevenson backed his close friend, John C. Breckinridge. In 1865 he was a delegate to the National Union convention in Philadelphia.

John W. Stevenson was installed as lieutenant governor on September 8, 1867, having been elected on a pro-Andrew Johnson ticket. Just five days later, he became Kentucky's chief executive when the new governor, John L. Helm, died. At a special election in August 1868 Stevenson was elected governor for the remaining three-year term by 115,560 to 26,605 over Republican R. Tarvin Baker. In February 1871, however, he resigned the governorship to enter the United States Senate.

Throughout his tenure as governor, Stevenson wrestled with the problem of uncontrolled mob violence in a state sharply divided by racial antipathies and Civil War hatreds. A month after assuming office, in 1867, Stevenson dispatched the state militia to several central Kentucky counties to quell renegade bands. The governor summoned troops to the same area again in 1869; the following year, when blacks were first allowed to vote in the state, he warned that violence against the freedmen would not be tolerated. That time, however, he deferred to local authorities for the preservation of order, only offering a reward for the arrest of perpetrators of election-related violence against blacks once it had occurred.

Governor Stevenson strongly opposed efforts by the federal government to interfere with state policies toward former Confederates or blacks. In an early address to the legislature he condemned Congress for failing to seat Kentucky's entire legislative delegation—several members of the group had been charged with having Confederate sympathies. In 1868 the governor complained that federal attempts to protect and expand the rights of blacks was a violation of the rights of the states. Stevenson favored the immediate removal of political disabilities from former Confederates and remained silent when the state legislature: refused to ratify the Fifteenth Amendment, conspired to prevent blacks from voting by altering local town boundaries and changing election dates, and defeated a proposal that would have allowed black testimony against whites.

Public education in Kentucky moved dramatically forward during the Stevenson administration. The governor strongly supported a successful referendum that levied an additional tax for school purposes. School funds were raised, however, on a racially segregated basis, and the meager assets of most blacks yielded little revenue for their education. In 1870 the legislature complied with Stevenson's request to establish a state bureau of education.

In an era of escalating expenses and fixed revenues Governor Stevenson took steps in 1870 to avoid an impending fiscal crisis. He ordered a formal study of state finances and declared that the state should cease covering its short-term indebtedness with bonds. He intensified his effort to collect Kentucky's Civil War claims against the federal government—an effort that was partially successful. Stevenson also pressed for the creation of a state bureau of immigration and statistics to stimulate interest in the state. His proposal was killed, however, by the legislature in 1870. The governor did persuade the lawmakers to begin important reforms in the state's prisons and asylums.

In late 1869, Governor Stevenson became embroiled in a major political controversy when he charged two of Kentucky's congressmen with having endorsed Stephen G. Burbridge for a federal post in the Grant administration. Burbridge, a northern Kentuckian, had been vilified for his alleged heavy-handedness while serving as the Union military commander in his home state during the Civil War. The governor, apparently desiring a United States Senate seat, sought to embarrass major contenders for the post with his charge that they had been soft toward Republican "radicals" like Burbridge. Stevenson was elected senator by the legislature for a term beginning in March 1871.

In Washington he was politically conservative, opposing federal spending on internal improvements and favoring a strict interpretation of the United States Constitution. In 1877 Stevenson returned to Kentucky to practice law and to teach at the Cincinnati Law School.

83

He remained interested in politics, however, and was chosen chairman of the Democratic party's national convention at Cincinnati in 1880. Four years later, he served as president of the American Bar Association. Governor Stevenson, an active Episcopalian, died in Covington on August 10, 1886, and was buried at Cincinnati, Ohio.

SUGGESTED READINGS: *American Annual Cyclopedia and Register*, vols. 7-10 (1867-1871); Jennie C. Morton, "Governor John W. Stephenson [*sic*]," *Register* 5(May 1907), 13-15; George Lee Willis, *Kentucky Democracy* (1935) 3 vols.

TOM OWEN

## 1871-1875
# PRESTON HOPKINS LESLIE
## 1819-1907

Preston Hopkins Leslie was born on March 8, 1819, in Clinton (then Wayne) County, Kentucky, the second son of Vachel and Sally Hopkins Leslie. Raised on a farm, the boy received a limited education. He worked at many occupations (stagecoach driver, laborer, ferryman, and store clerk) before studying law under Judge Rice Maxey. Admitted to the bar on October 10, 1840, Leslie became deputy clerk of Clinton County court. In 1841 he moved to Tompkinsville, the seat of Monroe County, where he practiced law and farmed. In 1842 he was elected county attorney. An ardent admirer of Henry Clay, he entered politics as a Whig and was elected to the legislature in 1844. He lost his bid for the state Senate in 1846 by one vote, but was elected to that body in 1850 where he served until 1855. With the death of Clay, like so many Southern Whigs, Leslie became a Democrat. In 1859 he moved to Glasgow in Barren County where he achieved a reputation for "sound judgment and good common sense."

Leslie was married twice: in 1841 to Louisa Black of Monroe County by whom he had seven children (Martha, Bedford, Sarah, Joseph, Valera, Jerry, and Evans) and, upon her death in 1858, to Mrs. Mary Kuykendall of Boone County, Missouri, in 1859, by whom he had three children (Isabel, Robert, and Emily).

By 1861 Leslie had acquired land and slaves and was relatively prosperous. Ambitious, he secured land in Texas and in December set out for his new property, accompanied by his eldest son, twenty-six slaves, and a large part of his possessions. After establishing his household, he returned to Kentucky, leaving his Texas estate in the hands of his son.

Before the Civil War, Leslie was known as a "strong Union man," but with the outbreak of the conflict Leslie's sympathies were with the South. However, he did not believe that the South should secede, but rather should negotiate its differences. Leslie refused military service and pursued his law practice and his farming.

With the end of the war, Leslie again became active in politics, and in 1867 he was elected to the state Senate where he was chosen president. When Gov. John W. Stevenson was elected by the General Assembly to the United States Senate in February 1871, Leslie as president of the Senate became acting governor.

As the Democrats convened to select a gubernatorial candidate in May 1871, the party was divided into Bourbons, Standpatters, and New Departure Democrats. Since Leslie had objected to the Fourteenth and Fifteenth amendments as well as the Southern Railroad bill, his candidacy was opposed by Henry Watterson, editor of the Louisville *Courier-Journal*. Despite Watterson's efforts, Leslie was nominated with a vague, reactionary platform. The Republicans chose a former Whig and Louisville lawyer, John M. Harlan, and drafted a rather progressive platform. Harlan proved an able campaigner, and as a result Leslie began voicing New Departure principles. His supporters argued that Leslie was "sober, conservative, and safe," thereby winning over the state's tobacco and railroad interests. The vote in this first gubernatorial election with Negro suffrage was one of the largest in the state's history: Leslie received 126,089 votes to 89,083 for Harlan.

In his inaugural address at Frankfort on September 5, 1871, Leslie insisted that he would ask the legislature for increased appropriations for schools and internal improvements, as well as for laws admitting Negro testimony into the courts, reforming the system of revenue collection, and ending the violence that troubled the state. However, when the General Assembly met in December, its members were more concerned with the Southern Railroad bill than with Leslie's proposals. This bill would permit the building of a railroad, backed primarily by Cincinnati capital, which would run through central Kentucky into Tennessee where it would connect with thousands of miles of Southern railroad. This proposed railroad would challenge the monopoly of Southern trade by the Louisville and Nashville Railroad. Leslie was unenthusiastic about the Southern Railroad bill, but he refused to veto it since it would open up the trade of central Kentucky. At his urging the legislature passed a bill legalizing the admission of Negro testimony into the courts.

Early in his administration Leslie was faced with a serious lawlessness that plagued the state. Bands of bushwackers, known as Regulators, moved freely throughout the state, and local authorities were unable to suppress their activity. Leslie declared it was his firm purpose to suppress this violence and issued a proclamation urging the people to bring pressure to bear upon their courts and sheriffs to put down these local disorders. The legislature responded with a stringent law that helped end the violence.

Meanwhile Leslie was becoming more progressive. Addressing the legislature in December 1872, he again asked for increased assistance for the insane and revision of the revenue laws, but most important, provision for a geological survey that would determine the natural resources of the state.

After adopting resolutions condemning the scandals in Washington, the legislature amended the revenue laws, increased the assistance to the state's eleemosynary institutions, provided strict penalities for anyone interfering with the suffrage, and appropriated funds for a geological survey. Leslie named a native son, Harvard professor Nathaniel Southgate Shaler, to head this important work.

The legislative session of 1873-1874 was not as productive. At the governor's urging, the General Assembly provided for a referendum regarding constitutional revision, passed laws regulating the sale of liquor, created a board of pharmacy, established a "uniform system of common schools for the Colored Children" and again increased appropriations for the insane asylums and reformatories.

Leslie never permitted liquor to be served at state functions, but he and Mrs. Leslie gave "festive celebrations" in the executive mansion and Mrs. Leslie was considered to be "an ideal hostess." She was also known for her charities, and it was said that no needy person ever appealed to her in vain. Both Leslie and his wife were devout Baptists. When Leslie retired from the governorship, the Good Templars of Kentucky presented him with a silver service in appreciation for his support of their cause.

As governor, Leslie was not popular with the press, which did not consider him a "forceful leader." Yet during his administration some important steps were taken that placed Kentucky in the vanguard of other states. His efforts to suppress violence were sustained by the people, Negro testimony was admitted in the courts, sound fiscal policy was instituted, and important educational improvements were achieved, including a provision for the education of blacks. The state's mental, deaf, and blind asylums were improved, as were the correctional institutions. The Southern Railroad opened up central Kentucky to northern and southern markets, and the geological survey uncovered a wealth of natural resources.

In 1875 Leslie returned to Glasgow where he resumed his practice of law. He became circuit judge of his district in 1881 and served until his appointment by Pres. Grover Cleveland as territorial governor of Montana in 1887. As he arrived in Helena, he was referred to by the press as "vigorous," and because of his temperance advocacy, as the "Coldwater Governor" of Kentucky. As governor, Leslie pressed the territorial legislature for a Sunday blue law, fiscal reforms, and improved facilities for the insane and the incarcerated, but he was no match for the machine politics that dominated the territory. Again the press proved hostile, particularly when he pardoned a prostitute convicted of grand larceny because the penitentiary was not able to accommodate women. When in 1889 he applied the pocket veto to an appointment bill, the Republicans demanded that Pres. Benjamin Harrison replace him.

Leslie remained in Helena and opened a law office. In 1894 President Cleveland appointed him United States district attorney for Montana, a post that he held for four years. In 1906 he visited Kentucky. Addressing the legislature, Leslie recalled that as governor he had made every effort to assist Kentuckians to adjust to the "new order" following the Civil War. Upon his return to Montana he died of pneumonia on February 7, 1907, and was interred in Forestvale Cemetery.

SUGGESTED READINGS: Jennie C. Morton, "Sketch and Picture of Governor Preston H. Leslie," *Register* 5(September 1907), 13-16; John W. Wade, "Hon. Preston Hopkins Leslie, A Short Sketch of His Life," in *Contributions to the Historical Society of Montana* (1966), 202-14.

ROSS A. WEBB

1875-1879
1911-1915
# JAMES B. McCREARY
1838-1918

Two-term governor James Bennett McCreary was born on July 8,
1838, in Madison County, Kentucky, to Dr. E.R. and Sabrina Bennett
McCreary. A Presbyterian, he received his bachelor's degree at Centre
College in Danville and LL.B. from Cumberland University in Tennessee in 1859. During the Civil War he served in the Confederate
army as cavalry major and lieutenant colonel. At the conclusion of the
war he reestablished his law practice and in 1867 married Kate
Hughes of Lexington. McCreary, affable and handsome, was an active
Democrat who served three successive terms, 1869-1875, representing Madison County in the state House of Representatives, his last
two terms as speaker.

At the Democratic state convention of 1875 McCreary won the
gubernatorial nomination on the fourth ballot over John Stuart Williams of Mount Sterling. In the ensuing campaign McCreary stumped
the state, attacking the abuses of the Grant administration and its reconstruction policy. McCreary and his opponent, Republican John
Marshall Harlan, waged strenuous campaigns that featured joint debates. Although McCreary received a smaller majority than any other
Democrat on the state ticket, he easily defeated Harlan by 130,026
votes to 94,236. McCreary won despite predictions to the contrary
because of a Republican infusion of money and stump speakers in the
closing days of the campaign.

In his inaugural address McCreary tried to put to rest reconstruction politics and to emphasize reconciliation. Because of large Democratic majorities in both houses of the legislature representing
Grange-minded farmers new to politics, relief for farmers suffering
from the depression was a significant issue. McCreary's first message
to the new legislature, however, suggested that his term would reflect
Southern Democratic conservative orthodoxy. It also reflected the tradition of a relatively weak executive branch that did not forcefully advocate and draft legislation for consideration. This lack of executive
leadership, the brief length of the regular biennial session (sixty days),
and agrarian concern with taxation meant that few of the more than
one thousand bills passed were significant. Most were local or private

bills with no statewide impact. McCreary called for the establishment of normal schools to train teachers, opposed the taxation of corporations by municipalities, advocated a change in the insurance law to assure beneficiaries would be promptly paid, and urged the legislature to consider general bills rather than clog the session with purely local bills. The major legislative achievements of the biennial session were extremely modest—a reduction of the legal rate of interest from 10 to 8 percent, a 12½ percent reduction in property taxes, and some legislation concerning eleemosynary institutions.

Again in 1878 the heavily Democratic legislature met and was greeted with a generally optimistic, bland, and conservative message from the governor. He again stressed economy, support for improvement of schools, and prison reform, as well as appropriations for improving navigation of the Kentucky River. This last suggestion grew out of recommendations from the Kentucky River Navigation Convention of 1877 and was popular enough to win the governor's support. The legislature responded to pressure for the Kentucky River project with a weak bill of little significance. It passed a number of agriculture-related measures supported by the governor, including a further reduction in the interest rate from 8 to 6 percent, assessment for tax purposes of railroad property at the same rate as other real estate, and disassociation of the Agricultural and Mechanical College from Kentucky University. Another bill also established a state board of health with responsibility for "public health, vital statistics and sanitary inspection, inquiries respecting the causes of diseases, death, epidemics, conditions, food, water, habits of people, health books for schools, and associated matters." The legislature also elected John S. Williams to the United States Senate over McCreary and two other Democratic nominees.

Thus McCreary's first term was not distinguished by much legislative activity. Rather than advocate legislation, McCreary devoted some of his energies to suppressing violence, particularly mountain feuds such as those in "bloody Breathitt" County. While he tended to downplay the challenge to lawful authority that these feuds represented, he nevertheless used a show of force to assure order.

Following his term as governor, McCreary returned to his law practice but stayed active politically. In 1885 he won election to the United States House of Representatives and served successively terms until 1897. Then in 1902 he won a term in the United States Senate. During his years in Congress he represented the state's agricultural interests, advocated free coinage of silver, and secured passage of a bill to convene an international monetary conference. In 1891 Pres. Grover Cleveland appointed McCreary to the five-member delegation to the monetary conference, where McCreary spoke in favor of bimetallism.

By the time McCreary ran for governor a second time he was in his midseventies. McCreary campaigned only briefly before the 1911 primary, relying on his established reputation to guarantee a victory. Early in the Democratic race, moreover, he pictured himself as a progressive candidate, contending that he was a consistent backer of progressive political goals. His support for progressivism, then at high tide nationally, contrasted with his earlier conservatism. In both instances he mirrored prevailing sentiments. The former governor had apparently read public opinion correctly: He coasted to an easy 25,000-vote majority over William Adams in a light state vote. In the party's state convention, McCreary supporters successfully defeated the Beckham prohibitionists, voting for continuance of the county unit option and a host of progressive reforms including direct election of United States senators, a direct primary,a corrupt practices act, an anti-lobby law, a public utilities commission, a uniform system of accounting, and a workmen's compensation law. With an eye toward the farmers who had been fighting the tobacco trust, Democrats added a plank defending farmers and laborers against the trusts and favoring the "enactment of such constitutional laws as will protect them from the greed and oppression of the trusts and monopolies of the country." And on the subject of tax reform, they went on record as "opposed to any law the effect of which would be to lighten the burdens of taxation on the wealthy and on corporations at the expense of the poor, the farmer or the laboring man."

Throughout the campaign McCreary sparred with his Republican opponent, Judge Edward C. O'Rear, who ran on a moderately progressive platform. Whether the two candidates' views on progressive issues affected the outcome of the election is moot, but for the first time both candidates for governor discussed progressive reform as an important part of their legislative programs. McCreary easily defeated O'Rear 226,771 to 195,436.

At his inauguration the following month McCreary reiterated the Democratic platform as his legislative program. He favored revision of the tax system, establishment of a department of banking, women's suffrage in school elections, and standard progressive reforms, all called for in his party's platform. Then in his first biennial message McCreary reminded fellow Democrats that they had run on a progressive platform and urged them to begin immediately to redeem their pledges. The first major progressive bill that he advocated and that became law was a mandatory primary election law. McCreary had less success with other reforms he advocated, such as an extensive corrupt practices act and a law to regulate lobbying at the capitol. Although neither bill reached his desk during the session, legislators showed some sensitivity to the governor's plea by agreeing to stricter rules governing those who would be allowed in the house and senate chambers when they were in session. The new rules restricted access to members of the General Assembly, a few departmental heads, and some elected officials. Until that time, lobbyists frequented the chambers while the legislature was in session.

Although both parties had called for the creation of a public utilities commission, division over rival bills concerning form, size, and duties of the commission, as well as opposition from key Democrats and public service corporations, effectively stalled the bill. The Democratic platform had also called for a revision of the antiquated tax laws of the state. The legislature partially redeemed that pledge when it passed a House resolution providing for the appointment of a state tax commission. The governor approved a five-member commission which began its investigation of the state's revenue system and those of other states. The commission submitted a lengthy report in 1914, and McCreary incorporated many of its recommendations into his second biennial message. Meanwhile, McCreary directed the Board of Assessment and Valuation to make a thorough investigation of the real value of corporate property. When the board reported that many corporations were undervalued, he ordered them to be revalued and taxed accordingly.

The legislature agreed to submit a tax revision scheme to the voters; it also created a Department of State Banking under the control of a bank commissioner, passed a law permitting women to vote in school elections, and adopted a local or county unit option law to deal with prohibition. Also in that year, the State Highway Department was established.

When Governor McCreary next sent his biennial message to the General Assembly in 1914, he advanced another progressive idea, a compulsory school attendance act. The governor believed that increased school attendance and a longer school term, perhaps eight months, would "be a long step toward bringing our school system to that state of efficiency that would make it equal to the demands of a more enlightened and intelligent public opinion." Under McCreary's administration, per capita expenditures for schoolchildren increased 25 percent, even though attendance increased substantially under the Compulsory Attendance Act.

Another educational issue, and a perennial center for political contention, was that of uniform textbooks. In 1910 the Republicans took the lead in repealing the uniform textbook law and replacing it with an optional system that permitted each city, county, and school district to purchase its own texts at whatever price it could get. This new system was to become effective in June 1914. McCreary succeeded in convincing the legislature to modify the new law to create a textbook commission.

The governor again, as he had two years earlier, called for full disclosure of the source and disbursement of campaign contributions. Although the legislators considered several similar bils, none passed. On the platform pledge for a uniform system of accounting, however, McCreary succeeded in 1914 where he had failed in 1912.

McCreary consistently favored a workmen's compensation law, and so in his final message to the General Assembly he renewed his plea for an extensive law to protect the laborer who sustained injury. The legislature passed a compromise bill that was a patchwork of amendments inadequately considered. The governor signed the bill before leaving office, but the state courts soon ruled the law unconstitutional.

Governor McCreary also advocated the establishment of a permanent state tax commission. Although he agreed with the findings of the special tax commission that many corporations did not bear their fair tax burden, he advocated no new legislation. He did, however, ask the Board of Valuation and Assessment to increase the value of corporate property for taxation, a move unsuccessfully challenged by large corporations in the courts.

At the conclusion of his term as governor, McCreary unsuccessfully sought his party's nomination to the United States Senate, losing to J.C.W. Beckham. For the next three years, until his death in Richmond on October 8, 1918, he continued to work as a private attorney.

SUGGESTED READINGS: Nicholas C. Burckel, "From Beckham to McCreary: The Progressive Record of Kentucky Governors," *Register* 76(October 1978), 285–306; Roscoe C. Cross, "Public Life of James Bennet McCreary" (M.A. thesis, University of Kentucky, 1925).

NICHOLAS C. BURCKEL

# LUKE PRYOR BLACKBURN

Luke Pryor Blackburn, the father of prison reforms in Kentucky, is the only physician who has served as governor of the commonwealth. Born in Woodford County on June 16, 1816, Blackburn was the son of Edward (Ned) and Lavinia Bell Blackburn. He received his medical degree from Transylvania University in March 1835 and a few months later married Ella Gist Boswell of Lexington. To them was born one son, Cary Bell. Shortly after his wife's death in 1856, Blackburn married Julia Churchill of Louisville.

Most of Blackburn's early professional life was spent in Versailles, but in 1846 he and his family moved to Natchez. There, the doctor won acclaim during the 1848 and 1854 yellow fever epidemics for establishing the first effective quarantines in the Mississippi Valley. In the early months of the Civil War, Blackburn served as a civilian agent for the Confederates, but in 1863 the governor of Mississippi sent him to Canada to collect supplies for blockade runners. With other rebels in Canada he planned a variety of schemes to cause panic among Union residents, and he instigated and carried out an unsuccessful plan to infect northern cities with yellow fever. The plot was revealed in April 1865, and the Bureau of Military Justice charged the doctor with conspiracy to commit murder and ordered his arrest. Living in Canada and beyond United States jurisdiction, Blackburn nevertheless was detained by Montreal authorities and was tried and acquitted by a Toronto court for violating Canadian neutrality.

Returning to Kentucky in 1872, Blackburn soon gained a reputation as a philanthropist by giving aid to victims of yellow fever during the 1873 epidemic in Memphis and the 1877 outbreak in Florida. In March 1878 the doctor announced his candidacy for governor of Kentucky. Local politicians scoffed at his chances, for his only experience had been gained as a Whig representative to the 1843-1844 Kentucky legislature. Nevertheless his ministrations to the people of Hickman, Kentucky, during the 1878 yellow fever epidemic gained for him thousands of supporters. The Hero of Hickman easily won the Democratic nomination and was elected governor over Republican Walter Evans of Hopkinsville by 125,790 to 81,882.

As the commonwealth's first citizen Blackburn recommended to the legislature a variety of fiscal, judicial, and educational reforms, which they endorsed. They increased property taxes, revamped the district court system, established a superior court to hear some appeals cases, set salaries for judges and prosecuting attorneys (whose pay previously had depended on the number of cases heard and won), re-organized the Agricultural and Mechanical College, and created a "people's college"—the University of Kentucky. The lawmakers also gave minimal emergency powers to the infant Board of Health, and Blackburn's appointee to the board, Joseph McCormack of Bowling Green, served for nearly forty years as its dynamic executive officer, drafting and enforcing legislation that advanced the course of public health.

Blackburn's major gubernatorial contribution came out of his crusade to improve conditions at the Kentucky Penitentiary at Frankfort. Other influential figures had from time to time unsuccessfully urged change at the eighty-year-old institution, but Blackburn made the prison an issue the lawmakers could not ignore. Using the only weapon at his command—his executive pardon—he tried to alleviate some of the suffering at the overcrowded prison. He released the very young, the aged, the infirm, and those he believed were victims of injustice. Some Kentuckians speculated that "lenient Luke" might open the prison gates and expel everyone from "Kentucky's Black Hole of Calcutta."

At his urging committees of legislators investigated the Frankfort facility. Their grim reports contained descriptions of filthy and over-crowded cells, insufficient and unwholesome food, defective heating and ventilating systems, harsh treatment, and excessive illnesses caused by the abominable conditions. But improvements would be expensive, and the legislators feared that spending the voters' tax dollars on felons could be political suicide. Thus the solons investigated, resolved, argued, and postponed action. As they delayed, convicts sickened and the governor issued pardons. Newspapers across the state ridiculed the wrangling lawmakers and praised and damned the governor for his leniency. Residents of areas to which the "cutthroats and thieves" returned cried out that their lives were in danger and complained of rising crime rates. Because of the increasing pressures, the 1880 legislature drew up and submitted to the governor for his signature two bills that incorporated most of his recommendations.

A commission composed of the governor, secretary of state, attorney general, and auditor were to serve as the prison directors. Their

94

duties included making monthly visits to the facility and appointing an assistant warden, a full-time physician, and a part-time chaplain, who also served as a teacher. The legislature selected the warden whose supervisory and administrative duties were carefully defined. Unlike the lessees who had managed the prison since its creation, this administrator and the members of his staff received salaries but gained nothing from the profits derived from the convicts' labor.

To relieve the overcrowded conditions at the prison, plans were made for a new facility. A committee of three, appointed by the governor, was to study existing prison systems across the nation and to select a site and plan for the proposed branch penitentiary. Until the new prison opened, however, the law recommended that all inmates in excess of six hundred be hired out to labor on public works. The contractors would feed, clothe, house, guard, and provide medical care for the convicts in their charge. Blackburn opposed this portion of the law, believing it encouraged all of the evils of the old leasing system, but to gain the other reforms he was forced to accept it. When the law went into effect, nearly four hundred convicts left the prison to work for railroad contractors. Blackburn and the other directors visited the railroad camps on numerous occasions and then pleaded in vain with the legislature to repeal the law. To rescue these men from inhumane conditions at the camps, Blackburn made liberal use of his pardoning power.

With the implementation of the new laws and appointment of able men, conditions at the prison improved. Nevertheless, Blackburn continued to push for a new facility where felons could be rehabilitated rather than punished. The committee of three recommended that a branch penitentiary be built at Eddyville, a healthy area in immediate proximity to the resources needed to build and maintain it. A Louisville firm drew plans for the facility and estimated its cost at $565,000, a figure that might be reduced by half with the use of convict labor. The 1881-1882 General Assembly refused to appropriate the money. Nevertheless, the public outcry against convicts competing with free laborers forced the 1884 legislature to reconsider the measure and to approve funds for the new penitentiary. The reformatory at Eddyville was a great improvement over the Frankfort prison, but it never became the kind of facility Blackburn recommended—one that would "teach and train the prisoner in such a manner that on his discharge, he may be able to resist temptation and inclined to lead an upright and worthy life."

Blackburn had entered the executive office in 1879 on the wave of popularity and gratitude, and as governor he achieved the first major reforms in more than twenty years. But he left office in 1883 embittered by the criticisms and derisions heaped on him. Many of his former supporters, who had lauded his political inexperience, laughed at his naivete. Newspapers gave exaggerated counts of his pardons (he issued about one thousand) or accused him of selling them. Politicos had assumed the doctor would be their puppet and were therefore appalled at his independence and feared his campaign for an unpopular cause would harm their careers.

In the autumn of 1883 Blackburn returned to his profession and briefly operated a sanitarium in Louisville. He died in Frankfort on September 14, 1887, and was buried in the Frankfort cemetery on a hillside overlooking the Kentucky River. His monument, erected by the state, contains a bronze bas-relief depicting the parable of the Good Samaritan, a salute to the man who defied disease and disapproval to help those unable to help themselves. In 1971 the commonwealth named the state's newest minimum security facility the Blackburn Complex for Kentucky's father of prison reforms.

SUGGESTED READINGS: Nancy Disher Baird, *Luke Pryor Blackburn: Physician, Governor, Reformer* (1979); Baird, "Luke Pryor Blackburn's Campaign for Governor," *Register* 74 (October 1976), 300-313; Baird, "The Yellow Fever Plot," *Civil War Times Illustrated* 13 (November 1974), 16-23.

NANCY DISHER BAIRD


1883-1887
# J. PROCTOR KNOTT
1830-1911


Born on August 29, 1830, in Marion County, Kentucky, the son of Joseph Percy and Maria Irvine Knott, James Proctor Knott received his education there before moving to Missouri in 1850. Admitted to the bar in 1851, he practiced law in Scotland County, Missouri, and served in the circuit and county clerk's offices, as well as in the Missouri legislature. In 1852 he married Mary E. Forman who died in childbirth the next year. In 1858 Knott married a cousin, Sarah R. McElroy of Bowling Green, Kentucky. In 1858 he was appointed to fill the unexpired term of the attorney general and was elected to a full term as the Democratic candidate for that office in 1860. A moderate secessionist, Knott refused to swear allegiance to the Union and resigned his office in 1862. After a short period of imprisonment, he returned to Kentucky in 1863 to practice law in Lebanon. Following the Civil War, he served six terms in the United States House of Representatives (1867-1871, 1875-1883) where he opposed reconstruction and protectionism and delivered a famous speech on January 27, 1871, ridiculing federal aid to a railroad proposed to terminate at Duluth, Minnesota.

Failing in his attempt in 1871 to secure the Democratic nomination for governor, Knott made a successful effort in 1883. More controversy characterized Knott's campaign for the nomination than his run in the general election. Delegates to the Democratic gubernatorial convention battled for seven ballots before narrowly choosing Knott over four other aspirants. On the last ballot only two candidates remained, Knott and former Congressman Thomas L. Jones from Newport. At the conclusion of the balloting, Jones had a lead of nine and one-fifth votes, but rather than promptly announcing the result, the presiding officer after some delay recognized the chairman of the Owen County delegation. The Owen County chairman switched five of his delegation's votes from Jones to Knott, giving the latter a lead of four-fifths of a vote. Immediately thereafter the chair recognized other delegations who switched their support from Jones to Knott, producing a stampede that ultimately resulted in Knott's nearly unanimous nomination. Jones's supporters protested that their candidate had been undermined by illegal tactics, but the state committee refused to change the decision of the convention and Knott's campaign progressed generally unaffected by the event. The general election proved to be a much easier affair for Knott who overwhelmed his Republican rival, Thomas Z. Morrow of Somerset, 133,615 to 89,181. To their credit both candidates fully discussed the issues, sometimes in head-to-head debate.

Seizing upon several major issues of the campaign in his first annual message to the legislature, Knott called for reform of the tax assessment system and state finances in general, the construction of a branch penitentiary, and an overhaul of the system of public education. Citing the "grossest disparity" between the market value of taxable property and its assessed value, with the problem especially severe in rural areas, Knott called for the creation of a state agency to equal-

97

ize tax assessments. He also urged the elimination of tax immunities granted to corporations, the taxation or abolition of lotteries, and the transfer of certain expenses to the counties. The General Assembly responded positively to the first request, creating a state Board of Equalization empowered to make tax assessments more uniform and realistic, but failed to pass legislation on tax immunities, lotteries, and county expenses. The legislature also approved construction of a branch penitentiary to relieve chronic overcrowding at the main facility in Frankfort and enacted a comprehensive overhaul of the public education system. The latter reform appears to have been less the result of Knott's efforts than those of a state central committee of prominent Kentuckians which had earlier presented a detailed report to the governor calling for specific changes, many of which the legislature adopted after the report was referred to it. Among other things, the school law provided for a more uniform system of public education, defined the length of the school year and the duties of state and county school boards, regulated the course of study, authorized a state teachers' association, replaced county school commissioners with popularly elected superintendents, and created a state board of education.

Citing a continuing deficit of nearly $500,000, Knott asked the second and final legislature of his administration for further revisions of the system of tax assessment, consisting primarily of provisions strengthening the powers of the state Board of Equalization. The legislature met this request, but once more failed to adopt his recommendations for the transfer of certain expenses to county governments and the revocation of corporate tax immunities. Also, despite his urgings, the General Assembly failed to create a uniform pay scale for local public officials, whose salaries varied widely due to dependency on fees and to variations in the amount of available business. The legislators also failed to heed Knott's call for the establishment of a state board of charities and for the empowerment of the state railroad commission to equalize the rates for long-short haul traffic.

Although he seemed cognizant of the commonwealth's major problems, Knott was myopic about Kentucky's difficulties with crime. Despite the notorious penchant of his constituents for committing homicide (at a rate probably twice that of 1980), Knott denied the existence of an epidemic of murder and went so far as to whitewash the issue in his first state of the commonwealth message. The outbreak of a three-year war in Rowan County and his unsuccessful efforts to terminate it (including the appointment of a special prosecutor, the negotiation by his emissaries of a truce, and the dispatching of the state guard) severely undermined his credibility if not his performance on this issue (the war was appropriately concluded by vigilante action).

Knott also praised the condition of the penitentiary, alleging that it maintained a "superb sanitary condition" despite evidence to the contrary. Most significantly, after exercising initial restraint, he succumbed to the tendency of his predecessors to pardon criminals too freely, even though the Republicans constantly made the practice a campaign issue, especially in the election that sent Knott to the executive mansion. It was difficult for Knott to temper his actions in pardoning criminals because of the large number of convicts, the absence of a parole board, and the importance of the pardoning power, which Knott's successor called "the great labor of the office."

In sum, Knott ranks as one of the most effective governors of the postwar nineteenth century. He secured badly needed tax reform and presided over educational change. He drew attention to a number of other deficiencies in the state's financial system, including the tendency of certain counties to siphon off large amounts of state money by means of excessive, even fraudulent claims. His attitude toward corporate power, increasingly a major issue in the state, remained ambivalent throughout his administration. In his initial message to the legislature he expressed misgivings about the need for a state railroad commission, but in a subsequent document he endorsed empowering that agency to regulate long-short haul rates. He also vetoed a bill granting a five-year tax immunity to new railroad construction, which was overridden by the legislature.

Always a fiscal conservative, Knott guarded the state treasury against untraditional assaults, successfully opposing, for example, an attempt to provide public compensation for losses suffered by farmers in a bovine pneumonia epidemic. While endorsing a strong system of public education, he contended that the bulk of its expenses should be born by local government. He likewise denied that significant law enforcement responsibilities should be assumed by the commonwealth and blamed lawlessness on defective local peacekeeping. Although critical of special and local legislation, he was not as vigilant in vetoing the more scandalous examples of it as his successor, Governor Buckner, would be.

After his term as governor, Knott practiced law in Frankfort for five years. From 1887 to 1888 he was special assistant to the state attorney general, and in 1890 he was elected delegate to the constitutional convention. Knott then served as professor of civics and economics at Centre College. In 1894 he and the college president organized a law department, Knott becoming its first dean and professor. His teaching and educational administration earned great praise. Forced to retire in 1902 for reasons of ill health, Knott spent the rest of his life in Lebanon. He died on June 18, 1911, and was buried in Lebanon.

SUGGESTED READINGS: Hambleton Tapp, "James Proctor Knott and the Duluth Speech," *Register* 70 (April 1972), 77-93.

ROBERT M. IRELAND

1887-1891
# SIMON BOLIVAR BUCKNER
1823-1914

Simon Bolivar Buckner was born on April 1, 1823, at Glen Lily, the family estate nine miles east of Munfordville in Hart County. His parents, Aylett Hartswell and Elizabeth Ann Morehead Buckner, were both of Virginia ancestry. Aylett Buckner was moderately successful in farming and the iron business before moving to Arkansas. Young Bolivar remained in Kentucky and attended schools in Greenville and Hopkinsville before entering West Point on July 1, 1840. The handsome cadet, six feet tall with a powerful physique, made steady progress and in 1844 graduated eleventh in a class of twenty-five. Mathematics, history, and drawing were his best subjects, and he excelled in gymnastics.

After a stint of routine garrison duty, Buckner taught at West Point in 1845-1846 before joining the army in Mexico. Most of his active duty was served with Gen. Winfield Scott, who became Buckner's hero. Buckner received a slight wound and was brevetted to captain. He left West Point after a year of postwar teaching because of his objection to compulsory Sunday chapel. On May 2, 1850, he married Mary Jane Kingsbury, daughter of an army officer who had made extensive real estate investments in Chicago. Five years later Buckner resigned his commission to help his father-in-law with business affairs. Buckner returned to Kentucky in 1858, the year his daughter Lily was born.

Buckner was active in both the Illinois and Kentucky militia, and in 1860 he became Kentucky's inspector general, head of the state militia whose reorganization he had planned. In 1861 Buckner represented Governor Magoffin in negotiations with Union and Confederate officials in an effort to preserve Kentucky's neutrality. He declined a Union commission to brigadier general in August but accepted one from the Confederacy in September. Buckner occupied Bowling Green in September and became one of Gen. Albert Sidney Johnston's trusted subordinates. After a comedy of leadership errors left him in command, Buckner surrendered Fort Donelson to his friend Gen. U.S. Grant in February 1862. Exchanged in August, Buckner was promoted to major general and joined Gen. Braxton Bragg's army for its ill-fated invasion of Kentucky. Later assignments carried Buckner to Mobile and then to east Tennessee where he did his most effective work of the war. Ordered back to Bragg, he engaged in a bitter controversy with that irascible commander. In May 1864 Buckner was sent to Gen. Kirby Smith's trans-Mississippi department. Promoted to lieutenant general in September, Buckner surrendered the trans-Mississippi army for Smith on May 26, 1865.

Forbidden to return home, Buckner wrote newspaper editorials in New Orleans before turning to commercial and insurance enterprises. When he returned to Kentucky in early 1868, he wrote editorials for the Louisville *Daily Courier* and started the law suits that finally recovered most of his and his wife's prewar property. Now wealthy, Buckner engaged in a number of business undertakings. His wife died in 1874, and in 1885 Buckner married twenty-eight-year-old Delia Claiborne of Richmond, Virginia. Their only child, Simon Bolivar, Jr., was born in 1886.

Buckner was deeply interested in politics, and as early as 1867, friends urged him to run for governor. He withdrew his name from nomination at the 1883 Democratic convention, but in 1887 he was nominated easily. Buckner was a better writer than orator, but he made an impressive platform appearance, and his clear, factual speeches won votes. In a close race, he defeated Republican William O'Connell Bradley, 143,466 to 126,754.

Buckner's administration was noted for honest, efficient service and for his extensive use of the veto to kill private interest bills. The governor personally examined all requests for pardons and rejected most of them. Surprisingly progressive in several areas, he was unable to get legislative approval for most of his advanced ideas. He failed to secure the creation of a department of Justice, the regulation of trusts, closer supervision of turnpike companies, greater local support for education, and measures for the protection of forests. He did secure the creation of a state board of Tax Equalization, a parole system for convicts, enlargement and completion of the prison at Eddyville, and codification of school laws. Buckner saw immigration as essential to the state's economic development, and he sought to encourage it without great success. Much of his time and energy was devoted to curbing east Kentucky feuds and to jurisdictional disputes with the governor of West Virginia.

The major scandal of Buckner's administration involved James W. Tate, state treasurer since 1868. In 1888, when the governor ordered a routine auditing that had been neglected for years, "Honest Dick" disappeared, leaving a shortage reported to be $247,128.50. Most of the money was recovered, and the state's ultimate loss may have been about $40,000. Buckner took swift steps to prevent any future loss.

Buckner boasted of not having sought a tax increase, but he believed in fiscal responsibility, and one of the few bills passed over his veto came in 1890 when the legislators reduced the general fund's share of the state property tax from twenty cents to fifteen cents per one hundred dollars assessed value. Pointing out that they had already voted appropriations that would exceed revenue, the governor rebuked their irresponsible action in a stinging message. By mid-June the treasury was empty, and the state could not pay its bills. Acting quietly without publicity, Buckner arranged to lend the state enough money from his own resources to keep it solvent until taxes started coming in. Buckner never revealed the interest-free total, but it was probably in the range of fifty to seventy-five thousand dollars.

As a delegate from Hart County, Buckner had an active role in the 1890-1891 constitutional convention. However, he failed to get the governor's appointing power extended to minor state officials or taxes levied on churches, clubs, and schools that made profits. Buckner accepted the completed document as the will of the majority, but he was not enthusiastic about it.

When Buckner left office on September 7, 1891, he had given the state four years of honest, efficient government and had lent integrity and dignity to the office. He surprised many Kentuckians with his progressive ideas, but few of those ideas were implemented. While Buckner cannot be considered one of Kentucky's greatest governors, his performance was well above average.

When he left Frankfort, Buckner returned to the simple country life that he loved with his family, his friends, his corncob pipe, and his books. At eighty, when cataracts threatened to blind him, he memorized five of Shakespeare's plays so he could "Read in the Dark," but operations saved his sight. He entered the 1895 race for the United States Senate, but the Democrats were badly divided on the money question, and Buckner, a Gold Democrat, soon withdrew. He left the Democratic party in 1896 to protest over William Jennings Bryan and free silver and accepted the vice-presidential slot on the Gold Democrat ticket with Gen. John M. Palmer. Buckner campaigned extensively, and the Palmer-Buckner ticket may have helped defeat Bryan. Buckner remained a political independent for the rest of his life.

As long as he could travel, Buckner attended Confederate encampments. After 1908, he was the only surviving Confederate of lieutenant general rank. He was delighted when his son entered West Point in 1904, and he enjoyed a visit in 1909 to his old Mexican War battlefields. His health failed rapidly after 1912, and after a week's illness the "Sage of Glen Lily" died at home of uremic poisoning on January 8, 1914. He was buried at Frankfort.

SUGGESTED READING: Arndt M. Stickles, *Simon Bolivar Buckner: Borderland Knight* (1940).

LOWELL H. HARRISON

1891-1895
# JOHN YOUNG BROWN
1835-1904

John Young Brown was born in Elizabethtown, Kentucky, on June 28, 1835. His father, Thomas Dudley Brown, attained some prominence as a local politician, serving in the legislature and the state constitutional convention of 1849-1850. He influenced his son to pursue an active political career. John's mother was Elizabeth Young Brown. After graduating from Centre College in 1855, Brown commenced the study and practice of law in Elizabethtown. In 1857 he married Lucie Barbee who died the next year; in September 1860 Brown married Rebecca Hart Dixon. In 1859 he was elected to Congress as a Democrat despite his admission that he was underaged, a fact that delayed his being seated by the House. During the Civil War he grew progressively disenchanted with the Union, so much so that the House refused to seat him for alleged disloyalty following his election to that body in 1866. He was elected once more in 1872 and served three successive terms in the House, retiring in 1879 to practice law in Henderson.

In 1891 Brown came out of political retirement to wage a successful campaign for the Democratic nomination for governor. His nomination appears to have been a compromise between the party's agrarian and corporate factions, which had been vying for party control for several years. Brown received most of his initial support from agrarians in western Kentucky, center of protest against corporate power, and ultimately and decisively from the corporate Louisville and Nashville Railroad, which perceived him as a moderate on the issue of reform. Because of division within the party, the nominating convention avoided mentioning the newly drafted constitution of 1891, which would also be voted on in the August election. Instead it concentrated on national issues such as the tariff and the free coinage of silver, advocating reform of the former and adoption of the latter, positions shared by Brown. The Republicans nominated Andrew T. Wood of Mt. Sterling, a lawyer who had lost in previous bids for Congress and state attorney general. Running on a slightly more relevant platform that included endorsement of the new constitution, Wood lambasted Brown for evading the question and accused him of being in league with the monopolists and the L&N. With approximately six weeks to go in the campaign and sensing that popular support heavily favored the new charter, Brown announced he favored the constitution of 1891. Nevertheless, Wood continued his attacks on Brown and his alleged conspiracy, but to no avail as the latter triumphed at the polls 144,168 to 116,087 (the Populist candidate drew 25,631 votes and the Prohibitionist 3,292). Voters overwhelmingly ratified the new constitution by a margin of nearly three to one.

Brown's legislative record as governor was mixed. He advocated and secured statutes tightening state control over foreign corporations, suppressing lotteries, increasing penalties against delinquent tax collection, reforming state printing contracts, transferring certain governmental expenses to the counties, empowering the governor to fill vacated offices, and clarifying laws on asylums and charitable institutions. Of more dubious benefit, he secured termination of the geological survey, contending it was an unnecessary expense. He failed in his attempt to secure legislation increasing the powers of the railroad commission and requiring greater railroad safety, reforming prison management, creating a separate prison for adolescents, establishing a state bank inspector and a superintendent of public printing, and abolishing the recently constituted parole board, an institution he vowed to ignore. Emancipated by the new constitution from most of the evils and irrelevancies of local and private legislation, which had preoccupied the assembly for over forty years, the legislature spent much of its time carrying out the mandate of the new frame of government. Unfortunately the legislature enacted several principal statutes, including massive ones on revenue, private corporations, and cities, without having requisite majorities, forcing Brown to veto the laws and convoke a special session to rectify the body's collective negligence. His veto of the revenue bill of 1892 elicited a lengthy address of protestation from a group of offended legislators. The General Assembly also passed significant legislation not expressly advocated by Brown, including a separate coach law (the comprehensive enforcement of which he endorsed), a married women's property act, a law prohibiting collusive bids on leaf tobacco, a primitive coal mine safety act, an act regulating grain warehouses, a comprehensive common school statute, and a "free" turnpike statute.

As governor, Brown failed to preserve the party compromise that his nomination represented. During his administration he antagonized two of the most powerful corporate interests in the commonwealth, the Louisville and Nashville Railroad and the Mason and Foard Company, which leased convict labor and employed it in the construction of railroads. Closely allied with several leading Democrats, including former governor Simon B. Buckner and former state auditor Fayette Hewitt, Mason and Foard denounced changes in prison administration engineered by Governor Brown. Ultimately, Brown publicly alleged that Buckner had illegally permitted Mason and Foard to lease convict labor, a charge Buckner hotly denied.

Brown responded erratically to the railroad problem and thereby alienated the railroad and members of his own party. In his first message to the legislature he argued that a five-year tax exemption granted for new railroad construction was invalid, but several months later he vetoed a revenue bill that would have increased railroad taxes. In 1894, perhaps embittered because of the failure of the L&N lobby to support his unsuccessful campaign to secure for himself the United States senatorial seat vacated by John G. Carlisle, Brown helped prevent the railroad company from acquiring the Chesapeake, Ohio and Southwestern line, alleging that the proposed acquisition violated the state constitution. Brown also alienated influential legislators by his vetoes and the state auditor and the attorney general by his criticism of their official conduct. Such actions split the Brown administration asunder, causing the auditor, treasurer, and lieutenant governor to form a coalition against him and forcing Brown and his appointed ally, the secretary of state, into a minority position on the sinking fund commission and other important boards. With his control of valuable patronage, state auditor Luke C. Norman formed a powerful political machine that ultimately outflanked Brown's position within the Democratic party.

During the last year of his term, Brown made another attempt to secure a seat in the United States Senate by promoting the candidacy of Cassius M. Clay, Jr., for the Democratic nomination for governor. As governor, Clay could promote Brown's senatorial candidacy in 1896. The assassination of his philandering son by an irate husband prompted Brown to lose interest in the race. Clay's candidacy likewise aborted as the anti-Brown forces at the nominating convention implicitly repudiated Brown by refusing to bless his administration and by nominating his rival, P. "Wat" Hardin, to head the 1895 ticket. Disillusioned by these and past slights, Brown refused to endorse Hardin, despite their mutual support for free silver, and watched silently as Hardin went down to defeat by his Republican challenger, William O. Bradley.

Following the election, Brown practiced law in Louisville. In 1896 he ran unsuccessfully for the United States House of Representatives. In 1899 he reconciled with the L&N and received its support as the candidate of the anti-Goebel Democrats for governor, a quest that only deprived Goebel of a plurality of the votes. Brown served as a defense counsel for Caleb Powers in his first trial for the murder of Goebel. Brown died on January 11, 1904, in Henderson and was buried there.

SUGGESTED READINGS: John Edward Wiltz, "The 1895 Election—A Watershed in Kentucky Politics," *FCHQ* 37 (April 1963), 117-136; Nicholas C. Burckel, "William Goebel and the Campaign for Railroad Regulation in Kentucky, 1888-1900," *FCHQ* 48 (January 1974), 43-60; Franklin T. Lambert, "Free Silver and the Kentucky Democracy, 1891-1895," *FCHQ* 53 (April 1979), 145-176.

ROBERT M. IRELAND

# WILLIAM O'CONNELL BRADLEY
1847-1914

Born March 18, 1847, near Lancaster in Garrard County, Kentucky, William O'Connell Bradley was the youngest child and only son of Robert McAfee Bradley, a noted land lawyer, and Nancy Ellen Totten. The family later moved to Somerset where W. O. Bradley received schooling through age fourteen. Filled with military ardor in 1861, the youngster unsuccessfully sought to fight for the Union. He did serve as a page in the Kentucky House that year. Devoting those wartime days to self-education, Bradley was given permission by special act of the 1865 legislature to be examined for the bar, even though he was only eighteen years old. Successful in his attempt, he began practicing law in Garrard County. On July 13, 1867, he married Margaret R. Duncan, a grand-niece of a chief justice of the state Court of Appeals. They had a son, George Robertson, whose death in 1892 deeply hurt the parents, and a daughter, Christine. Bradley's nephew, Edwin P. Morrow, would serve as Kentucky governor from 1919 to 1923.

Bradley's early misfortune was to be a Republican in a Democratic region and state. His early career was chiefly marked by defeats. In 1870 at age twenty-three he was elected county attorney, but that was followed by two losses in congressional races. Milton J. Durham defeated him 10,736 to 10,063 in 1872; four years later the outcome was the same, but the margin increased 15,484 to 12,654. Yet Bradley clearly was a promising young politician. His party honored him with its support for senator in hopeless balloting in the Democratic-controlled General Assembly in 1876. On three other occasions similar actions brought similar results. Bradley turned down several other nominations in the 1870s. He personified that first generation of Republicans who came to maturity in the postwar period, men who suffered numerous defeats before finally tasting political success much later.

During the 1880s Bradley became the state's leading Republican. On the stump he was a powerful figure. Stockily built, five feet, eight inches tall and 235 pounds, Billy O. B. had a fine, fluent voice that carried well. His dark beard, which he would later shave off, contrasted with the white Alpine hat that became his trademark. All this, together with a sharp wit, an excellent memory, and a simple love of politics, made Bradley a strong candidate. In 1880 he attended the first of his seven Republican national conventions and seconded U.S. Grant's nomination for a third term. Bradley also was selected to serve on the Republican National Committee, 1890–1896.

In 1887 he ran for governor against former Confederate general Simon Bolivar Buckner. In his campaign Bradley emphasized the need for better education, increased mineral development, and a stronger protective tariff. The Republican also attacked what he saw as Democratic financial extravagance in creating a Bureau of Agriculture and in building a new penitentiary. As in all his races, he attracted great support from Kentucky blacks. The final results showed Bradley's strengths but also the continued dominance of the Democrats: Buckner won with 143,466 votes to Bradley's 126,754. But it was the closest Republicans had come to victory. At the national convention the next year Bradley received numerous votes for vice-president.

By 1895 the time seemed ripe for Republican victory. Although factionalism divided his party, Bradley was nominated for governor in a harmonious convention, and he assailed the Democratic candidate, former attorney general P. Wat Hardin, for his part in past political scandals. He next capitalized on divisions in the opposition party, where a bitter convention fight had left many political scars. The presence of a third party, the Populists, led by Thomas S. Pettit, drew votes from Democrats in western Kentucky. Hardin's support of free silver also aided Bradley, as many conservative, sound money Democrats, especially in Louisville, went to the Republicans.

Billy O.B. further split the Democratic ranks by courting the vote of those sympathetic to the American Protective Association (APA), a secret, nativist, anti-Catholic organization of significant strength, particularly in urban areas. A depressed national economy, a state drought, and other economic factors also helped the Republicans. The chief obstacle to GOP victory was Hardin's appeal to Democrats to vote for their party to stop "Negro domination" by Republicans. This was overcome, however, and Bradley won the election, with 172,436 votes to Hardin's 163,524 and Pettit's 16,911. In December 1895 W. O. Bradley was inaugurated as the state's first Republican governor.

The new chief executive faced a difficult task. Politically his hands were tied, for the House was Republican and the Senate Democrat. On joint ballots the votes were almost equally divided. This stalemate was painfully evident in the United States Senate race of 1896. The Republicans nominated W. Godfrey Hunter and the Democrats chose

J.C.S. Blackburn. But the money issue kept Gold Democrats from casting their ballots for Blackburn, a silverite, and no candidate received a legislative majority. Moves to unseat several members of the General Assembly brought threats of violence. Bradley called out the militia, a move angrily denounced by the Democrats. Adjournment quieted the furor. Finally, in a March 1897 special session, William J. Deboe's name was presented in place of Hunter's and on the 112th ballot Deboe became the state's first Republican senator. The Democrats had remained divided to the end.

That defeat, coupled with a very narrow Republican victory in the presidential election of 1896, strengthened Democratic resolve in the General Assembly. In what supporters saw as a reform measure and opponents as a dangerous attempt to control elections, the so-called Goebel bill was introduced. Supported by future governor William Goebel, the measure gave control over contested elections to a three-man commission. Bradley's veto was overridden in 1898.

Away from politics, the question of violence demanded much of Bradley's time. Feuds still plagued eastern Kentucky and the so-called tollgate wars over free roads dominated the interests of central Kentuckians. But the chief concern of the time was the Spanish-American War. Four Kentucky regiments eventually served in that conflict, but confusion, equipment problems, and bureaucratic delays hindered their effectiveness.

When Bradley left office in 1899, he could point to few accomplishments other than some political victories. A weak compulsory education act had passed, two houses of reform for children were set up, and a pure food and drug act went into effect without the governor's signature. But rising party feelings had left less and less room for compromise as his term passed. Consequently little legislation came out of the divided General Assembly.

Retirement from the governor's mansion did not end Bradley's involvement in politics, however. He moved to Louisville and immediately became a major advisor to William S. Taylor in the gubernatorial election of 1899. In 1900 he lost 75-54 in a bid for the United States Senate, and four years later he seconded the nomination of Theodore Roosevelt for president. The Republican gubernatorial victory in 1907 brought hopes that the party might elect a senator, and in 1908 Billy O.B. was offered to the legislature by the Republicans. Again the Democrats were divided, this time over the liquor question, and the contest continued for twenty-nine ballots. Finally four "wet" Democrats cast their votes for Bradley, and his sixty-four votes beat "dry"

J.C.W. Beckham's sixty. As United States senator, Bradley was better known for his oratory than for his legislative accomplishments. He died at age sixty-seven in Washington on May 23, 1914, before he had served a full term. He was buried in Frankfort.

SUGGESTED READINGS: Hambleton Tapp and James C. Klotter, *Kentucky: Decades of Discord, 1865-1900* (1977); Maurice H. Thatcher, *Stories and Speeches of William O. Bradley* (1916); John E. Wiltz, "The 1895 Election: A Watershed in Kentucky Politics," *FCHQ* 37 (April 1963), 117-36.

JAMES C. KLOTTER

1899-1900
# WILLIAM SYLVESTER TAYLOR
1853-1928

William S. Taylor was born October 10, 1853, in a log house near Morgantown in Butler County, Kentucky. When his parents married on July 28, 1853, his father, Sylvester, was a middle-class farmer, forty-one years of age, and his mother, Mary G. Moore, was seventeen. Their first child worked on the farm early in life and did not begin formal schooling until age fifteen. He then excelled, however, and won local fame as an orator. In 1874 William began teaching school, a profession he would follow until 1882. He later received training in the law and became an attorney, but he continued to operate a farm. On February 10, 1878, Taylor married Sara (Sallie) Belle Tanner. Their union would produce nine children, including seven who lived past age five: daughters Tyler F., Alma Kline, Anna Belle, Aldian, Letha Belle, and Mabel, and son Wendell Sylvester.

Taylor's quest for political office began in 1878, when he ran and was defeated in the county clerk race of that year. Two years later he supported the Greenback party in the presidential election; not until 1884 did he join the Republican party he followed thereafter. In 1882 Taylor won election as county clerk of Butler County. He served a four-year term and then won two terms as county judge from 1886 to 1894. Rising quickly in his new party's councils, he attended the 1888 and 1900 Republican national conventions and sat on several important state committees. In 1895 he ran for attorney general on the successful ticket led by William O. Bradley and served until 1899.

A determined man who had to work hard to rise in his party, Taylor had modest statewide recognition, limited financial resources, and little polish. Opponents attacked him on these counts when he sought the Republican gubernatorial nomination in 1899. Furthermore he represented the western, "lily-white" branch of a party that depended heavily on black votes. That stance would not help in certain circles. Yet Taylor was a quietly successful politician with a spotless record, a man who early gained the backing of United States Senator William J. Deboe and numerous local delegations. While Governor Bradley supported another candidate for governor and important central Kentucky Republicans favored a third, Taylor had a clear majority of delegates and was unanimously nominated at the convention. When the party saw that it had an excellent opportunity to win over the divided Democrats, the various factions, including Bradley's, united behind the forty-six-year-old nominee.

It was William S. Taylor versus Democrat William Goebel in the 1899 election; a small third party completed the field. The campaign was unusually bitter, even for Kentucky, with each side charging the other with bad faith, corruption, and machine rule. Taylor, under fire for his party's past administration and present ties to the railroads, focused his attacks on his opponent's controversial election law and "bossism", and on the Democrats' party divisions. He defended the Republican state administration, praised the prosperity of the national administration, and supported the territorial acquisitions arising from the Spanish-American War. All this appealed to some conservative Democrats, but their added votes probably only offset those of blacks who left Taylor. A close vote was expected.

The election returns, as certified by the Board of Election Commissioners, showed Taylor the victor by only 2,383 votes—193,714 to 191,331—with some 15,000 cast for other parties. On December 12, 1899, Taylor was inaugurated as the state's second consecutive Republican governor. Within three weeks, however, the election results were challenged by the General Assembly. The Democratic majority voted to investigate charges that certain ballots were not legal and that the militia had coerced voters in Louisville. An eleven-man committee, made up of ten Democrats and one Republican, heard testimony and prepared to issue a recommendation.

Taylor's party feared they would be voted out of office, as had happened in Tennessee in the election of 1894. In this charged atmosphere, the brief presence in Frankfort of numerous armed men, mostly Republicans from eastern Kentucky, added to the tensions. Then on January 30, 1900, Democratic aspirant Goebel was shot just in front of the capitol. Governor Taylor declared a state of insurrection, called out the militia, and ordered the legislature to reconvene in London, a Republican area. Democrats, who refused to comply with what they argued were unconstitutonal acts, met secretly, declared enough of Taylor's votes invalid to make Goebel governor, and swore him in. Republicans rejected these moves as illegal. Another militia appeared, and two governments, each with its own army, existed.

Goebel's death on February 3, 1900, eased tensions somewhat, and both sides agreed to let the courts decide the outcome. Taylor lifted the ban on the legislature's assembling in Frankfort, and it reconvened with two sets of officers. In March a circuit court ruled in favor of the Democrats; the next month the state Court of Appeals in a nonpartisan vote agreed; and on May 21, 1900, the United States Supreme Court refused to overturn the lower court decisions. Taylor, under indictment as an accessory to Goebel's murder (a politically inspired move), left the state immediately and went to Indianapolis. Officially he had served 50 days as chief executive; unofficially he had held the office for 110 more. Other than some minor appointments and pardons, virtually all his time had been devoted to the election question.

Almost penniless, Taylor lived for a time under armed guard. Shortly after their arrival in Indiana, his wife of twenty-two years died. To add to his problems and fears, Kentucky Democrats several times sought to extradite him. Indiana governors refused. On at least one occasion, in 1901, there was an abortive attempt to abduct Taylor by force. Finally on April 23, 1909, he received a pardon from Republican Gov. Augustus E. Willson, but even then he seldom returned to Kentucky. One of those occasions came in 1912, when he married Nora A. Myers in her old family home in Jamestown. They would have one child, Charles Linden. Taylor rebuilt his life and became vice-president and general counsel of the Empire Life and Accident Company. He died in Indianapolis of heart disease on August 2, 1928, and was buried there.

SUGGESTED READINGS: Hambleton Tapp and James C. Klotter, *Kentucky: Decades of Discord, 1865-1900* (1977); R. E. Hughes, F. W. Schaefer, and E. L. Williams, *That Kentucky Campaign* (1900).

JAMES C. KLOTTER

# WILLIAM GOEBEL

## 1856-1900

William Goebel was born on January 4, 1856, in Sullivan County, Pennsylvania. His German-born parents, William and Augusta Greenclay Goebel, had immigrated in the 1850s, married on April 19, 1855 (according to a note in the family papers), and made their home in a log cabin. The first of their four children, William, grew up in a German-speaking environment, reportedly not using English until his fifth year. The family was relatively poor, a fact Goebel would use to advantage in later years. His father held several jobs, including cabinetmaker, store worker, and general laborer, before his death in 1877. The continual search for better opportunities prompted the family to move to Covington, Kentucky, after the father returned from Union service to the Civil War. But the mother's influence on young William was apparently more important. Her death in 1880 came as a great shock to him.

Intelligent, hard-working, and thorough, Goebel graduated from Cincinnati Law School in 1877 and became a partner at separate times with two prominent northern Kentuckians—one-time governor and senator John White Stevenson and John G. Carlisle, who later became Speaker of the United States House and secretary of the treasury. Their political and legal contacts provided crucial early support for attorney Goebel. His specialty of corporate and railroad law earned him great wealth but also the enmity of those interests.

Goebel was ambitious; neither friend nor foe would argue that. But controversy swirled around the means he used to achieve his aims. Over time, critics would portray him as a cold, power-hungry man who catered to the masses publicly, while behaving like a dictator privately. Allies, however, presented Goebel as a rare reformer in a conservative state, a caring man who dared attack the old guard and the old ways.

Whether demagogue or reformer, Goebel climbed steadily up the political ladder. He first worked in ward politics, developed a powerful urban-oriented regional organization, and in 1887 won election to the state senate where he would serve until 1900. After 1896 he was also Senate president pro tempore and a spokesman for the younger leaders. Throughout those legislative years Goebel worked for extended railroad regulation, restriction of toll roads, abolition of lotteries and poolrooms, and expansion of laborers' rights. He also favored greater civil rights for women and blacks and an end to monopoly in the sale of textbooks. As an often absent delegate to the 1890-1891 state constitutional convention, he worked to include passages dealing with labor, urban, and railroad concerns.

Goebel seemed to attract controversy in every field. His involvement in local politics eventually resulted in a face-to-face encounter and his killing of John Sanford, a prominent politician, in 1895. Goebel went free. His strong stands for increased business and railroad regulation and his later support for free silver alienated many of the Democratic party's old leaders, including Goebel's former partner Carlisle. Goebel's methods of attaining power—what his supporters called a talent for organization and his opponents termed bossim—angered others. His background of northern birth, immigrant parents, and his father's Union army service created some division. Even Goebel's life-style differed from the political norm, for he was a reserved, private man with limited interests outside of politics and the law. Romantically close to few if any women, Goebel was the only Kentucky governor who never married. In public he cared little for mingling with the masses at political rallies and was no orator or charismatic personality. Yet he took forceful stands on reforms that many sought and these, together with his talent for behind-the-scenes organizing, won him great support.

The controversy began to increase in 1898 when the legislature passed the so-called Goebel election law. Designed as a reform measure to insure fair elections, it centralized powers under an election commission, which was manned by three allies of Goebel. Bitter criticism followed. Then in 1899 Goebel announced for governor and won the nomination in a divisive convention fight that led to the formation of a third party made up of disgruntled Democrats led by former governor John Y. Brown. Republicans nominated William S. Taylor, the state attorney general from Butler County. In a closely contested race, the Board of Election Commissioners decided by a split vote (2-1) that Taylor had 193,714 votes, Goebel 191,331, and Brown 12,040. Taylor was inaugurated in December. But when the General Assembly met in January, the Democratic-controlled body decided to investigate the contest. Republicans feared that they would be voted out of office, as had happened earlier in Tennessee. The presence of armed pro-Taylor protestors from the mountains added to the tension.

In this atmosphere on January 30, 1900, Goebel was shot once, in front of the capitol by an unknown assassin. Taylor declared an emergency, called out the militia, and ordered the legislature to reconvene in London, Kentucky. The Democrats, holding a majority and quorum in each house, refused to leave the capital. They met secretly in a Frankfort hotel, declared certain votes illegal, and voted Goebel in as governor, moves that Republicans refused to recognize. Meanwhile, on February 3, 1900, Goebel died of his wounds, and his lieutenant governor, J.C.W. Beckham, took over the reins of office for the Democrats. Two legislatures, two governors, and two militias vied for power, and civil war seemed possible. Cooler heads prevailed, however, and the courts finally decided in May that the Democratic majority's actions were legal. Taylor fled the state. Three men, including the Republican secretary of state, were later convicted of murder or conspiracy in a series of trials and upper court rulings not noted for bipartisan fairness. Eventually all three were pardoned, and the identity of the assassin remains uncertain.

William Goebel died at age forty-four, the only governor in American history to die in office of wounds inflicted by an assassin. He had served as chief executive but three days, and his only official action was to order the existing militia dissolved. A controversial figure in life, he would remain so in death.

SUGGESTED READINGS: James C. Klotter, *William Goebel: The Politics of Wrath* (1977); Urey Woodson, *The First New Dealer* (1939); Thomas D. Clark, "The People, William Goebel and the Kentucky Railroads," *Journal of Southern History* 5 (February 1939), 34-48.

JAMES C. KLOTTER

1900-1907
# J. C. W. BECKHAM
1869-1940

John Crepps Wickliffe Beckham, son of William Netherton and Julia Tevis Wickliffe Beckham, was born into a Presbyterian family on August 5, 1869, in Bardstown, Kentucky. He was also born into a political family; his maternal grandfather, Charles A. Wickliffe, had been governor and postmaster general, and his uncle had been governor of Louisiana. He attended Roseland Academy in Bardstown and Central University (later Eastern Kentucky University) in Richmond before returning to Bardstown to serve as principal of the public schools from

1888 to 1893. During that same period he studied law and was admitted to the bar in 1889, beginning a law practice in 1893. He began his political career as president of the Young Democrats' Club of Nelson County. In 1894 he was elected to the first of three successive terms in the state House, where he served as speaker in 1898. He married Jean Raphael Fuqua in 1900; they had two children.

Beckham came to the governorship through a peculiar concatenation of events. When Democrats assembled in Louisville in 1899 to select the gubernatorial candidate who would reclaim the governorship from the Republicans, the major battle was among 1895 gubernatorial nominee P. Wat Hardin, ex-Confederate soldier William J. Stone, and president of the state Senate William Goebel. Goebel nearly declined to accept Beckham as his running mate because Beckham's native county was already pledged to Hardin. Friends convinced Goebel that Beckham would loyally serve him, and Beckham thus became the youngest nominee for lieutenant governor when Goebel won his party's nomination. Goebel and Beckham apparently narrowly lost the election to Republican Attorney General William S. Taylor. Subsequently the Democratic-controlled legislature contested the election, declaring Goebel the winner. Goebel's victory was short-lived, however, because he died of an assassin's bullet within days of being declared governor.

Thus J.C.W. Beckham, barely old enough to assume the office, became governor on February 3, 1900. In a special election for governor held on November 6, 1900, he won election in his own right over Republican John W. Yerkes 233,052 to 229,363. As Goebel's successor, Beckham appeared to be the ideal person to reunite a divided Democratic party. In his inaugural speech Beckham sought to settle emotions rather than to stir them. He not only avoided references to Goebel's assassination, but also unexpectedly indicated he would seek accommodation rather than reform. His address emphasized noncontroversial issues, such as keeping the state militia in first-rate condition while subordinating it to civilian control.

In his first biennial message he recommended little in the way of political reform. His more liberal suggestions, which caused no ferment in the legislature or business community, included the development of additional roads, more concern with charitable and penal institutions, and improvement of the quality of education. The only obviously progressive measure was the suggested taxation of nonresident corporations. Perhaps because of the closeness and bitterness of the Goebel-Taylor election, Beckham could not have worked harder for reform if he had wanted to, since he had first to unite fellow Democrats and mollify Republicans.

Beckham had no serious rival within the party for renomination in 1903. His support for revision of the controversial Goebel election law undercut Republican criticism to a degree, and he concentrated on his record of educational reform and gradual retirement of the state's debt. Consequently the majority party returned Beckham to Frankfort by a vote of 222,014 to 202,764 over Republican M. B. Belknap.

Although they passed a uniform textbook bill during the 1904 session, the legislators, in the absence of strong executive leadership, showed little initiative in proposing reform. At the opening of the 1906 session the governor urged the assembly to regulate insurance companies operating in the state, an issue popularized by Charles Evans Hughes in New York. In particular Beckham recommended the reduction of deferred dividends, which allowed insurance companies to accumulate large surpluses that could become ready sources of cash for illegal purposes. To keep some of the money out of the major financial centers like New York, Beckham advised that insurance companies doing business in the state be required to invest part of their earnings in the state. This would bolster the state's economy and offer policyholders some protection against fraud. Because of complaints of exorbitant fire insurance rates, Beckham had investigated the issue and recommended that the legislature create an office of fire marshal to be financed by the insurance companies. The marshal would act as a check on incendiary losses and thereby reduce fire insurance rates. The legislature imposed some taxes on the insurance companies but provided less regulation than the governor had requested.

Throughout his term as governor, Beckham seemed ambivalent about the railroads. He never attacked them directly and bitterly as Goebel had or defended them as conservative Republicans would have. Most of the impetus for regulation of the railroads came from the state Railroad Commission and involved Beckham only indirectly. He also was unwilling to deal with the violence growing out of attempts by militant farmers, known as night riders, to keep tobacco from being sold to the American Tobacco Company.

Although Beckham as governor was not noted for reform or significant political leadership, he did build a new state capitol and expand educational aims and facilities, while reducing the state debt. He supported the establishment of Eastern State Normal School at Richmond and Western State Normal School in Bowling Green in 1906. Beckham took an unequivocal stand on only one controversial issue of the era: He strongly and consistently spoke in favor of prohibition. Although he did not emphasize it, he opposed women's suffrage.

Beckham's aspirations for the United States Senate in 1908 were dealt a crippling blow by Louisville Democrats who were upset with his involvement in the reform efforts of Mayor Robert W. Bingham in dealing with the liquor interests, long a force in city and state politics. After retiring from the governor's office, Beckham returned to private practice. In 1914 he became the state's first popularly elected senator, defeating another former governor, Augustus E. Willson, by 32,000 votes. Although renominated without opposition in 1920, his support for Woodrow Wilson's policies and particularly his advocacy of prohibition cost him the election. He lost to Republican Richard P. Ernst by fewer than five thousand votes. Again in 1927 Beckham made a bid for the Senate. He succeeded in winning the Democratic nomination but lost to Republican Judge Flem D. Sampson, again because of opposition within the Democratic party. From 1900 to 1920 Beckham was an active participant in Democratic national conventions.

Beckham supported Albert B. Chandler for governor in 1935. Chandler in turn appointed Beckham to the Public Service Commission the following year. Beckham also served as chairman of the state Government Reorganization Commission, but failed to win his party's nomination for the Senate in 1936. He died on January 9, 1940, at the age of seventy-one and was buried in the state cemetery at Frankfort.

SUGGESTED READINGS: Nicholas C. Burckel, "From Beckham to McCreary: The Progressive Record of Kentucky Governors," *Register* 76 (October 1978), 285-306; Glenn Finch, "The Election of United States Senators in Kentucky: The Beckham Period," *FCHQ* 44 (January 1970), 38-50.

NICHOLAS C. BURCKEL

1907-1911
# AUGUSTUS EVERETT WILLSON
1846-1931

Unlike some twentieth-century chief executives in Kentucky, Augustus Everett Willson could not boast of forebears who had long been prominent in state politics and society. His parents, Ann Colvin Ennis and Hiram Willson, both of New England, migrated in the early 1840s from Allegany County, New York, to Maysville, Kentucky, where the future governor was born on October 13, 1846. Within the year Hiram Willson, a lumberman and mill operator, moved his family to nearby Covington. In 1852, before he had reached his sixth birthday, young Gus and his parents left Kentucky for New Albany, Indiana.

Orphaned at the age of twelve, Willson moved east with his younger sister and brother to live first with their grandmother in New York State and then with their older brother, Forceythe, a poet of some distinction, in Cambridge, Massachusetts. In his brother's home Gus profited from exposure to men of letters, including Emerson, Holmes, Lowell, and Longfellow, who often gathered there to discuss poetry. In 1869 he received the baccalaureate degree from Harvard University, where he subsequently spent several months reading law. Willson returned to New Albany in 1870 to live briefly with Indiana Congressman Michael C. Kerr.

Armed with a letter of introduction from Kerr, a future Speaker of the House, Willson applied for a position in the Louisville law firm of renowned attorney John Marshall Harlan, who later described the applicant as "one of the brightest young fellows I ever met." The two men forged a professional and personal bond that lasted a lifetime; their deep friendship did not diminish with Harlan's appointment in 1877 to the United States Supreme Court. Indeed, Harlan's fervent devotion to Republicanism proved contagious. His youthful protégé embraced partisan politics with a convert's zeal.

On five occasions between 1879 and 1892, Republicans in Kentucky tapped Willson as their nominee for public office. Although a polished orator and graceful campaigner, the Louisville attorney failed to be elected to the Kentucky Senate in 1879 and to the United States House in 1884, 1886, 1888, and 1892. In each contest Willson could not surmount the handicap of being a Republican in a predominantly Democratic state. Undaunted, he continued to advance the cause of Republicanism in Kentucky, especially in Louisville. In appreciation of his tireless efforts Republicans nominated the sixty-year-old Willson as their candidate for governor in 1907, despite the fact he had never before held a major appointive or elective office.

A bitter campaign ensued that revolved around the emotional issues of temperance and alleged Republican misrule. Both Willson and his Democratic challenger, State Auditor Samuel Wilber Hager, advocated the adoption of a uniform local option law, with the county as the governing unit—in the political jargon of the period, "county unit extension." Hager, the handpicked candidate of incumbent governor J.C.W. Beckham, repeatedly asserted that Democrats deserved full credit for passage of earlier temperance legislation. "I am most seriously and unrelentlingly opposed to intemperance," the Republican nominee countered, "whether in the man who parades as a temperance reformer, or in the victims of the habit or temptation." Denouncing politicians who masqueraded behind a "sham, grand-stand temperance," Willson charged that Democrats were attempting to "deliver the goods to both sides" on the liquor question. While Hager preached temperance "in the quiet valleys and country towns," Willson maintained, the Democratic candidate for mayor of Louisville openly proclaimed his intention to repeal Sunday closing laws. On the defensive, Hager often resorted to waving what had become the bloody shirt of Kentucky politics, the assassination of William Goebel. He further charged that during the administration of Gov. William O. Bradley Republicans had almost plunged the commonwealth "into a whirlpool of anarchy."

On November 5, Republicans emerged victorious in each of the statewide contests. The leading vote-getter was Willson, who captured the governorship with an absolute majority of 4,910 votes, winning by 214,481 to 196,428 over Hager. Willson owed his victory largely to overwhelming support from Louisville and Jefferson County. His winning margin in his home county—approximately 8,970 votes—provided almost half of the 18,053 votes by which he defeated Hager statewide. Willson also enjoyed the backing of a united Republican party, while his Democratic opponent was handicapped by intraparty factionalism and opposition to the Beckham "machine."

Republicans benefited as well from a relatively low turnout of voters. Confused by last-minute allegations of a Democratic sellout to the brewers, many dry Democrats apparently chose to remain home, while wets in both parties supported Willson, whom they considered more conservative on the liquor issue than Hager. In truth, the Democratic ticket fell victim to a curious combination of antagonistic wets and apathetic drys.

As Willson prepared to assume office on December 10, 1907, civil unrest in the western tobacco fields reignited with particular fury. The Black Patch War, named for western Kentucky's dark leaf tobacco region, had erupted two years earlier when independent tobacco growers established cooperatives to halt the price fixing of the so-called tobacco trust, a monopoly of American and European tobacco companies. The cooperatives could control the tobacco supply and drive up prices only if every producer joined in the effort. When some growers refused to participate, the so-called night riders resorted to violence and intimidation, including lynchings, horsewhippings, and crop burnings, to force compliance.

In his inaugural address Governor Willson vowed to protect the lives and property of the citizens of western Kentucky and to prosecute swiftly those who violated the law. During December 1907 his administration arranged meetings among the American Tobacco Company, the producers, and the residents of tobacco-growing areas. Frustrated when his efforts at mediation failed and convinced that local authorities were unable or unwilling to quell the unrest, Willson declared martial law in troubled areas and sent in the National Guard. Night rider activity declined quickly as civilians helped the guard suppress violence. Nonetheless, Willson was criticized for imposing martial law without a request from local authorities.

Although talented and well intentioned, Willson proved unsuccessful in getting his legislative program enacted. Throughout his term, the Democratic majority in the General Assembly refused to accept his leadership, but could not agree on a legislative agenda of their own. At the core of the Democrats' disagreement lay the volatile liquor issue, for Beckham had become the foremost political advocate of the dry cause. In 1908 the Democrats brought the work of the General Assembly to a virtual standstill as they battled over the election of a United States senator and the proposed extension of the county unit law. After seven weeks and twenty-eight ballots, four Democrats abruptly defected from Beckham—their party's senatorial nominee—to Republican William O. Bradley, ensuring Bradley's election. The enraged dry Democrats charged that the bolting Democrats had sold out to the "whiskey trust." Although a county unit extension bill easily passed the House in 1908, the measure was defeated by parliamentary legerdemain in the Senate. Two years later the liquor question again dominated the General Assembly, and Senate wets succeeded in forestalling a vote on county unit extension through "indefinite postponement." Because of partisan rancor and factionalism, few pieces of progressive legislation were enacted during the Willson administration. Indeed, the legislative sessions of 1908 and 1910 were among the least productive in the history of the General Assembly. The vexing problems of redistricting, tax reform, and civil unrest in the tobacco fields were but three issues that remained unaddressed. Allegedly because of the liquor interests, school suffrage for women likewise was not achieved.

Upon leaving office in December 1911 Willson resumed the practice of law in Louisville. In November 1914 he was defeated by former governor J.C.W. Beckham for a seat in the United States Senate. Although Willson never again sought public office, he maintained a keen interest in politics and civic affairs. His alma mater, Harvard University, honored him with election to its board of overseers (1910-1918). He died in Louisville on August 24, 1931, at eighty-four, and was buried at Cave Hill Cemetery. He was survived by Mary Elizabeth Ekin Willson, his wife of a half century. Their only child, a son, had died in infancy.

SUGGESTED READINGS: Glenn Finch, "The Election of United States Senators in Kentucky, The Beckham Period," *FCHQ* 44 (January 1970), 38-50; Robert K. Foster, "Augustus E. Willson and the Republican Party of Kentucky, 1895-1911" (master's thesis, University of Louisville, 1955); Thomas H. Appleton, Jr., "'Like Banquo's Ghost': The Emergence of the Prohibition Issue in Kentucky Politics" (Ph.D. dissertation, University of Kentucky, 1981); James O. Nall, *Night Riders of Kentucky and Tennessee, 1905-1919* (1939); Christopher R. Waldrep, "Augustus E. Willson and the Night Riders," *FCHQ* 58 (April 1984), 237-52.

THOMAS H. APPLETON, JR.


1915-1919
# AUGUSTUS OWSLEY STANLEY
1867-1958

Augustus Owsley Stanley was born on May 21, 1867, in Shelbyville, Kentucky, the son of William Stanley, a Disciples of Christ minister, and his wife Amanda Owsley, a niece of former governor William Owsley. Having attended Gordon Academy in Nicholasville, young Stanley enrolled first at the Kentucky Agricultural and Mechanical College in Lexington and later at Centre College in Danville, where he received a baccalaureate degree in 1889. After teaching in several Kentucky towns, Stanley read law in the Flemingsburg office of Gilbert Cassiday. Admitted to the bar in 1894, Stanley suffered one of his few political defeats three years later when he lost in his bid to become Fleming County attorney.

Struggling financially, Stanley moved in 1898 from Flemingsburg to Henderson and quickly rose in Democratic councils in western Kentucky. In 1902 the thirty-five-year-old attorney won the first of six terms in the United States House. As congressman from Kentucky's Second District, Stanley championed the cause of the tobacco growers and encouraged the formation of cooperatives to curb price fixing by the tobacco trust. Leadership in the fight for repeal of the six-cent tax on leaf tobacco made Stanley virtually unbeatable in his district. An unrelenting opponent of trusts, the Kentucky congressman gained national notoriety in his committee's investigation of the United States Steel Corporation. Many of the committee's recommendations were later incorporated into the Clayton Antitrust Act.

In 1914 Stanley decided to forego certain reelection to a seventh term in the House and announced his candidacy for the United States Senate, his lifelong ambition. Vying for their party's senatorial nomination were three of the state's most popular Democrats—Stanley, former governor J.C.W. Beckham, and incumbent governor James B. McCreary. However, the primary soon evolved into a two-man race between Beckham and Stanley. Beckham, the undisputed leader of the dry faction in his party, hit hard at his opponent's career-long defense of the whiskey industry. Stanley, in turn, repeatedly disparaged Beckham's sincerity on temperance. A celebrated wit, Stanley quipped on one occasion: "Beckham's as dry in the country as a dusty road; in the cities he's so wet you can catch him by the head and feet and wring water out of him." Yet Stanley could not surmount the public feeling that Beckham "deserved" the seat in the Senate that had been denied him six years earlier. On August 1, 1914, Beckham garnered 72,677 votes to Stanley's 65,871 and McCreary's 20,257.

Stanley decided to seek the governorship as a vehicle for furthering his senatorial goal. In January 1915 Stanley announced his candidacy for the Democratic nomination. He pledged to build better roads, to abolish the prison and contract labor system, and—most important— to enforce the county unit law and oppose statewide prohibition. His chief opponent was Henry V. McChesney of Frankfort, an ardent prohibitionist closely allied with the Beckham forces. In primary balloting Stanley emerged victorious in a field of four gubernatorial candidates with 107,585 votes to McChesney's 69,722.

In the general election the following November, Stanley faced Republican Edwin P. Morrow of Somerset, a nephew of Gov. William O. Bradley. Morrow condemned the alleged extravagance and inefficiency of the Democratic state administration and advocated "a general housecleaning" for Frankfort. He emphasized his own longstanding support for county unit; unlike his opponent, Morrow said, he had not been forced to embrace county unit "by the exigency of political conditions."

The Stanley-Morrow campaign was one of the most colorful and memorable in Kentucky history. Their warm friendship notwithstanding, the two candidates verbally attacked each other without mercy. Yet in private they enjoyed dining and drinking together, and they were once observed walking with their arms around each other's shoulders. Stanley eked out a meager 471-vote plurality over Morrow, 219,991 to 219,520.

As governor, Stanley enjoyed solid Democratic majorities in both houses of the legislature. Yet the 1916 session witnessed frequent carping and sniping between administration and antiadministration forces. The liquor issue was the principal cause of contention. Despite the jubilant cries of "Prohibition is dead!" that had greeted Mc-Chesney's defeat, dry legislators attempted to pass a constitutional amendment establishing prohibition. When both chambers rejected the amendment, angry drys held Governor Stanley responsible. Stanley himself showed little willingness to assuage the ire of temperance leaders. He complained publicly that legislators frivolously wasted 75 percent of their time debating the question, "Am I dryer than my neighbor?" But the governor rejoiced at the passage of virtually all of his program, which included a corrupt practices act, an antitrust law, a workman's compensation measure, and a convict labor bill. Left unresolved was a revision of the state tax structure.

In February 1917 Stanley convened the legislature in special session for the sole purpose of enacting "a just, progressive and modern" system of taxation. To rectify a "grossly inadequate" tax structure that "excessively burdened" agricultural interests, Stanley strongly advocated additional levies on intangible property. During sixty days of often rancorous debate, legislators accepted several bills, the most important of which established a three-member tax commission to supervise the administration of tax laws and property assessments.

Prohibition, however, remained the foremost political question. Like other Kentuckians, Stanley grew weary of the chronic acrimonious debates over prohibition and declared in July 1917 that the voters themselves should decide its fate. When the General Assembly convened in 1918, legislators quickly agreed to a prohibition amendment to the state constitution and scheduled a referendum on its adoption for November 1919. Drys exulted further when, by a combined vote of 94-17, Kentucky became the first wet state to ratify the proposed Eighteenth Amendment establishing national prohibition. The vexing liquor issue behind them, legislators debated and passed several measures advanced by the Stanley administration, including the first redistricting bill in twenty-five years and an act establishing the commonwealth's first budget system. Stanley provoked much criticism when, in the midst of World War I, he vetoed a bill that would have banned the teaching of German in Kentucky public schools.

Throughout his years as governor, Stanley continued to aspire to the United States Senate. When incumbent senator Ollie M. James, a fellow Democrat, died in August 1918 while a candidate for reelection, Stanley was immediately selected to replace him. Stanley entered the campaign a clear favorite. Senator Beckham, his erstwhile factional opponent, closed ranks behind the nominee. The Republican candidate, Dr. Ben L. Bruner, criticized the "undemocratic" manner of Stanley's nomination and accused the governor of being un-American in his veto of the German language bill. In November, Stanley won by a narrow 5,600-vote majority. He resigned the governorship in May 1919 to assume his seat in the Senate, but his tenure in the chamber to which he had so long aspired was short-lived. As a freshman Democrat in a Republican Senate, he enjoyed little influence, and in November 1924 he fell victim to the Coolidge landslide and was defeated by Republican Frederic M. Sackett.

Returning to private life in March 1925, Stanley made his home in Washington, where he resumed the practice of law. In 1930 he accepted an appointment by President Hoover to the International Joint Commission, which mediates disputes along the United States-Canadian border. Named chairman of the commission three years later, Stanley held that position until 1954, when he resigned under pressure from the Eisenhower administration.

Stanley died in Washington on August 12, 1958, at the age of ninety-one and was buried in the state cemetery at Frankfort. His wife, the former Sue Soaper, whom he had married in 1903, survived, as did two of their three sons, William and Augustus Owsley Stanley, Jr.

SUGGESTED READINGS: Thomas W. Ramage, "Augustus Owsley Stanley: Early Twentieth Century Kentucky Democrat" (Ph.D. dissertation, University of Kentucky, 1968); Nicholas C. Burckel, "A.O. Stanley and Progressive

Reform, 1902-1919," *Register* 79 (Spring 1981), 136-161; Thomas H. Appleton, Jr., "Prohibition and Politics in Kentucky: The Gubernatorial Campaign and Election of 1915," *Register* 75 (January 1977), 28-54.

THOMAS H. APPLETON, JR.

1919
# JAMES DIXON BLACK
1849-1938

James Dixon Black was born September 24, 1849, nine miles from Barbourville on Big Richland Creek in Knox County, the son of John C. and Clarissa Jones Black. He attended rural and subscription schools in and near Barbourville and in 1872 received his bachelor's degree from Tusculum College near Greenville, Tennessee. In 1911 his alma mater conferred on him an honorary LL.D. degree. After finishing college, Black returned to Knox County where he spent two years as a public schoolteacher. In the meantime he studied law and in 1874 was admitted to the bar. On December 2, 1875, he married Nettie Pitzer of Barbourville. They had three children, Pitzer D., Gertrude D., and Georgia.

Black soon entered politics, serving one term (1876-1877) in the Kentucky house. In 1879 he and several other Barbourville citizens purchased stock to fund a new college. Black insisted on naming the institution Union College in the hope that it would unify the community. Always interested in education, he became the superintendent of the Knox County public schools in 1884. He returned to his law practice the following year. In 1893 Black served as Kentucky's commissioner to the Chicago World's Fair. He continued to play an active role in the development of Union College, serving as its attorney, as a fundraiser, and as its president from 1910 to 1912.

In 1912 Black returned to politics, becoming Kentucky's first assistant attorney general. He next sought and won the Democratic nomination for lieutenant governor in 1915. A dry, he conveniently balanced the ticket with the gubernatorial nominee, A.O. Stanley, who was a wet. When Stanley became a United States senator in May 1919, Black succeeded to the governorship to serve out the remaining seven months of the term. He was still not accepted by the Stanley rank and file, yet his association with the administration had cost him the support of many drys. Since the legislature did not meet during his brief tenure, his administration was spared some potential conflicts.

Besides being a man without a faction, Black immediately had to face allegations of extravagance, corruption, and poor appointments by his predecessor. It is generally believed that Black had promised to keep Stanley appointees in office for the remainder of their terms, some believed in exchange for Stanley's support in the gubernatorial election. The Louisville *Courier-Journal* pointed out that he could make new appointments for positions filled by Stanley since the last legislative session, because those appointments had not yet been confirmed by the senate. Black chose to defend the Stanley administration instead.

Under special attack was the School Textbook Commission appointed by Stanley, which was accused of selecting books that had not been completed and, in general, of making poor selections. After the court of appeals ruled that the commission had not abided by the law in selecting books submitted in dummy form, Black called on the commissioners to resign. When they refused, he dropped the matter, saying he had no authority to remove them except for fraud or corruption. Also under attack was the Stanley administration's compromise settlement on back taxes owed by L.V. Harkness before his death. At the governor's direction, the attorney general investigated the matter and filed suit, but the case was not decided while Black was governor.

Another issue facing Black was Stanley's appointment of three special attorneys to collect inheritance taxes from the estate of Mrs. Robert Worth Bingham. Although Black indicated he would like them to resign, thereby saving the state their large fees, he refused to remove the attorneys, citing their "solemn contract" with the state. One of them, James Garnett, was an important member of Black's campaign staff.

In a bitter struggle for the Democratic gubernatorial nomination Black defeated his opponent, Judge John D. Carroll, by about 16,000 votes. During the campaign Black admitted writing a letter as assistant attorney general to an official of the Louisville and Nashville Railroad asking that William Tye of Barbourville be allowed to keep his pass but denied implying that Tye could influence jurors in favor of the railroad.

Black's Republican opponent, Edwin P. Morrow, declared that the Stanley administration was the main issue in the general election. Morrow capitalized on charges brought out during the primary. A few days before the election the Republicans disclosed that the state Board of Control had entered into a contract with A.S.J. Armstrong for cloth at twice the material's actual value. Black temporarily halted his campaign and ordered an investigation but refused to remove the members of the Board of Control. Armstrong proved to be a Louisville plumber, while the real bidder for the contract was his brother-in-law, Eugene Ray, former secretary of the state Prison Commission. The incident climaxed charges of partisan mismanagement of the state's institutions. In the election Black was swamped by Morrow's majority of more than 40,000 (254,490 to 214,114).

Black blamed his defeat on the liquor interests, pro-Germans, the Armstrong cloth mystery, President Wilson's handling of the coal strike, and his own failure to remove certain Stanley appointees. On the latter issue, he maintained that he had no authority to remove such persons. He spent his last days in office clearing up appeals for pardons and executive clemency. On December 1 he pardoned Henry Youtsey who had been paroled from prison the previous year after serving eighteen years for conspiracy in the assassination of Governor Goebel.

In 1920 Black became chief prohibition inspector in Kentucky. He later resumed his law practice and became president of the National Bank in Barbourville. He was serving as Sen. Alben Barkley's campaign manager in the Ninth Congressional District when he contracted pneumonia and died on August 5, 1938.

SUGGESTED READINGS: Erwin S. Bradley, *Union College 1879-1979*, edited by W.G. Marigold (1979); Thomas W. Ramage, "Augustus Owsley Stanley: Early Twentieth Century Kentucky Democrat" (Ph.D. dissertation, University of Kentucky, 1968); Robert F. Sexton, "Kentucky Politics and Society: 1919-1932" (Ph.D. dissertation, University of Washington, 1970).

MELBA PORTER HAY

1919-1923
# EDWIN PORCH MORROW
1877-1935

Edwin Porch Morrow was born November 28, 1877, at Somerset, Kentucky, the son of Thomas Zanzinger and Catherine Virginia Bradley Morrow. His father had been one of the founders of the Republican party in Kentucky and the party's unsuccessful candidate for governor in 1883. His mother's brother, William O. Bradley, was Kentucky's first Republican governor.

Morrow was educated in the public schools of Pulaski County until 1891 when he entered St. Mary's College near Lebanon. Two years later he entered Cumberland College in Williamsburg, Kentucky, where he distinguished himself in the debating society. In 1895 he took an active part in his uncle's gubernatorial campaign. With the advent of the Spanish-American War, he enlisted as a private in the army on June 24, 1898, and was mustered out as a second lieutenant on February 12, 1899, never seeing active duty. In 1900 he entered law school at the University of Cincinnati where he received the LL.B. degree in 1902.

Morrow then opened a law practice in Lexington. He established his reputation by defending William Moseby, a black man accused of murder. Morrow proved that his client's testimony had been extorted and that other testimony against him was untrue. Moseby was acquitted on September 31, 1902.

In 1903 Morrow moved back to Somerset and on June 18 married his childhood playmate, Katherine H. Waddle. They had two children, Edwina and Charles Robert. In 1904 he began a four-year term as Somerset city attorney. From 1910 to 1913 he served as United States district attorney for the eastern district of Kentucky. He was selected as the Republican candidate for the United States Senate in 1912 but was easily defeated by Democrat Ollie M. James.

In 1911 Morrow declined to be a candidate for governor, but in June 1915 he easily won his party's nomination for that office. Although opposed in the August primary by Latt F. McLaughlin, he won handily. He faced the Democratic nominee. A.O. Stanley, in the November election. In a rollicking campaign the two great stump orators often traveled together, denounced each other fiercely on the platform, and then went off to dinner together. Both parties endorsed similar progressive legislation, calling for an antilobby law, a corrupt practices act, a law to prevent railroads from issuing free passes to government officials, and approval of the county unit or county option law, as opposed to statewide prohibition. Morrow questioned Stanley's sincerity on the latter issue, since Stanley had long been known as a wet. On November 2, in the closest gubernatorial election in the state's history, Stanley defeated Morrow by 471 votes (219,991 to 219,520) out of more than 440,000 cast. Morrow declined to challenge the election despite charges of fraud, an act that greatly enhanced his popularity.

The Republican convention in June 1919 nominated Morrow for governor by acclamation. His Democratic opponent was Gov. James D. Black, who as lieutenant governor had succeeded to the governorship in May 1919 when Stanley went to the United States Senate. Morrow focused his campaign on the alleged graft, corruption, and poor appointments of the Stanley administration and on Black's failure to clean house. He called for better roads, elimination of politics from and improvement of schools, a nonpartisan charitable and penal board, and a nonpartisan judiciary. Although he opposed United States entry into the League of Nations, he avoided the question by saying it was not a party issue. He strongly supported the federal woman suffrage amendment and less enthusiastically the prohibition amendment. He promised to make better appointments to state boards and commissions and to remove special attorneys hired to represent the state in the tax case involving Mrs. Robert Worth Bingham's estate. Shortly before the election Morrow's campaign manager disclosed that the state Board of Control had granted a contract to a nonexistent corporation, A. S. J. Armstrong and Company, for inferior cloth at an excessive price. Black's refusal to remove the members of the board for its action simply capped the Republican charges of inefficiency and corruption. Despite the active campaigning of A. O. Stanley, Alben Barkley, and William Jennings Bryan on Black's behalf, Morrow won the governorship by 254,490 to 214,114.

In his message to the state legislature on January 6, 1920, Morrow called for abolition of useless offices and consolidation of boards and commissions whenever possible, a variety of new laws to improve public and higher education, an act to remove charitable and penal institutions from politics, a nonpartisan judiciary, the creation of a Department of Labor, road improvement, and a revision of property tax laws. With a legislature in which the Republicans controlled the House by a safe margin and the Democrats controlled the Senate by two votes, Morrow realized most of his requests and fulfilled virtually all of his campaign promises. Improvements in school textbook selection, creation of the state Board of Charities and Corrections, and centralization of the administration of highway work are among the most important achievements of his administration.

Morrow strongly supported enforcement of the laws. He announced that the eight-year-old law against carrying concealed weapons would be enforced in an effort to reduce homicides in the state. He instituted stiffer rules for the granting of pardons; his pardon of bank robber Frank Blair, however, became the strongest weapon of his political opponents. Although he signed the syndicalism and sedition bill passed in 1920, he later regretted his action and announced that he would not enforce section 10 because it violated the constitutional right of free speech. Morrow also spoke out forcefully against the Ku Klux Klan and became noted throughout the nation for his opposition to lynching. In February 1920 he called out the National Guard to protect Will Lockett, a black on trial for murder in Lexington. Lockett was convicted and later executed. A year later, Morrow removed the jailer of Woodford County from office because he had failed to prevent the lynching of Richard James, a black accused of killing two distillery guards in Midway. In addition, he offered a $25,000 reward for information leading to the arrest and conviction of the lynchers. In 1922 he sent the National Guard to Newport to quell disturbances resulting from a mill strike.

Morrow was frequently mentioned in 1920 as a possible vice-presidential candidate. Keeping a campaign promise not to seek another office while governor, he withdrew his name from consideration. He did, however, in a speech at Northampton, Massachusetts, on July 27, officially notify Calvin Coolidge of his nomination for that office. As a delegate to the Republican National Convention in 1920, Morrow had supported the Illinois governor, Frank O. Lowden, for president. Nevertheless he campaigned vigorously in Kentucky for Warren G. Harding and Coolidge.

In his message to the legislature in January 1922 Morrow called for more reforms in the educational system, for repeal of section 10 of the syndicalism and sedition law, for the repeal or modification of all laws to grant equal legal status to men and women, and increased expenditures for all state institutions, including prisons, reform schools, the feeble-minded institute, hospitals for the mentally ill, and the state university and normal schools. He recommended that the General Assembly submit to the people a large bond issue to finance improvements in state institutons and a $50 million bond issue to finance a modern highway system. The legislature, controlled now by Democrats, rejected virtually all his recommendations, although it created two new normal schools, one at Murray and one at Morehead. Morrow in turn vetoed a number of bills passed by the legislature.

After leaving the governorship in 1923, Morrow became an active member of the Watchmen of the Republic, an organization formed to promote a spirit of harmony and toleration by eradication of class, religious, and racial prejudice. From 1924 to 1926 he served on the United States Railroad Labor Board and from 1926 to 1934 on its successor, the United States Board of Mediation. He remained a popular Republican campaigner and was frequently touted as a candidate for various offices. In 1934 he sought the Republican nomination for Congress in the Ninth District but was defeated by John M. Robsion. He then made plans to move to Lexington and resume the practice of law. On June 15, 1935, while temporarily living at a cousin's home in Frankfort, he died unexpectedly of a heart attack. Funeral services were held at his cousin's home, followed by burial in the Frankfort Cemetery.

SUGGESTED READINGS: Willard Rouse Jillson, *Edwin P. Morrow—Kentuckian* (1921); Thomas H. Appleton, Jr., "Prohibition and Politics in Kentucky: The Gubernatorial Campaign and Election of 1915," *Register* 75 (January 1977), 28-54.

MELBA PORTER HAY

1923-1927
# WILLIAM JASON FIELDS
1874-1954

William Jason Fields was born in Willard, Kentucky, on December 29, 1874, the son of Mr. and Mrs. Christopher C. Fields. He married Dora McDaniel in 1893. A graduate of the University of Kentucky, Fields entered politics after working for several years as a drummer for an Ashland grocery company. In 1910 he made a bid for the Ninth District congressional seat. Using the slogan "Honest Bill from Olive Hill," he barely won the contest and became the first Democrat elected in that district in two decades. His constituents returned him to Congress for seven consecutive terms, and he eventually became the ranking minority member of the Military Affairs Committee. During World War I Fields became the ranking member of the subcommittee that handled the vast new appropriations needed to finance the war effort.

The 1923 Democratic gubernatorial primary brought out some of the bitterest factionalism in years when Alben Barkley challenged A.O. Stanley's followers. J. Campbell Cantrill, with the support of the

Kentucky Jockey Club and the coal interests, narrowly defeated Barkley for the nomination. However, in early September, with nearly two months remaining in the race, Cantrill died. Barkley, perhaps already intent on running for the United States Senate in 1926, declined consideration for the gubernatorial nomination. On September 8, the Democratic Central Committee chose Fields as the substitute candidate, a sign of the ascendancy of James B. Brown, a Louisville banker, as a coequal power broker with Stanley and Lexingtonian Billy Klair.

Owing to the state's displeasure with the administration of Republican Gov. Edwin Morrow and the strength of the Brown-Stanley-Klair triumvirate, Fields swept into office in one of the largest Democratic landslides in Kentucky history. He defeated Republican Charles I. Dawson 356,035 to 306,277. For the first time in seven years Democrats carried Louisville and Jefferson County. "Kentucky is a Democratic State and this is a Democratic Year," the Louisville *Courier-Journal* lamented, after having taken no stand during the general election.

A Methodist and a prohibitionist, Fields maintained a rather austere atmosphere at the governor's mansion and banned dancing. However, his code of conduct did not forbid nepotism, and he appointed his eldest son as state examiner and added several other kinfolk to the state payroll. He also repaid the political debt to Brown with an appointment to the state Tax Commission.

In Fields' opening message to the 1924 session of the General Assembly, he proposed a $75 million highway bond issue, urged the development of normal schools at Morehead and Murray, and asked for an increase in the gasoline tax to three cents per gallon. Moreover he indicated a desire to pay off the floating public debt, otherwise known as the state warrant system. The *Courier-Journal* reacted unfavorably, distrusting the intentions of the Highway Commission as well as the powers behind the scenes in Frankfort politics.

The Haly-Bingham forces threw down the gauntlet for the remainder of the session, challenging the Fields administration on nearly every substantive item to come before the legislature. These issues included the bond controversy, a bill to end pari-mutuel betting, and investigations of the state Board of Charities and Corrections. Bingham claimed that the "interlocking, bipartisan machine" of Republican Maurice Galvin and Democrat Klair worked to use the above issues for self-seeking purposes. Near the end of the session Fields and Bingham engaged in a spirited debate published by the *Courier-*

*Journal* and the Louisville *Herald* and *Post*, two papers recently purchased by James B. Brown.

At the end of his first legislative session Fields could point to at least one victory. The proposed bond issue passed the General Assembly and went to the people for approval in the 1924 general election. After the final legislative bargaining, the bond program was split into two parts with $50 million to go for highway construction and $25 million to be divided among educational, penal, and charitable institutions.

The *Courier-Journal* led the fight against the bond issue, joined by the state Efficiency Commission and the Pay-As-You-Go organization. Bingham claimed that the bonds would not fund enough miles of roads to warrant such indebtedness, which would be paid for by Kentucky farmers, and he suspected that the spoils system would be used to decide where the highways would be built. The pro-bond forces, led by Governor Fields, the Kentucky Good Roads Association, and Desha Breckinridge, editor of the *Lexington Herald*, emphasized the need for modernization of the state's road system and charitable institutions. Fields devoted nearly ten weeks to the campaign and traveled extensively across the state. Election day brought victory for President Coolidge and Republican senatorial candidate Fred Sackett but defeat by more than 90,000 votes for the bond issue.

After his defeat on the bond vote, Fields concentrated on the administration of state government. He remained an active executive during his last two years in office and presented an extensive legislative program to the 1926 General Assembly. It considered and passed more bills than any previous legislature. Many of the new laws related to government reorganization. However, Fields won an increase in the gasoline tax to five cents per gallon, a move designed to generate more funds for highway construction and maintenance. In addition, the General Assembly created three major departments to streamline government regulation and operation, including the state Department of Bus Transportation and the state Purchasing Commission. Fields failed to get an educational bond on the ballot. The Bingham faction continued its opposition to the Fields administration throughout the session.

The record of Governor Fields is mixed. For each sign of progressivism there is evidence of reversion to the old spoils system. Fields apparently had a genuine desire to economize and to serve his state honestly. However, charges of corruption continually tarnished his image. If not a confidant of the bipartisan combine of Klair and Galvin, Fields nonetheless appeared subservient to their wishes. Like most Kentucky governors of this era, he abused the power to pardon criminals. Moreover he could not pull diverse factions together, and the state Democratic party continued to be divided in most elections. While the Democrats generally united behind Barkley in his victorious Senate race in 1926, Republican Flem Sampson easily defeated Beckham in the 1927 gubernatorial election.

After Fields left Frankfort, he failed to win back his old congressional seat. In 1927 he was admitted to the bar and served briefly as commonwealth attorney for the Thirty-seventh District. Governor Chandler appointed him to the state Workmen's Compensation Board, a position he held through the first months of the administration of Republican Gov. Simeon S. Willis. Fields moved to Florida in the 1940s, but later returned to Carter County to practice law and to farm, dying there on October 21, 1954.

SUGGESTED READINGS: Paul Hughes, "William J. Fields," *Courier-Journal Magazine*, July 2, 1950; Robert F. Sexton, "Kentucky Politics and Society: 1919-1932" (Ph.D. dissertation, University of Washington, 1970); Woodson D. Scott, "The Work of the 1926 Legislature," *Kentucky Law Journal* 15 (November 1926), 52-54.

WILLIAM E. ELLIS

1927-1931
# FLEM D. SAMPSON
1875-1967

Sampson was born on January 25, 1875, near London, Kentucky, the son of Joseph, a farmer and trader in lumber, and Emoline Kellum Sampson. The ninth of ten children, as a candidate Sampson would later boast his humble origins and that he had "trapped skunks in the piney woods of Laurel County" to buy his schoolbooks. He attended school in Laurel County and by sixteen was a teacher in the local Indian Creek School. He attended Union College in Barbourville and then Valparaiso University where he received his law degree (LL.D.) in 1894. In 1897 he was married to Susie Steele and became the father of three daughters—Pauline, Emolyn, and Helen Katherine.

Returning to Barbourville with his law degree, Sampson practiced law, served as city attorney, and then as the young president of the First

National Bank of Barbourville. His Horatio Alger-like rise gave him a good base for politics. One of his law partners was Caleb Powers, accused assassin of William Goebel, and Sampson's friendship with the martyred Powers gave him a good claim on eastern Kentucky Republicans. In 1906 he ran for and won the county judgeship of Knox County as a Republican in heavily Republican territory. In 1911 he was elected circuit judge of the Thirty-fourth Judicial District and was then reelected in 1916.

With a reputation for toughness on crime and liquor law violators, he was elected judge of the Kentucky Court of Appeals in 1916 and reelected in 1924. He served as chief justice of that court in 1923-1924. Over the years Sampson built a strong alliance with powerful eastern Kentucky Congressman John M. Robsion and together they built an eastern Kentucky faction of the Republican party.

Sampson's major, and successful, venture into statewide politics came in the 1927 governor's election, largely the result of division and bickering among the state's Democrats. Since the early 1920s, Democrats had been split by a movement with prohibitionist and fundamentalist leanings to outlaw pari-mutuel gambling on horse racing, including racing at Churchill Downs, and to levy a severance tax on coal. The Democratic primary in 1923 had been a contest between young Congressman Alben Barkley, dubbed the reform or antigambling candidate, and William Jason Fields, the candidate supported by the Kentucky Jockey Club and many members of the Democratic machine. One biased newspaperman observed: "Kentucky is in the grasp of a national organization of coal operators . . . and an international syndicate of race-track gamblers." Fields won, but did not reunite the party.

By 1927 the antigambling movement peaked while the coal severance tax movement disappeared. With the support of Robert Worth Bingham, publisher of the Louisville *Courier-Journal*, and Percy Haly, legendary Lexington political organizer, former governor J. W. C. Beckham captured his party's nomination for the antigamblers or reformers. A sincere reformer or not, Beckham's nomination split the party widely and publicly. James Brown, Billy Klair, Johnson Camden, James E. Cantrill, Desha Breckinridge, and other Democratic powers from Louisville and Lexington sympathetic to the horse and liquor industries bolted the party.

By throwing their support to Republican Sampson they seemed to confirm the impression that a "bipartisan combine" of pro-Jockey

Club power brokers controlled the state. The campaign became bitterly personal. Sampson, alluding to his opponent's personal drinking habits and his own personal purity on the gambling issue, said he himself "never smoked, chewed, drank, gambled—not even bet on an election." (Democrat A.O. Stanley asked, "I wonder if he'd suck an egg?") Sampson promised to protect horse racing, build better roads, provide free textbooks, and enforce national prohibition. Beckham's supporters in return picked up the label "Flim-Flam" for Sampson, first used by Sampson's opponent in the Republican primary.

Sampson's victory with a sizable margin of 32,000 votes, 382,306 to 350,796, especially with every other Republican on the ticket losing, sealed the impression that power brokers indeed controlled the state. In assessing the mandate Sampson carried into office, the *New York Times* said the campaign had been "a dull confusion of personalities, unpleasant revelations about candidates, inconsistency and hypocrisy on both sides. . . . Both campaign committees represent temporary alliances of hostile factions. . . . Students of democracy will find little to encourage them in the whole spectacle."

As Sampson entered office he faced a hostile Democratic General Assembly with a weak political base of his own. His free textbook plan was adopted, but the General Assembly provided no appropriation to pay for it. His efforts to create a Kentucky Progress Commission (the forerunner of the Kentucky Department of Commerce) and to add to the state parks system were more successful.

But Sampson soon wound up in trouble. He allied closely with traditional power groups in southern politics—the utilities and the textbook manufacturers. A sniping Frankfort grand jury indicted him for receiving gifts from textbook manufacturers, but the indictment was dismissed. Perhaps most controversial was his support for building a hydroelectric plant at Cumberland Falls and rejection of a $230,000 gift from the DuPont family to buy the falls and convert the area to a park.

Meanwhile the depression came to Kentucky with a vengeance. Severe drought prevailed in 1930 and eighty-six counties applied for federal assistance. In the depressed coalfields the United Mine Workers made their first substantial inroads as unemployment there reached about 40 percent. And by 1930 the Banco Kentucky, a Louisville financial empire, closed its doors.

In the 1930 General Assembly, when Sampson vetoed the bill accepting the DuPont gift for Cumberland Falls, it was passed over his veto. Riding what the newspapers called a tidal wave of anti-Sampson feeling, Democrats moved to regain power, especially over patronage, through the legislative branch.

In Sampson's most humiliating defeat the legislators "ripped" him of much statutory authority and gave it to a three-member committee that included Sampson and two Democrats—the lieutenant governor and the attorney general. The lieutenant governor became de facto governor. With no substantial allies, Sampson had lost control of the state government.

When he left office in 1931 Sampson returned to Barbourville to practice law and to participate in civic activities. He died in Louisville on June 25, 1962.

SUGGESTED READINGS: Robert F. Sexton, "Kentucky Politics and Society: 1919-1932," (Ph.D. dissertation, University of Washington, 1970); Sexton, "The Crusade Against Pari-mutuel Gambling in Kentucky: A Study of Southern Progressives in the 1920s," *FCHQ* 50 (January 1976), 47-57.

ROBERT F. SEXTON

1931-1935
# RUBY LAFFOON
1869-1941

Ruby Laffoon was born in Madisonville on January 15, 1869, the son of John Bledsoe and Martha Earle Laffoon. He attended public schools in Madisonville and a private school in Hopkins County. In 1890 he received his law degree from Washington and Lee University and established a practice in Madisonville. On January 31, 1894, he married Mary Nisfet. Laffoon soon became involved in state politics as a Democrat. He failed to win races for state treasurer in 1907 and state auditor in 1911, but he won appointment as chairman of the first Insurance Rating Board in 1912. He was elected circuit judge in 1921 and 1927.

At the onset of the Great Depression Kentucky state politics changed abruptly. For the first time since the tumultuous 1899 Music Hall Convention the Democratic party did not use an open primary to choose candidates for statewide office. New alliances formed in the party, and the bipartisan combine did not tamper with the two-party system as it had in the elections of the twenties. Though he had little previous contact with state government, Laffoon found support among such important party leaders as Ben Johnson, Allie W. Young, and Thomas Rhea in his bid for the Democratic party's gubernatorial nomination.

In early May 1931, 120 county conventions selected delegates who met a few days later in Lexington. The Laffoon canvass far outdistanced all other hopefuls, and he swept the Democratic convention. Capitalizing on the poor state of the economy, Laffoon vowed to rid Frankfort of all remaining Republican officials. He enjoyed old-fashioned stump speaking, often sprinkling his electioneering with passages from the Bible. Though crippled from a childhood accident, Laffoon waged a vigorous campaign. The *Courier-Journal* gave lukewarm support to the Republican candidate, former Louisville mayor William B. Harrison, primarily because of Laffoon's campaign style. On election day Laffoon swept into office with a poll of 446,301 votes to 374,239, the largest majority for a gubernatorial victor up to that time. However, old Ed Morrow, the survivor of many a Kentucky political bloodletting, forecast that the alliance between the "terrible Turk from Madisonville and the unbending Benjamin [Johnson] from Bardstown" would not last long.

Soon after taking the oath of office, Laffoon paid his debt to Johnson with an appointment to the Highway Commission. In his inaugural address the governor made the obligatory pledges to improve education, highways, and charitable and penal institutions. "Retrenchment and reform shall be the watchword of this administration," he intoned. The problems facing the state and its new governor appeared insurmountable as revenues plummeted with the deepening depression. Just before the opening of the 1932 session of the General Assembly Laffoon promised to end the old discredited warrant system used for paying state debts and to initiate a full audit of previous administrations.

Morrow's prediction of an impending break between Laffoon and Johnson was not long in coming. When the governor proposed a sales tax measure during the 1932 session, an antiadministration faction coalesced, led by Highway Commissioner Johnson and Lt. Gov. Albert B. Chandler. As presiding officer of the Senate, Chandler worked diligently to keep the sales tax from gaining support. The session ended with the party bitterly divided. In retaliation for Democratic defections Laffoon vetoed a cut in the state property tax and $7 million in legislative appropriations.

During Laffoon's second year as governor, the election of Franklin

D. Roosevelt overshadowed the state administration. The sales tax issue, however, lingered near the surface of Kentucky politics. In March 1933, just prior to the Roosevelt inauguration, Laffoon declared a bank holiday, an act reflecting the near collapse of Kentucky's economy. Late in the year he also closed the burley tobacco markets after farmers complained of low prices and violence threatened to erupt throughout the tobacco belt.

The Great Depression and the advent of the New Deal social programs radically changed traditional federal-state relationships, exerting great stress on the already impoverished treasury of the Commonwealth of Kentucky. Throughout much of 1933-1934 Laffoon and Harry Hopkins, head of the Federal Emergency Relief Administration, sparred over Kentucky's inability to come up with its share of matching relief funds. As a result, Kentucky lagged behind most other states in administering aid to the needy.

With the state in dire financial straits Laffoon never gave up on the idea of raising funds through a sales tax, a plan also being considered by the United States Congress at the time. Before leaving on a trip to the nation's capital, Laffoon assured the press that he would not introduce a sales tax measure into a special session of the General Assembly, undoubtedly a ruse to keep antiadministration forces off guard. On his return he called an emergency meeting of the legislature and proposed a "gross receipts tax," eschewing the now divisive name of sales tax. The battle lines formed, with the Kentucky Retail Merchants' Association voicing opposition. Again the Chandler-Johnson faction was too strong, and the Laffoon tax program went down to defeat. The issue did not die, and it ruptured party unity as completely as it had been a decade before when the Beckham and Stanley groups often waged suicidal warfare.

After the 1933 legislative races Tom Rhea worked on a new coalition in the Senate and finally wrested control from Allie Young. When the 1934 regular session of the General Assembly met, Laffoon's forces, with the aid of Republicans, rammed through a reorganization bill stripping Chandler and his ally, State Auditor J. Dan Talbott, of most of their powers. Moreover another statute gave the governor power to remove summarily an appointed state official. Having neutralized his adversaries, Laffoon now moved to set the stage for passage of the sales tax. At his request the General Assembly cut the automobile and state property taxes, Laffoon's strategy being to make passage of the sales tax the only alternative.

This time, confident of quick success, the governor quickly called a special session in July. Administration supporters orchestrated a pro-sales-tax parade with several thousand educators, schoolchildren, and college students marching the streets of the capital. The Chandler-Johnson forces could still muster enough votes to stall procedures for weeks, but the battle ended when a 3 percent sales tax bill barely passed the Senate. Laffoon predicted that Kentuckians would soon be praising the virtues of the new tax.

Near the end of his term, Laffoon appeared to be more powerful than at any time since taking office. Though action under the dismissal law was delayed by an appeal, the governor finally replaced Johnson with Rhea, grooming him to run as the next Democratic gubernatorial candidate. Laffoon and Rhea understood that the stand of Chandler against the sales tax had made him a hero. To keep the lieutenant governor out of the gubernatorial race, Laffoon and Rhea had worked against a compulsory primary law during the 1932 and 1934 regular sessions and dissuaded the state Democratic committee from adopting an optional primary in early 1935.

At this point one of the most crucial and fateful turnabouts in Kentucky politics occurred. President Roosevelt requested an explanation for the lack of a Democratic primary in Kentucky and Laffoon and Rhea made preparations for a trip to Washington. As soon as their train crossed into West Virginia, Chandler as temporary governor of the commonwealth called a special session of the General Assembly to study a primary bill. Laffoon and Rhea rushed back to the state and asked the Court of Appeals to disallow the meeting. After being denied this request, the governor agreed to a dual, double-barreled primary system, one with a runoff election if no candidate had a clear majority in the first poll. Rhea won the first primary but not by a majority. In the second battle Chandler won the war, defeating Rhea by a substantial margin. Laffoon and Rhea bolted the party, but Chandler won handily in the general election against Republican judge King Swope.

Being governor during one of the most critical periods of Kentucky history, Laffoon stayed the course with his sales tax idea. As has happened with many other governors, he ran afoul of Kentucky Democratic factional politics and finally lost not only party control but his cherished sales tax as well.

Laffoon could display a fiery temper, but he also had a sense of humor. He collected original drawings of political cartoons in which he was caricatured. The Terrible Turk often suggested prison reform measures and continually complained about the great expense of operating the penal system. Before he left office in December 1935, Laffoon pardoned more prisoners than any previous governor. After leaving the capital, he resumed law practice in Madisonville, dying there on March 1, 1941.

SUGGESTED READINGS: Vernon Gipson, *Ruby Laffoon, Governor of Kentucky, 1931-1935* (1978); Willard Rouse Jillson, *Governor Ruby Laffoon* (1932).

WILLIAM E. ELLIS

1935-1939
1955-1959
# ALBERT BENJAMIN CHANDLER
1898-

Albert Benjamin Chandler, twice governor of Kentucky, is the state's real-life Horatio Alger hero. Like the boys of Alger's novels, Chandler rose from poverty to dazzling success. He was born July 14, 1898, the son of Joseph Sephus and Callie Saunders Chandler, on a tiny farm near Corydon in western Kentucky. Rejected and abandoned at age four by his mother, he was reared by relatives and by his father. The young Chandler worked almost from infancy; by the time he was seven or eight he was virtually supporting himself by selling newspapers and doing other chores in Corydon. A lifelong friend of his says the kind citizens of the little town assumed the role of mother to him.

The adversities of Chandler's childhood forged a character with unusual strength and resilience. He mastered all hardships and grew up cheerful, buoyant, and self-assured, an outstanding athlete and a popular young man known among friends as Irish Chandler, either because of his presumably Irish disposition or, as he supposes, because he reminded them of the lad in the Alger story, *Only an Irish Boy*. Chandler never forgot his earlier experiences, and this memory powerfully influenced his views on public policy throughout his career. In 1935 his wife wrote to someone who had commented on his kindness to a group of little boys, "He had a bitter struggle with never enough to eat and never enough clothes to keep him warm. The sight of a small boy selling papers on the street never fails to remind him of his own past." During Chandler's first term as governor he wrote a petitioner saying: "You are correct in assuming that I am interested in the welfare of every under-privileged man, woman and child in the Commonwealth. . . . I might mention that I have known the pinch of poverty and that I have been dependent upon my own resources from my very earliest years. I would be sympathetic with any program that would give poor children an opportunity to enjoy the necessities of life." He wrote this as a politician seeking to impress a constituent, but it truly represented his feelings toward all of the more unfortunate citizens of Kentucky.

Chandler went from the Corydon High School in 1917 to Transylvania University in Lexington. His list of the possessions he brought with him is a permanent part of Kentucky folklore. He says, "I had a red sweater, a five dollar bill, and a smile." He made his way through college much as he had made it through his previous years—by doing such jobs as baby-sitting, washing windows, and serving tables at a boardinghouse. He was a star athlete, captain of the baseball and basketball teams, and quarterback of the football team. His grades were adequate but not outstanding, mostly Bs and Cs. Besides his formal education, he acquired something else at Transylvania that later would be of immense value to him. He acquired the nickname Happy, an accurate reflection of his outlook on life.

In 1922 Chandler enrolled in the Harvard University Law School, but a year later he transferred to the University of Kentucky Law School, from which he graduated two years later. He supported himself through law training by coaching high school athletics, first at Wellesley, Massachusetts, and later at Versailles, Kentucky, which became his permanent hometown. After graduation he established a law practice there, but he also continued his high school coaching and took on the added duty of scouting college football games for Coach Charles Moran of the famed Centre College team.

In 1925 Chandler married Mildred Watkins, a young woman from Virginia who was a teacher in the Margaret Hall girls' school in Versailles. Both bright and charming, she possessed extraordinary insights into the nature of people and politics. Chandler affectionately called her "the Secretary of War," but she eventually became known throughout Kentucky as "Mama." She has been a devoted wife and an invaluable advisor and associate.

Chandler entered politics soon after his marriage. He became active in the Woodford County Democratic organization, and in 1929 he won a seat in the state Senate. Two years later he was elected lieutenant governor on the ticket with Gov. Ruby Laffoon. Chandler soon broke with Laffoon over the state sales tax, which Chandler opposed. The Laffoon forces in the Senate retaliated by enacting a series of so-called ripper bills that stripped Chandler of his customary prerogatives as president of the body. In 1935, guided by his friend and political mentor, State Auditor J. Dan Talbott of Bardstown, Chandler made the most daring step of his career. While the governor was in Washington, Acting Governor Chandler called a special session of the legislature for the purpose of enacting a law requiring party primaries instead of conventions for the nomination of candidates. The state Court of Appeals validated the call, and the legislature eventually passed the act.

In recounting the episode of calling the special session, Chandler quotes with relish the famous line that Shakespeare put in Brutus's mouth: "There is a tide in the affairs of men which taken at the flood, leads on to fortune." Certainly, Chandler's action in getting a primary law led him directly into the governor's mansion. It brought an instant outpouring of enthusiastic mail from all over the state. The most penetrating comment came from a Newport attorney and state legislator who urged Chandler to run for governor in the forthcoming election, saying: "You may not realize it, but now you are a different man in the realm of reputation than you were a few weeks ago. Comparatively few people knew you well enough [then] to appreciate you; they considered you a likeable young man more or less on a political lark. They liked you, but they would not have supported you for Governor. Since your dramatic victory over the machine a few weeks ago, you have emerged as a young political leader conspicuous for courage and brains. You are a field-general now."

Chandler entered the 1935 Democratic primary and won the party nomination in a runoff election. He then overwhelmingly defeated his Republican opponent King Swope, 556,262 to 461,104. One of the first acts of his administration was to carry out his most effective campaign pledge by repealing the state's 3 percent sales tax. Widely hailed at age thirty-seven as the "boy governor," he now launched a vigorous program of administrative reorganization and reform, frugality, and fiscal responsibility; at the same time, he sponsored significant improvements in the state's roads, schools, and health, welfare, and penal institutions. He raised the revenue required for these measures by increasing the state's excise and income taxes. The levy on whiskey was especially important, as the repeal in 1935 of the Kentucky prohibition amendment created a great source of fresh income for the Chandler administration. He was able to inaugurate his program by exercising a remarkable degree of control over the legislature, a feat accomplished through a combination of suasion, organizational discipline, political horse-trading, and the skillful application of patronage. He also made effective use of the radio to exert pressure on recalcitrant legislators by addressing the electorate directly. An admirer from Covington wrote, "Your ability to line up members who would like to oppose [your program] is almost uncanny."

Perhaps the most important measure Chandler sponsored was the Government Reorganization Act of 1936, which drastically reduced the number of departments and clearly defined the responsibilities of each. It was a long step in the direction of imposing modernity and order on what had been an outmoded and chaotic administrative arrangement. As a result of this streamlining, accompanied by the appointing of capable and conscientious department heads and other officials, the Chandler administration was able to cut by more than three-fourths the state's outstanding debt of $28.5 million, thus achieving a great saving in interest payments and making possible the redemption at face value of the state's warrants of indebtedness, which had been selling at a heavy discount.

Chandler also significantly increased the state's support of its public schools and colleges and its university. His administration provided the first funds to make free textbooks available to pupils in the public schools. Near the end of his term he started the state's teachers' retirement system, though the first money for it was to be supplied by his successor. Because of these and other progressive measures, Dr. Frank L. McVey, president of the University of Kentucky, was moved to write him, ". . . in the year in which you have been in office much more has been accomplished than would have been thought possible."

The Chandler administration in 1936 inaugurated the state's rural roads program with a $2 million appropriation for this purpose. The administration also enacted the state's first Rural Electrification Act to take advantage of the federal government's rural electrification program. Chandler sponsored the initial appropriation of funds for old-age assistance, a measure that had been authorized in 1935 by a constitutional amendment. He persuaded the legislature in 1938 to put before the voters another amendment adding dependent children and the needy blind to the assistance rolls.

Chandler's record in dealing with the state's hospitals and penal institutions was particularly noteworthy. He built a number of new and thoroughly modern facilities, and he staffed them with persons of genuine professional competence. The most dramatic episode of his gubernatorial career occurred at the time of the great 1937 flood; at one point he risked his own safety in supervising the removal of prisoners from the partly inundated Frankfort penitentiary. Writing to congratulate him on his behavior in the entire flood crisis, university president McVey said: "Your leadership has been one of the highest possible. You have shown courage, administrative capacities and a grim cheerfulness that has set an example for all. You have done a great piece of work."

Chandler was naturally sympathetic to the laboring classes. He protected the Harlan County miners in their efforts to unionize, and he sponsored a law prohibiting company mine guards from serving as deputy sheriffs. He also took the lead in establishing a state Department of Industrial Relations, and he appointed as its commissioner a man who was endorsed by the unions. Chandler supported the legislature's ratification of the proposed child labor amendment to the United States Constitution. But he intractably opposed the practices of the sit-down strike and the closed shop. During both of his administrations he incurred the condemnation of labor leaders and their friends by sending the National Guard into turbulent Harlan County to protect strikebreaking workers and keep the mines open.

Chandler's record of accomplishments, along with his forceful address and winning personality, made him the hero of a majority of the citizens of Kentucky and gained him national recognition as well. Expressions of confidence, gratitude, and praise were showered upon him by people from all areas, classes, and conditions. If Chandler was not the greatest governor the commonwealth ever had, certainly his administration from 1935 to 1939 deserves to be credited as among the best in the state's history.

Urged by a multitude of his supporters, Chandler now made a move that brought the first reverse of his meteoric political career. He challenged Sen. Alben Barkley, majority leader of the United States Senate, in the 1938 Democratic senatorial primary in Kentucky. Chandler lost in a campaign of accusations and counteraccusations, a campaign in which Pres. Franklin D. Roosevelt felt obliged to come to Kentucky to speak in direct support of Barkley. Chandler had undertaken too much in his bid to oust a popular and accomplished incumbent who was also a formidable campaigner and who had the backing and patronage of an adored president.

The fates nevertheless soon placed Chandler in the United States Senate. In October 1939 the junior senator from Kentucky, M. M. Logan, died suddenly. Chandler now resigned the governorship in favor of Lt. Gov. Keen Johnson who, by prearrangement, appointed Chandler to the vacant place in the Senate. The next year Chandler won a special election to serve out the remainder of Logan's unexpired term, and in 1942, in another campaign filled with recriminations Chandler defeated a former political ally, John Y. Brown, Sr., for a full senatorial term.

In the Senate, Chandler associated himself closely with a coterie of Southern conservatives who were led by Sen. Harry Flood Byrd, Sr., Chandler's warm, friend and political idol. But Chandler never wore any one political brand; he was the quintessential maverick who insisted upon following his own head. Usually he supported the measures of the Roosevelt administration, though he never forgave Roosevelt for interposing himself in the 1938 Kentucky senatorial campaign, and Chandler opposed what he considered to be spendthrift ways of Roosevelt's New Deal.

The most burning issues of Chandler's Senate years were those of military preparedness and the waging of World War II. Appointed through Byrd's influence to the Military Affairs Committee, he shared the deliberations and activities of this important body. He was one of a set of committee members who circled the globe in 1943 inspecting American bases, troops, and operations. He backed the nation's war measures with unstinting devotion, though he disagreed vociferously with the strategy of making its primary mission the defeat of Germany instead of Japan.

In the fall of 1945 Chandler surprised his acquaintances, and himself too, he says, by suddenly resigning his seat in the Senate to accept the job of National Commissioner of Baseball. Serving in this position for six years, he presided over the adoption of a number of the most significant measures in the history of the sport, including the establishment of a players' pension fund and the admission of black players into the major leagues. But his forceful actions alienated many of the team owners, and in the summer 1951 when they refused to reappoint him he returned to Versailles and reentered his frequently interrupted practice of law.

Nobody expected him to remain very long on the political sideline, and in 1955 he successfully challenged the Democratic machine in the state by winning the governorship a second time. That he could return to politics after apparently "burning all his bridges" and defeat the formidable party organization was a tribute to his past accomplishments. It was also a tribute to his art as a campaigner, in which he had few peers and no superiors. In this role, perhaps more than any other, he became a Kentucky folk figure, a living legend. His strength lay partly in his perceptiveness in identifying and elaborating those issues of deepest concern to the citizens: tax relief, for example. Just as important, his strength lay also in his skill at infusing the appeal for votes with the verve and color of his own personality. He loved a campaign. There was a saying that he enjoyed running for office more than he enjoyed occupying the office. Vehemently denying accusations of favoritism and corruption during his career in the Senate, he mounted an offensive against his opponent by promising to take the incumbent governor "off the public teat and turn him out into the cornstalks, where [Chandler said] he would bellow like a young bull calf." Chandler appealed to the electorate to "Be like your pappy and vote for Happy." A majority of the voters did just that. Chandler won the Democratic primary in a close election; he won the general election over Edwin R. Denney by the greatest margin ever polled in Kentucky to that time, 451,647 to 322,671.

Chandler's second administration lacked the youthful reforming zeal that had marked his first term. It attracted a drumfire of criticism from the state's traditionally liberal voices, including the *Louisville Courier-Journal*, which had been a strong Chandler supporter early in his career. But there were many positive accomplishments, particularly in road building and the financing of schools and other public institutions. Chandler sponsored appropriations bills to increase the support of the public schools' minimum foundation program and the teachers' retirement program. He also sponsored a $100 million bond issue to finance the construction of federal and state highways in Kentucky.

The most spectacular and far-reaching accomplishments of his second administration were his enforcement of the United States Supreme Court's desegregation decision and his preeminent role in founding the University of Kentucky medical school and hospital. When in 1956 angry mobs threatened to prevent black pupils from enrolling in two formerly white schools, Chandler sent the State Police and the National Guard in with tanks to protect the blacks and keep the schools open. In building the medical school, he was obliged to overcome the opposition of many of the state's most influential physicians. The establishment deservedly was named the Albert B. Chandler Medical Center. Chandler says its creation was the greatest achievement of his entire public career.

Three times again Chandler sought the state's highest office (1963, 1967, 1971), all in vain. He has been out of political office since his second term as governor. These have, nevertheless, been full years for him. He has been active on the political scene, sometimes in opposition to the Democratic candidates. In 1967, for example, he threw his support to the victorious Republican candidate for the governorship.

Chandler has also been engaged in various business and public enterprises. He has served on the athletics board of the University of Kentucky and on the boards of trustees of both his alma maters, Transylvania University and the University of Kentucky. The embodiment of the Kentucky spirit, he is the state's most enthusiastic booster, its ambassador at large. When he says Kentucky is God's country, and he says it often, the words come from the heart. When he sings "My Old Kentucky Home," which he says is the most beautiful song ever written, the words, notes, and tears come from the heart.

In his own mind Chandler is at peace with the world, including his rivals and critics of the past—most of them, at least. In the summer 1982 one of his keenest ambitions was fulfilled: he was inducted into the baseball Hall of Fame. He is secure in the knowledge that his individual efforts will leave Kentucky and, to some extent, the entire nation a legacy of better health, education, well-being, and contentment. In 1985 his long love affairs with Mama and with life are still going strong. He says he lives every day as if it were his last day on earth and sleeps every night as if he were going to live forever.

Chandler's door in Versailles is open to all. His telephone number is listed in the directory. He is besieged with requests for favors or assistance from fellow Kentuckians and non-Kentuckians of all ranks and descriptions. To these petitioners, nothing seems impossible if he sets his mind to it. At eighty-seven his eyes still twinkle; his handshake is still viselike; he is still ready to flex a bulging arm muscle and invite the caller to feel it. He keeps himself informed and holds strong opinions, which he will freely share, on almost any imaginable subject. Above all else, he is still Happy.

SUGGESTED READINGS: J. B. Shannon, "'Happy' Chandler: A Kentucky Epic," *The American Politician*, edited by J. T. Salter (1938); Orval W. Baylor, *J. Dan Talbott, Champion of Good Government: A Saga of Kentucky Politics from 1900 to 1942* (1942); Stephen D. Boyd, "The Campaign Speaking of A. B. Chandler," *Register* 79 (Summer 1981), 227-239; Walter H. Hixson, "The

1938 Senate Election: Alben W. Barkley, 'Happy' Chandler, and the New Deal," *Register* 80 (Summer 1982), 309-329.

CHARLES P. ROLAND

# 1939-1943
# KEEN JOHNSON
## 1896-1970

Keen Johnson, one of four children of Robert Johnson, a circuit-riding Methodist minister, and Mattie Holloway Johnson, was born on January 12, 1896, at Brandon's Chapel, Lyon County. He was named for John S. Keen, a native of Adair County and a family friend. Johnson married Eunice Nichols of Higbee, Missouri, on June 23, 1917.

After receiving his elementary education in the public schools, Johnson graduated in 1914 from Vanderbilt Training School, a Methodist preparatory school in Elkton. He entered Central College, Fayette, Missouri, where he studied until 1917 when he enlisted in the army. Johnson began military service at Fort Riley, Kansas, in May 1917. In August he became a second lieutenant in the infantry. After promotion to first lieutenant, he embarked in June 1918 for France where he served until his return to the United States in April 1919. He was honorably discharged October 31, 1919. After World War I, he enrolled in the University of Kentucky where he received a bachelor's degree with a major in journalism in 1922.

In 1920 with financial assistance from his father Johnson purchased a weekly newspaper, *The Mirror*, published in Elizabethtown, but he soon sold it to continue his education at the University of Kentucky. While a student, he was a reporter for the *Lexington Herald*. Following graduation, he became half-owner, editor, and publisher of the weekly Lawrenceburg *Anderson News*. In 1925 he became editor and co-publisher of the *Richmond Daily Register*. He was the only governor of Kentucky who was a journalist.

Johnson's political career began when he became secretary of the Democratic State Central and Executive Committee in 1932. He won the Democratic nomination for lieutenant governor in 1935 after defeating J.E. Wise and B.F. Wright, his principal contenders in the first primary, and Wise in the runoff primary. He defeated the Republican candidate, J.J. Kavanaugh, by more than 100,000 votes in the general election.

Johnson announced his candidacy for governor on May 17, 1939, and defeated John Young Brown, Sr., in the August primary. While engaged in the general election campaign, he unexpectedly became governor. United States Sen. Marvin Mills Logan died in early October. Gov. A.B. Chandler resigned on October 9; Johnson took the oath as governor and appointed Chandler to fill Logan's unexpired term. On November 7, Johnson was elected; he defeated Republican King Swope by more than 100,000 votes, 460,834 to 354,704.

Keen Johnson was a caring, conscientious, frugal man and governor. He was not gregarious and ebullient, but quiet and reserved. In his inaugural address he proclaimed his love for Kentucky and said that he would not be a spectacular governor but would try harder than any predecessor to be good and honest. He pledged to be "a saving, thrifty, frugal governor." In his valedictory address, he stated that he had great satisfaction in the knowledge that he had kept his pledges. He noted that the state debt, about $28 million at the beginning of the Chandler administration, had been cut to about $7 million by his inauguration. He was leaving office with Kentucky out of debt and with more than $10 million in the general fund, the first time the state had been out of debt since Governor Beckham left office with a $43,000 surplus.

Governor Johnson was especially interested in the rehabilitation of the mental and penal institutions, and he continued work begun during the Chandler term. He was bitterly disappointed that more was not accomplished, but World War II brought severe restrictions upon public construction. At the close of his term, he noted that these institutions were in the best condition they had been in for forty years and that he was leaving ample money to complete the program.

An outstanding accomplishment of his administration was the redistricting of the state legislature. The constitution requires the legislature to redistrict the legislative districts after each decennial census on the basis of population. In 1941 the districts were primarily the same as they had been in 1893 when the first districts under the present constitution were drawn. The governor requested the members of the 1942 General Assembly to adjourn early so that he could call them into special session for the sole purpose of considering redistricting. In his address to the special session, he told the legislators that they had a constitutional duty to pass a redistricting bill. Twenty days later he returned to the General Assembly and told the members that it was his duty to insist that a fair redistricting bill be enacted and it was their duty to pass one. They did.

A major issue in 1942 was Tennessee Valley Authority power. Legislation was needed to enable cities to purchase and distribute it. Johnson requested the necessary measure, and later when the General Assembly had not acted, he addressed the assembly on that issue. He emphasized the importance of TVA power to the future development and prosperity of Kentucky: "I have never had a stronger conviction on any question of public policy. . . . The principle involved is as correct as the Ten Commandments." The General Assembly then passed the bill.

World War II took priority during his administration. Johnson had to be concerned with the draft, gas and tire rationing, war production, scrap metal drives, and the prevention of strikes in coal mines and in war industries. Johnson also showed concern for the needy elderly, education, the highway system, and tobacco research. He increased the funding for old-age assistance and secured funds to finance the teachers' retirement system that had been authorized by the preceding administration. He supported a constitutional amendment to provide for a school equalization fund, and he increased funding for education in spite of his tight money policy. He obtained a modest increase of funds for the distribution of surplus food commodities. He enjoyed presiding over the elimination of tolls from highway bridges. He supported research on new uses for tobacco.

Johnson showed courage when he vetoed a bill in 1940 that would have permitted the sale of alcoholic beverages to surrounding states even if the laws of some states forbade it. Powerful interests had supported the proposal, and the measure had passed the House by 84-0 and the Senate by 31-3. Following his veto, the House reversed itself and sustained the veto 86-3.

The sesquicentennial of Kentucky's statehood fell during Johnson's term. While several events were held throughout 1942, at its close the governor indicated that the celebration had fallen short of his expectations because of the war.

Although Johnson continued an association with the *Richmond Daily Register* until his death, he was involved in other pursuits after his term as governor. He joined the Reynolds Metals Company as assistant to the president early in 1944 and became a vice-president in 1947 and a director in 1950, holding both positions until his retirement in 1961. During the Truman administration he served as under secretary of labor from 1946 to 1947. In 1960 he ran for the United States Senate and defeated John Young Brown, Sr., in the primary but lost to John Sherman Cooper in the general election. He was a member of the Democratic National Committee from 1940 to 1948.

Keen Johnson died February 7, 1970, in Richmond and was buried there. He succeeded in his goal to be a good, honest, frugal governor. He may have been overly penurious, but he loved Kentucky and served her well.

SUGGESTED READINGS: Willard Rouse Jillson, *Governor Keen Johnson: A Biographical Sketch* (1940); Frederic D. Ogden, ed., *The Public Papers of Governor Keen Johnson* (1982).

FREDERIC D. OGDEN

1943-1947
# SIMEON WILLIS
1879-1965

Born December 1, 1879, in Lawrence County, Ohio, Simeon Willis was the youngest of nine children of John H. and Abigail Slavens Willis. While the son for convenience later used an *S* as a middle initial, he never officially adopted that designation. His father, a Union army veteran and iron industry contractor, moved the family to Greenup County, Kentucky, when Simmie was about ten years old. After education in the public schools of both states, Willis took courses in a private normal school, passed the teacher's exam, and became an instructor in 1898 in the county system. He was principal of the three-room Springville (now South Portsmouth) grade school before the age of twenty.

While in the education field, Willis continued to study and work in other areas. He became involved in local Republican politics and briefly wrote and reported for the Portsmouth (Ohio) *Tribune* and the *Greenup Gazette*. But his attention increasingly turned to the legal profession. Prepared under the private tutoring of Republican county judge and later congressman Josiah Bentley Bennett of Greenup and William D. Corn of Ada University, Willis was admitted on November 11, 1901, to the Kentucky bar. Opening a private practice in nearby Ashland, he soon joined the important firm of Hager and Stewart and remained with them for six years. Thereafter he operated his own financially successful practice.

Politics continued to beckon but Simeon Willis's initial attempts for office resulted in defeats. In 1905 he ran for city attorney and lost. Eleven years later, in 1916, he sought the Republican nomination for a Court of Appeals seat, but finished third behind Flem D. Sampson, who also won the seat in the general election. When war came to America the next year, Willis served as a Selective Service appeals agent, as he would do again in World War II. Finally in 1918 he was chosen for a four-year term as city solicitor. Then he served from 1922 to 1928 as a member of the state Board of Bar Examiners.

Probably the turning point in Willis's political career came on December 31, 1927, when Governor Sampson appointed him to the Court of Appeals seat that Sampson had vacated when he became governor. An election victory the next year brought Willis both a four-year term on the bench of the commonwealth's highest court and statewide notice. His stature increased when he revised and rewrote the six-volume authority, *Thornton on the Law of Oil and Gas* (1932). Even an election defeat by Democrat Alex Ratliff in the Roosevelt year of 1932 did not erase the favorable impressions Willis had left. He was, in fact, "a lawyer's lawyer," well-versed in his profession and respected by his peers. When awarding a 1958 citation to Willis for outstanding service to the bar, then Chief Justice John R. Moremen remarked that, "If books and learning are the tools of a lawyer, then this man's mind is a crystalline library—and . . . whenever opportunity affords, I borrow a volume."

After leaving the court in 1933, Willis returned to private practice and to the quiet home life he so enjoyed. Marriage in 1920 to Idah Lee Millis, a deputy county clerk at that time, had brought an active advisor and fierce supporter into the Willis circle. In 1921, their only child, Sarah Lesley, was born. The private Willis enjoyed smoking his cigars, playing the violin in his natural left-handed manner, and reading poetry and history late into the night. While not charismatic, the six-foot, two-hundred-pound, white-haired Willis—whether standing before a jury or regaling friends—made a strong and favorable impression. This was the man who in 1943 became, as the *Courier-Journal* phrased it, "the Republican White Hope" for governor.

Nominated without opposition by his party, Willis faced a Democrat who had emerged from a bitter primary. J. Lyter Donaldson of Carrollton, the commissioner of highways under outgoing governor Keen Johnson, was not a strong candidate and did not handle criticisms of his earlier record well. Yet Republicans had not won the last three gubernatorial races and would not win the next five. Willis campaigned for income tax repeal and political machine destruction, plus further support for rural highways, education, and postwar planning. But his image as a dignified, reasoning man who transcended party was probably equally important in winning votes. He defeated Donaldson 279,144 to 270,525, brought into office his entire slate (except for a female secretary of state candidate), and gained national attention for his victory in the national off-year election. As a result, Willis gained considerable support for the office of vice-president in the 1944 Republican convention.

But Willis's chief focus was on state government. Although some quarter of a million citizens were absent because of the war, Willis located and appointed capable officials and, recognizing the need to retain knowledgeable officeholders, he did not institute massive dismissals. The latter policy did not improve his standing among office-hungry Republicans. Factionalism within the party would be a continuing problem for him; several constitutional officers (including the lieutenant governor and attorney general) increasingly opposed Willis as time passed. In turn, the Democratic legislative majority, divided between factions led by 1947 gubernatorial aspirants Harry Lee Waterfield and Earle C. Clements, did not institute massive "ripper" legislation, depriving Republicans of appointive powers, as had so often been done in the past.

The result was a considerable list of administration achievements. While tax receipts rose some 72 percent in the Willis years and federal aid increased, the support requested and given, especially in education, exceeded those figures. Teachers' average salaries increased 94 percent, from $782 to $1,325 a year; the education fund rose 94 percent; and the per capita student expenditure went from $13.49 to $25.66. The school term was lengthened from seven to eight months, the allowable maximum tax rate a county could levy was doubled, and an important education study, the Griffenhagen report, was issued. All this greatly aided an educational system that lagged far behind the national average.

In civil rights Willis appointed a black to the state Board of Education for the first time, created a Commission on Negro Affairs, and supported an act that made Lincoln Institute a state high school and teacher training center. The state also greatly increased the meager aid given to blacks who were forced to attend out-of-state professional schools.

Other accomplishments in the Willis years were removal of charges from twelve of thirteen toll bridges in the commonwealth, construction of five state tuberculosis sanatoriums and expansion of another, improvement in mine safety laws, and creation of a much more independent Game and Fish Commission. Old-age assistance increased 65 percent; aid to dependent children rose 72 percent; and in an expanded park system, revenue doubled. A Postwar Planning Commission aided in the readjustment that followed the war's end in 1945.

The years were not without disappointment for the chief executive, however. Not a strong party leader, the financially conservative Willis engaged in two bitter General Assembly budget fights, one of which was resolved by a special legislative session. In 1944 the governor, citing "uncertain and changing" economic conditions, did not ask for repeal of the income tax, which furnished 24 percent of state revenue. Two years later he fulfilled his campaign pledge by requesting the repeal but did not get it. And while expanded revenues allowed Willis to leave office with a very considerable surplus in the treasury, the compromise budget of 1946 far exceeded his recommendations.

The governor could leave office in 1947 both pleased and saddened. He had seen his candidate defeated in the Republican primary and his party's nominee crushed by Clements in the general election; he had experienced disappointments in financial matters; and he had not achieved all he had wished in other areas. Yet, he could take pride in successfully presiding over the commonwealth in an era of great change. Simeon Willis had not only fulfilled many parts of his platform; he had lived up to the image that had helped elect him—that of an honest, reform-minded conservative.

Returning to his Ashland law practice in 1946, Willis made only one other race—for a Court of Appeals seat that he lost to future Democratic governor Bert Combs in 1951. From 1956 to 1960 Willis served on the Public Service Commission, and from 1961 to 1965 on the state Parole Board. A Shriner and an Elk, an official in the Boys Clubs and member of the Kentucky Civil War Round Table, he continued to enjoy these activities, together with fishing and his ever-present reading. At eighty-five, Simeon Willis died April 2, 1965, and was buried in the Frankfort Cemetery.

SUGGESTED READINGS: Willard Rouse Jillson, *Governor Simeon S. Willis* (1944); *Your Kentucky Government, 1943-1947* (1947).

JAMES C. KLOTTER

# EARLE CHESTER CLEMENTS
1896-1985

Earle Chester Clements was born October 22, 1896, in Morganfield, in staunchly Democratic Union County. His father, Aaron Waller Clements, was a successful farmer and cattle producer who was active in local politics. His mother, Sallie Anna Tuley Clements, also a native of Union County, had been raised on a nearby farm. The couple had six children, four boys and two girls, the youngest of whom was Earle.

Although his father had served as a popular county judge and sheriff, Earle at first shunned a political career. He majored in agriculture and played varsity football at the University of Kentucky, leaving in 1917 to enlist for infantry service in World War I. The army, recognizing his leadership talents, trained him as a stateside professor of military science with the rank of captain. At war's end, Clements became bored and sought fortune and adventure as a rigger in the booming east Texas oilfields. However, in 1921 his father, whose health was rapidly declining, requested that Earle help him on the farm and become his deputy sheriff. Simultaneously, Earle became the volunteer football coach at Morganfield High; one of his teams tied for the state championship in 1928. In 1927 he married Sara Blue, his high school sweetheart.

Upon his father's death in 1922, Earle was appointed to serve the remainder of the term as sheriff and subsequently won election to that post. County leaders next urged him to run for county clerk. His eight years (1926-1934) in that post brought him much greater knowledge of county needs and politics and enhanced his popularity. In both 1933 and 1937 Clements won the race for county judge, a powerful political and administrative post that involved some judicial responsibilities. Although a poor stump speaker, he developed an enviable record for quietly getting things done. Despite the economic depression of the 1930s, the 123 miles of county roads paved during his administration exceeded the total mileage completed by all that county's previous judges.

In early 1935 party power broker Thomas S. Rhea, a supporter of outgoing governor Ruby Laffoon, unexpectedly asked Clements to serve as his gubernatorial campaign chairman. Clements agreed, but

157

several weeks later a closer boyhood friend, Albert B. ("Happy") Chandler, made the same request and was necessarily refused. Chandler won, and for most of the next thirty years Clements and Chandler led opposing wings of the Democratic party. There were periods of accommodation and alliance, but there were also bitter races between the Clementines and the Chandlerites. The former tended to be the political moderates or liberals, closely allied with Sen. Alben Barkley's supporters and more closely linked with the New Deal philosophy of Pres. Franklin Roosevelt than were their rivals.

After nearly twenty years in county offices Clements finally shifted his interest to statewide service, winning his 1941 state Senate race. By 1944 he was the Senate majority leader. After the regular legislature session failed to pass a budget bill, he virtually wrote the 1944 state budget, which greatly increased educational appropriations, and led his party in thwarting many of Republican governor Simeon Willis's more financially conservative programs.

Clements's successes in the 1944 legislative battles with the governor insured triumph in his November 1944 Second Congressional District race in which he ardently defended the New Deal. He won reelection in 1946, and his distinguished service on the Select House Committee on Food Shortages brought the Kentuckian into a close association with Pres. Harry Truman.

Congressman Clements voted to expand agricultural research, conservation and wildlife programs, REA funding, and federal parks. He endorsed the 1945 school lunch program and the reorganization of the Farm Security Administration. In addition, he supported civil rights proposals and bills banning lynching and poll taxes. His voting record included opposition to the Taft-Hartley and House Un-American Activities Committee (HUAC) legislation.

Turning down entreaties to run for the United States Senate in 1946, he campaigned for the governorship in 1947. Defeating former state House Speaker Harry Lee Waterfield by over 30,000 votes in the Democratic primary, Clements won 387,795 to 287,756, over the Republican contender, Att. Gen. Eldon S. Dummit.

As governor from December 1947, until December 1950, Clements pushed progressive "foundation legislation" through a conservative legislature. Most of this legislation has endured. Efficiency of operation, planning, and long-term economic development were the hallmarks of his administration.

During his administration only one state, New York, outspent the commonwealth in its $6 million outlay for state parks development. Twelve large parks and several smaller ones were involved, but Kentucky Dam Park was the cornerstone of this program. Between 1947 and 1950 tourism at Kentucky parks increased from fewer than 500,000 visitors to over 2,000,000.

Under Governor Clements, 3,800 miles of rural roads and 4,000 miles of primary roads were built or funded, and the state finally assumed the maintenance of some 6,000 miles of county highways. Work also began on the Kentucky Turnpike and on the Western Kentucky Parkway. Only Texas exceeded Kentucky in this period in building or contracting for road development. Kentucky farmers began to "come out of the mud."

Clements spurred a massive industrialization effort against strong resistance from many well-entrenched rural political groups. The Kentucky Agriculture and Industrial Development Board (AIDB), forerunner of the present state Commerce Department, was established, and within three years the AIDB claimed 250 new industries brought into the state and involvement in creating forty thousand new jobs. Similarly four hundred acres in Louisville were purchased to create a huge State Fair and Exposition Center, modeled after the famous Texas State Fair. The new center would be a showcase for disseminating modern concepts about industrial, economic, and agricultural development.

To assist the General Assembly in devising a more efficient governmental system, Clements had a nonpartisan Legislative Research Commission created. This body of permanent, full-time professionals from diverse disciplines would also do comparative governmental research.

Governmental operations were likewise enhanced by the creation of the Kentucky Building Commission (KBC), a central agency charged with managing and planning all of the state's buildings as well as the bonding requirements. The New Capitol Annex was one of the first projects of the KBC.

A strong, nonpartisan Kentucky State Police system, composed of trained professionals, was established. Clements abolished the weak, inept, and patronage-dominated highway patrol. He also reorganized the Kentucky Conservation Department and created a Water Resources Commission. And, with Gov. James Duff of Pennsylvania, he established the Ohio River Sanitation Commission (ORSANCO) to reduce the appalling pollution of that river and its tributaries.

Kentuckians also benefited from Clements's reorganization of the weak and inept Insurance Commission. A nationally prominent and independent expert was hired to rewrite the state's entire insurance code. His three-hundred-page proposal was adopted without amendment by the legislature, and industry fraud was thereby curtailed.

Nothing symbolized Governor Clements's concern for Kentucky's long-range needs more than a joint program he arranged with the federal government to map the state's 40,295 square miles as a priority for planning and developing the state's resources. The new 1/24,000 scale maps became the basis for industrial planning, highway and bridge construction, parks and conservation development, and myriad other public and private endeavors. These maps also became the basis for later subsurface soil and mineral mapping projects.

Clements spearheaded support for two constitutional amendments, which were adopted following special legislative session endorsement in 1949. One amendment increased the maximum salary for state employees from five thousand to twenty thousand dollars, making possible the retention of the most skilled officials and administrators. The other provided a 15 percent increase in the Minimum Foundation Program for assisting the very poorest school districts.

As governor he worked to stave off disaccreditation of the publicly funded colleges, when leading national accreditation groups sought to end gross political interference in the state's higher education system, and to secure reaccreditation of Morehead State Teachers College. Less successful were his attempts to initiate desegregation at the university and professional school levels. For the University of Louisville he supported successful 1948 legislation allowing blacks to pursue medical training there despite the segregationist Day law. But, as ex-officio chairman of the University of Kentucky Board of Trustees, he was thwarted by the Lexington school's governing body and administration. The federal district court in Lexington granted blacks admission in 1949 to programs that were not available at Kentucky State College or were not equivalent to those at the University of Kentucky.

Although Clements was an exceptionally strong governor who reunited the disparate factions in the state Democratic party, he nonetheless met some notable reverses. He failed in both the 1948 and 1950 legislative sessions to control strip-mining by requiring state performance bonds for reclaiming coal-mined lands. Of equal significance, his attempts at passing statewide pension and civil service statutes were unsuccessful. In addition, his sizable increases in public school funding were not sufficient to prevent a large group of teachers from organizing a troublesome protest march on his office in 1950. They insisted upon other measures and tax increases to raise another $10 million. Unexpectedly the outbreak of the Korean War in mid-1950 generated increased tax receipts, and the state's schoolteachers realized their goal after action by a special legislative session in 1951. Clements maintained that he intentionally allowed Lawrence Wetherby, his lieutenant governor and successor, to reap the credit for this appropriation.

By late 1950 Clements's interests had turned to the United States Senate, although his original intention had been to enter private business at the expiration of his term. He claimed that he entered the race when a suitable Democrat could not be found to assume Vice-Pres. Alben Barkley's former Senate seat, temporarily being held by interim appointee Garrett Withers. Clements resigned as governor on November 27, 1950, and he defeated conservative Republican Charles I. Dawson, a former federal judge, by more than 56,000 votes. A year later, he became assistant majority leader under Sen. Lyndon B. Johnson. His rapid rise among the Senate leadership included appointment to the chairmanship of the Senate Democratic Reelection Committee (1952-1954).

By 1954-1955 the split within the Kentucky Democratic party between the Clements and Chandler factions was acrimonious. Chandler, upon his return to the governorship in 1955, made sure his forces would not assist in Senator Clements's 1956 reelection campaign. Johnson's illness caused Clements to become more enmeshed in party and senatorial business in Washington, and so he campaigned relatively little in the commonwealth. Louisville Republican millionaire Thruston B. Morton defeated Clements by less than 7,000 votes.

From 1957 until 1959 Clements, upon Majority Leader Johnson's insistence, held a new position, executive director of the Senate Democratic Reelection Committee. The Kentuckian helped insure the election of a solid Senate Democratic majority of fourteen seats. The Democratic leadership consequently was able to modify greatly most of the proposals submitted by the Eisenhower administration.

After brief service in 1959-1960 as Kentucky highway commissioner under Gov. Bert Combs, who was a Clements protégé, Clements returned to Washington as a maritime lobbyist. His remaining career was spent in a series of executive posts in Washington at the Tobacco Institute. In 1981 he retired to a new home in Morganfield. His only child, Elizabeth (Bess) Clements Abell, who served as social secretary for Lady Bird Johnson and Vice-Pres. Walter Mondale, kept him abreast of Washington news and politics. After several years of ill health he died at home on March 12, 1985, and was buried at Morganfield.

SUGGESTED READINGS: Malcolm E. Jewell and Everett W. Cunningham, *Kentucky Politics* (1968); Gary Luhr and Thomas H. Syvertsen, "The Governor Who Broke New Ground," *Rural Kentuckian* 37 (May 1983), 8-12, 24; Willard Rouse Jillson, "Governor Earle C. Clements," *Register* 46 (January 1948), 375-379.

THOMAS H. SYVERTSEN

## 1950-1955
# LAWRENCE W. WETHERBY
1908-

It is an irony of Kentucky politics that the only governor native to the state's most populous county was Lawrence Winchester Wetherby. Born at Middletown in eastern Jefferson County on January 2, 1908, he was the son of Samuel David, a physician, and Fanny Yenowine Wetherby.

As a youth, Wetherby worked on his father's farms during school and in the summers. After graduating from Anchorage High School, he entered the University of Louisville's School of Law where he received his LL.B. degree in 1929, just four months before the stock market crash. Fortunately he was hired immediately by Judge Henry Tilford, and the two continued their association until Wetherby became lieutenant governor.

During the economically depressed early thirties, Wetherby took two momentous steps—he married and entered local politics. On April 24, 1930, he wed Helen Dwyer of Louisville. They eventually had three children. In 1933, already a Roosevelt New Dealer, he aligned himself with the Jefferson County political faction of Leland Taylor and Ben F. Ewing. When Ewing was elected county judge, he appointed Wetherby part-time attorney for the Jefferson County Juvenile Court, a position Wetherby held from 1933 until 1937 and again in 1942. This earlier work resulted in his appointment as the first trial commissioner of Jefferson County Juvenile Court in March 1943. Wetherby served as a judge until March 1947, when he resigned to make the race for lieutenant governor.

Wetherby was a member of the Democratic city and county executive committee when party leaders persuaded him to try for the lieutenant governor post. Wetherby ran without the endorsement of Earle Clements, Democratic candidate for governor, but with his tacit approval and clandestine assistance. Wetherby won in the primary, and the two men were then elected to office in November.

Clements and Wetherby constituted a political duo that held office for eight years and influenced state politics for many succeeding years. Much of their administrations' remarkable achievement resulted from their cooperative spirit. They genuinely admired and respected one another and agreed upon most major ideas. Indeed, it is often difficult to note where one administration ended and the other began simply by looking at their programs. As a result, some political enemies erroneously labeled Wetherby a puppet and a surrogate of Clements.

Clements's delegation of important responsibilities to Wetherby made him the first working lieutenant governor. Wetherby gained practical experience by preparing the budgets, attending Southern Governors' conferences, conducting Chamber of Commerce tours, and presiding over the Legislative Research Commission. Hence he was well prepared to assume the responsibilities of governor when Clements ran for and won the old Senate seat of Alben Barkley. On November 27, 1950, Clements was sworn in as senator, and the governorship was filled by Wetherby.

Within three months of taking office Wetherby called an extraordinary session of the General Assembly to convene on March 6, 1951. He proposed to allocate and spend a $10 million revenue surplus. He increased teachers' salaries, old-age assistance, and aid to the needy blind, dependent children, and wards of the state. He brought state and local employees under the United States Social Security Act.

This popular action made Wetherby a likely candidate for governor in 1951, although he seriously considered going to the Senate that year to fill the unexpired term of Virgil Chapman. His decision to seek the governorship was strengthened by his service as executive secretary of the Kentucky State Democratic Central Committee, a post in which he made many contacts and laid the foundation for his statewide race.

The campaign matched Wetherby against Republican Eugene Siler, a religious fundamentalist who accused the administration of immorality and corruption. Wetherby ran on his record and experience, defeating Siler by a vote of 346,345 to 288,014. Emerson "Doc" Beauchamp was elected lieutenant governor.

Wetherby's administration, lying between those of the innovative Clements and the flamboyant Chandler, is often overlooked for its record of solid progress. In the sphere of economic development, for example, Wetherby attempted the industrial diversification of a primarily agricultural state. He enticed many industries to the state by personally leading dozens of Chamber of Commerce tours. To assist in this effort, the Agricultural and Industrial Development Board was enlarged and carried out a mapping and aerial survey program to identify potential industrial sites. Wetherby's industrial program was particularly important to chronically depressed eastern Kentucky from which the governor wished to stem the increasing exodus. In 1954 he nevertheless stood by principle and favored enactment of the state's first anti-strip-mining legislation. That year he also demonstrated a prolabor stance by killing a right-to-work bill.

To further entice industry and to facilitate commerce, Wetherby encouraged the development of modern airports. He also led the movement for the canalization of the Big Sandy River and improved locks and dams on the Kentucky River.

In the realm of agriculture the governor established an agricultural council in 1952 to coordinate the work of numerous agencies and organized farm laborers. He suggested the diversification of crop production and supported the soil conservation and beef production measures of the Green Pastures Program. To save valuable farm lands, he acquired federal flood control programs for the watersheds of several rivers—Salt, Licking, Green, and Kentucky. To better display Kentucky's agricultural abundance, Wetherby completed a new state fairgrounds in Louisville.

Wetherby viewed tourism as good for the state's economy. To encourage it, he increased appropriations for the development of state parks and specifically called for the improvement of the Breaks of the Big Sandy area. He himself was an avid sportsman whose public romps in the field as hunter and fisher brought national attention to Kentucky as a sportsman's paradise. Yet he supported fish and wildlife conservation measures.

In part to facilitate tourism, Wetherby improved the highway system. He initiated the toll road between Louisville and Elizabethtown and ushered in an era of toll road construction. He advocated the building of a toll road from the Great Lakes to the Gulf and encouraged President Eisenhower to fund a federal interstate highway project. Recalling the deaths of his father and two brothers in automobile accidents, Wetherby organized a highway safety program.

Improved education was Wetherby's greatest challenge. His administration significantly increased school funding. To reach the rural areas, he called for the development of educational television and started the bookmobile project. An important improvement for those areas came in 1954 with the Minimum Foundation Act that attempted to equalize public school opportunities by basing the amount of funding on need. The act established minimum funding on two counts—per capita and equalization—while leaving school systems free to spend as much more as they liked.

In 1954 Wetherby publicly affirmed his support for the Supreme Court's decision in *Brown v. Board of Education of Topeka*, declaring it both the law of the land and right. He reaffirmed this position as chairman of the Southern Governors' Conference in 1955. To facilitate orderly desegregation, Wetherby appointed a biracial advisory council. Consequently Kentucky's schools were integrated with little acrimony.

In health and welfare Wetherby realized his two proudest achievements: the creation of a separate Department of Mental Health and the establishment of a Youth Authority that provided for the care, treatment, and rehabilitation of delinquent, dependent, and neglected children. In addition, he built fifteen county hospitals, thirty health centers, and new prison facilities. Wetherby supported a new medical school at the University of Kentucky.

In governmental reform Wetherby was unable to achieve a governor's right of succession, consolidation of the county units, or the short ballot. And the voting age was lowered to eighteen against his objections. But he secured passage of a new Registration and Purgation Act in 1952 to restore confidence in the integrity of the ballot and the appropriation of funds to purchase voting machines where their use was desired. In 1954 Wetherby modernized the probation and parole system and established a better and more orderly method of both grand and petit jury selection.

In the early 1950s organized crime and open gambling were rampant in the nation; Kentucky was not immune. Wetherby sent the state police on gambling raids into Campbell and Henderson counties in 1951. This unprecedented use of state power in local communities was made possible by the 1948 reorganization of the state police force. In 1952 he supported legislation that would revoke the alcohol licenses of establishments that permitted gambling. When labor unrest occurred in Central City in 1952 and later in the coalfields, Wetherby restored order with the police.

To pay for the costs of government, Wetherby, a financial conservative, put the income tax on a pay-as-you-go basis. The state's revenues were inflated by the Korean War, but by 1954 expenditures had to be drastically trimmed. To raise additional revenue, Wetherby approved that year an increase in "sin" taxes on cigarettes, alcoholic beverages, and pari-mutuel betting. He saw the need for a sales tax, and though unable to get it himself, he encouraged Bert T. Combs to secure its passage.

In 1955 Wetherby and Clements supported Combs as the administration's candidate for the gubernatorial nomination. In a primary campaign marked by great rancor, Combs was defeated by Albert B. Chandler. The latter attacked Wetherby's record as one of waste rather than concentrating on the neophyte Combs. Wetherby gave only nominal support to Chandler's election bid and retired to Anchorage after leaving office.

In 1956 Wetherby ran for the United States Senate. He lost to John Sherman Cooper, while Earle Clements was beaten by Thruston Morton, both Republicans being swept into office on Eisenhower's coattails. Governor Chandler's refusal to support his party's candidates was partly responsible for the results.

After the election Wetherby moved to Franklin County where he entered private law practice and served as a consultant to the Brighton engineering firm. In 1964-66 he was a member of the State Constitutional Assembly. He served two terms in the state senate in 1966 and 1968 and was its president pro tempore during the first session.

SUGGESTED READINGS: John E. Kleber, ed., *The Public Papers of Governor Lawrence W. Wetherby* (1983); Glenn Finch, "The Election of United States Senators in Kentucky: The Cooper Period," *FCHQ* 46 (April 1972), 161-178.

JOHN E. KLEBER

## 1959-1963
# BERT T. COMBS
## 1911-

Bert T. Combs's personality, background, and innate progressivism matched admirably the time in which he served. Deeply sincere and honest, and ruggedly tough beneath a mild-mannered exterior, Combs was proud of Kentucky and confident about the state's future. He recognized that the commonwealth had lagged economically behind most of the nation, and he believed improvements were long overdue. Fortunately the America of the early 1960s was a period of optimism and comparative prosperity, which made it possible to achieve the outcomes implicit in such attitudes. It mattered little that Combs did not know precisely how to accomplish all of his objectives; Kentucky was ready to move, and fortunately the means became available.

Combs was born August 13, 1911, in Clay County, the son of Stephen Gibson and Martha Jones Combs. A graduate of the local high school, he attended college and law school intermittently over a ten-year period before receiving his law degree from the University of Kentucky in 1937. He financed his studies by working at odd jobs and by serving full time for three years as a highway department clerk. Soon after graduation he began practicing law in Prestonsburg, Kentucky. He married Mabel Hall in 1937. After their divorce in 1969, he married Helen Clark Rechtin. With the advent of World War II, Combs volunteered for the army and rose from private to captain before his discharge in 1946. Returning to Prestonsburg, he expanded his law practice through a partnership with J. Woodford Howard. In addition Combs participated moderately in politics. He served as city attorney in 1950 and as commonwealth attorney of the Thirty-fourth District the following year. In April 1951 Gov. Lawrence Wetherby appointed him to fill a vacant seat on the Kentucky Court of Appeals. Later that year Combs won election to a full eight-year term.

In 1955 leaders of the dominant state Democratic faction plucked him from the court's relative obscurity to lead their ticket in the primary against former governor A.B. Chandler. During the campaign Combs learned much about politics, campaigning techniques, and the commonwealth, but Chandler's victory seemed to eliminate the eastern Kentuckian from future consideration for public office. Chandler, perhaps the premier Kentucky campaigner of his day, totally outclassed the inexperienced Combs. Chandler was eloquent, colorful, and entertaining; Combs campaigned like a judge in court, ticking off the points of his program without humor or emotion, affecting a delivery one observer described as "conversational." "Well, he ain't the best speaker in the world," another commented, "but he sure tells you where he stands."

Combs possibly was too candid about where he stood. Early in the campaign he boldly asserted that the state needed $25 million more than could be provided by existing revenues. It was a tactical mistake, and the wily Chandler knew it. Kentucky's revenue, he insisted, was more than adequate, if administered by an experienced former governor such as he. Waste and inefficiency within the Wetherby administration, which backed Combs, Chandler added, were responsible for persistent fiscal shortfalls. Chandler convincingly hammered away from one end of the state to the other on the point that if Combs won, there would be higher taxes; if Chandler won, effective use would be made of existing revenues. Combs's inability to persuade voters that Chandler was wrong lost the election (259,875 to 241,754) and apparently consigned the judge to political oblivion.

Yet the basis for Combs's later success lay in the 1955 experience. The state did need more money. Chandler got it by the imposition of various new excise levies and a sizable increase in the state income tax. Opposed vigorously by a group of Democratic legislators, the new taxes undermined Chandler's credibility. By contrast, Combs emerged as a symbol of courageous honesty.

Encouraged by legislative rebels who looked to him for leadership, Combs ran for governor a second time. More than anything else, Chandler's record made it possible. Even the judge's emotionless mountain twang proved pleasing, partly because voters were more accustomed to it and partly because they equated it with truthfulness and forthrightness. His primary opponent, Harry Lee Waterfield, had a pleasing personality but was identified with Chandler. Combs won the primary by 25,000 votes and went on in November to overwhelm his Republican opponent, John Robsion, Jr., with a record margin of 180,093 votes, 516,549 to 336,456.

During the 1959 campaigns Combs elaborated more fully on the program for progress that he had introduced earlier. Aware that some gains had been made, he believed that Kentucky needed to embrace progressivism. Kentucky had always been "too proud to whitewash and too poor to paint." It was time now, Combs felt, for some painting to begin. He insisted that funding for education had to be increased dramatically. The state also deserved better highways and parks, increased industry, airports, and a merit system for government employees. Such progress would open up untapped potential and benefit everyone. No longer would youthful Kentuckians leave their homes to find better opportunities elsewhere.

How to finance these ventures was a problem Combs had not resolved before his election. The public's acceptance of a referendum authorizing payment of a veteran's bonus, however, offered him a solution. The referendum provided for a sales tax to finance the payments. Knowing full well that a tax of only one cent would cover bonus costs, Combs obtained a three-cent sales tax that provided ample funds for every facet of his program. Gaining enactment of the sales tax, however, was only the first step. Combs knew he needed visible results to secure long-term acceptance of the levy. He not only made more money available for education, highway construction, state parks, industrial development, and human resources, but he also ensured that a full-scale public relations campaign accompanied every endeavor. The dedication of new schools, classrooms, highways, parkways, state parks, and industrial complexes always found the governor on hand to tell the public that the sales tax made it possible. Perpetuation of the levy would insure continued improvements, while repeal would signal retrenchment.

Combs impressed observers with a pattern of efficient, thoughtful, and trustworthy administration. The statutory merit system improved morale among state workers and attracted able newcomers to public service. Sensitive to the possibility that waste or graft might accompany the sizable increase in state expenditures, Combs cracked down on misconduct. In one instance he helped bring about early retirement of a powerful school superintendent, Herman McGuire of Carter County. In another, he effected the ouster of four local public officials in Campbell County. Though he might have avoided confrontation in either case, he persevered despite the fact his actions were politically damaging.

Combs took the lead among Southern governors in support of human rights by both word and action. He appointed the first Commission on Human Rights in Kentucky history, promoted the creation of similar commissions in local communities, and during the 1963 gubernatorial election desegregated by executive order all public accommodations in the state. Desegregation became an election issue and helped make the vote closer than expected. As always, however, Combs did what he deemed right.

Combs served from 1967 to 1970 as a federal court of appeals judge and watched Kentucky affairs with interest. In 1971 he tried to return to the governor's mansion, but lost to Wendell Ford in the primary. He resumed his law career, this time with the Louisville firm of Tarrant, Combs, and Bullitt. Never again a candidate for political office, Combs continued to provide advice and counsel when asked.

SUGGESTED READINGS: George W. Robinson, ed., *The Public Papers of Governor Bert T. Combs, 1959-1963* (1979); "Governor Bert T. Combs," *Register* 58 (January 1960), 3-5; John Ed Pearce, "Kentucky's Quiet Revolution," *Harper's,* 222 (January 1960), 45-50.

GEORGE W. ROBINSON

1963-1967
# EDWARD THOMPSON BREATHITT, JR.
1924-

Edward Thompson Breathitt, Jr., was born in Hopkinsville, Kentucky, November 26, 1924, the only child of Edward Thompson and Mary Wallace Breathitt. The Breathitt family had a long tradition of service to Kentucky. A distant ancestor, John Breathitt, was elected governor in 1832; James Breathitt, Sr., Governor Breathitt's grandfather, served as attorney general from 1907 to 1911; and an uncle, James Breathitt, Jr., was lieutenant governor from 1927 to 1931.

Breathitt was educated in the public schools of Hopkinsville. After graduation from high school in 1942, he enlisted in the army air force and served three years. Following the war, he enrolled at the University of Kentucky, completing requirements for his bachelor's degree in commerce in 1948 and his law degree in 1950. Breathitt's interest in Kentucky politics was apparent while he was a student. In 1947 Prof. Jack Reeves of the political science department and Prof. Thomas Clark, chairman of the history department, asked him to direct the campus campaign for a new state constitution. Breathitt accepted the assignment and also became actively engaged in the statewide campaign. Although the voters rejected the proposed constitution, Breathitt remained committed to constitutional reform.

In 1950 Breathitt returned to Hopkinsville and began the practice of law. Active in community affairs, Breathitt launched his political career in 1951 in a successful race for the Kentucky House of Representatives. He was reelected in 1953 and 1955. In the 1952 presidential campaign he worked as Adlai Stevenson's speaker chairman for the commonwealth, and two years later he campaigned to return former Vice-Pres. Alben Barkley to the United States Senate. From 1952 to 1954 he was president of the Young Democrats Club of Kentucky and served as a member of the national committee of the Young Democrats of America.

As a member of the state legislature Breathitt supported the adoption of Kentucky's first strip-mining legislation and improved registration and election laws. When Bert Combs was elected governor in 1959, he appointed Breathitt commissioner of personnel to draft legislation for a new merit system for state employees and to guide it through the legislature. Following the passage of the bill, Breathitt resigned as commissioner of personnel to accept membership on the Kentucky Public Service Commission.

In 1962, with Combs's endorsement, Breathitt entered the 1963 Democratic gubernatorial primary. Former governor A. B. Chandler was his opponent. In a bitterly contested primary that focused on the controversial 3 percent sales tax enacted during the Combs administration, Breathitt defeated Chandler by a landslide. Breathitt's opponent in the general election was Louie B. Nunn, a Republican from Glasgow. In the campaign Breathitt pledged to continue the popular initiatives of the Combs administration—improvements in education, highways, agriculture, state parks, and health and welfare programs. In addition, he promised a sustained economic development campaign to attract industry and create new jobs for Kentuckians. The Nunn campaign attacked recent Democratic state and national commitments in the field of civil rights. In particular, Nunn labeled Combs's controversial executive order prohibiting racial discrimination in all businesses licensed by the commonwealth "rule by executive decree." The introduction of race into the campaign and A.B. Chandler's last-minute endorsement of Nunn clearly hurt Breathitt. Many Chandler supporters in the Bluegrass apparently voted Republican and segregationists in western Kentucky stayed home. Breathitt's margin of victory, 449,551 to 436,496, portended difficulty with the legislature.

Breathitt was identified with a new breed of Southern Democrats, men who accepted the broad directions of the New Deal and Fair Deal, who viewed state government as a proper tool with which to address social, economic, political, and human problems, and who rejected the traditional demagoguery of race and states' rights. Breathitt believed in states' rights, but he also believed in state responsibility. The viability of state government, he frequently asserted, depended on its responsiveness to problems.

Breathitt's first session of the legislature was clearly a disappointment. His youth, the narrowness of his victory in 1963, the untimely death of Richard P. Maloney, Sr., a key legislative leader, and the lingering civil rights controversy combined to undermine his effectiveness with the 1964 General Assembly. Much of the session was devoted to wrangling over an unsuccessful effort to adopt a public accommodations bill. Breathitt secured a model purchasing law, improved teachers' benefits, and legislation regulating strip-mining. But, most important, he won legislative approval for a referendum on a $176 million bond issue that was vital to his administration.

Breathitt had pledged no new taxes during his administration, a pledge he wished to honor. Yet he wanted to continue the road building, park development, education, and social services programs initiated under Combs. The demand for physical facilities was particularly overwhelming in education. Moreover, Breathitt assumed office at a time when unprecedented sums were available from the federal government in generous dollar-matching programs. The combination of funding requests and dollar-matching opportunities far exceeded current state revenues. The answer was the $176 million bond issue that was structured to provide funds for capital improvements only. Most of the issue was designated for highway construction; however, funds for education, state parks, and other public facilities were also included. Breathitt carefully designed a campaign to win approval of the bond issue, and it passed by three to one despite the opposition of Harry Lee Waterfield and A.B. Chandler.

The 1964 General Assembly also adopted enabling legislation to draft a new state constitution. Thirty-eight distinguished Kentuckians worked for several months writing the new charter, and Breathitt, with the help of many eminent Kentuckians, mounted an impressive statewide campaign to secure its adoption. But the Kentucky voters rejected it by an overwhelming margin. Changes in the terms of constitutional officers, perceived threats to the independence of local governments, the apparent consolidation of power in Frankfort, and a historic aversion to constitutional change were the roadblocks to adoption.

In June 1965 the Court of Appeals rendered a decision that ordered the state to apply a previously unenforced constitutional provision requiring 100 percent assessment of property for tax purposes. Voters subjected Breathitt to immediate and overwhelming pressure to call a special session to deal with potentially skyrocketing tax bills. In the special July session he proposed a reduction in property tax rates in proportion to the increased assessment ratio. Other provisions of his plan provided for small increases in tax rates, primarily for the public schools. Breathitt's proposal was opposed by Lt. Gov. Harry Lee Waterfield, who submitted an alternative plan. Breathitt beat back the Waterfield challenge, secured adoption of his plan, and emerged from the special session with increased political prestige.

By 1966 Breathitt was a seasoned governor, and he dominated that year's session of the General Assembly. Several factors explain the change. Breathitt provided considerably stronger executive leadership than he had in 1964. His economic development program, spurred by an upturn in the national economy and the infusion of federal dollars into the state, generated an additional $100 million in state revenue. The 1966 budget, 27 percent higher than the previous one, included appropriations for most political districts. The budget won wide legislative support, and the elections of 1965 turned slender administration majorities in the legislature into comfortable majorities.

In rapid succession the 1966 General Assembly adopted the Breathitt budget, enacted a civil rights bill prohibiting discrimination in employment and public accommodations, adopted a strong strip-mining law, created an authority to regulate water, soil, and forest resources, enacted a controversial compulsory automobile inspection bill, tightened state regulations governing political contributions and expenditures by candidates, and adopted a Breathitt-sponsored congressional redistricting plan.

During his four years as governor Breathitt largely achieved the goals he outlined in his 1963 campaign. The road building program of the Combs administration was continued and expanded. In 1967, Breathitt's last year in office, Kentucky had more miles of highway under construction than any other state in the Union. Education also benefited. Teachers received real income increases; four state colleges were elevated to university status; a statewide vocational education program was expanded; needed physical facilities, including libraries, classroom buildings, and dormitories were constructed at record pace; a statewide educational television system was established; and the community college system was placed under the administration of the University of Kentucky. The state park system was also expanded, and the commonwealth joined the Tennessee Valley Authority in the development of the 170,000-acre Land Between the Lakes in western Kentucky. Agriculture also benefited, particularly through Breathitt's conservation efforts and his campaign to increase farm income.

The Breathitt years were a period of unprecedented prosperity in Kentucky, despite the poverty of Appalachia. Although the expansion of the national economy contributed much to that prosperity, so did the work of the Breathitt administration. A concerted effort to increase tourism generated substantial additional income and won the administration the coveted Midwest Travel Writers Association's award for the best state travel program. Breathitt's industrial development program produced 749 new industries or expansions of existing plants, 57,000 new jobs, and more than $1 billion in new plant investment. By 1967 manufacturing jobs increased by 23 percent and nonagricultural employment was up 20 percent. In 1964 his administration received the Society of Industrial Investors' award for the best state industrial development program. To deal with the problem of poverty in the eastern Kentucky mountains, Breathitt's administration aggressively pursued federally funded projects and programs. The result was a flood of construction, conservation, health, education, and welfare projects that would have been otherwise unavailable.

Following his term as governor Breathitt briefly returned to law practice in Hopkinsville, serving as special counsel to the Southern Railroad. In 1968 the Ford Foundation named him director of the Institute for Rural America to continue work he had begun as chairman of Pres. Lyndon Johnson's Commission on Rural Poverty. The institute drafted model legislation to establish state area development districts, conducted studies on rural problems, and suggested legislative remedies. Breathitt then served as chairman of the Coalition for Rural America, an organization he helped found that was designed to implement the work of the Institute for Rural America. He also was president of American Child Centers, a company formed to establish and promote private preschool education.

In March 1972 he was appointed vice-president of the Southern Railway System, the position he currently holds. He has remained active in the Democratic party and has served as a member of the Democratic National Committee and the Democratic Finance Council.

Governor Breathitt is married to the former Frances Holleman, and they are the parents of four children: Mary Fran, Linda, Susan, and Edward III. They reside in Washington, D.C.

SUGGESTED READINGS: Kenneth E. Harrell, ed., *The Public Papers of Governor Edward T. Breathitt, 1963-1967* (1984); Allan Trout, "The Breathitt Years, 'You Have to Lead,'" *Louisville Courier-Journal*, December 10, 1967; "Governor Edward Thompson Breathitt, Jr.," *Register* 62 (January 1964), 1-3.

KENNETH E. HARRELL

# LOUIE B. NUNN
1924-

Louie B. Nunn was born in the town of Park in Barren County on March 8, 1924, the fourth son of Waller H. and Mary Roberts Nunn. His father was a farmer and a merchant. In 1950 Nunn was married to Beula Cornelius Aspley, and they became the parents of two children, Jennie Lou and Stephen Roberts.

Nunn graduated from the Hiseville High School and later attended Bowling Green Business University. He left college to serve in the infantry from 1943 to 1945 and was discharged with the rank of corporal. He attended the University of Cincinnati and the University of Louisville, where he received his law degree.

In 1950 Nunn returned to Glasgow where he practiced law and was active in civic affairs, serving as chairman of the Board of Elders and Deacons in the First Christian Church and as an officer in several organizations, including the Rotary Club, the Chamber of Commerce, the Parent-Teachers Association, the American Legion, and the Junior Chamber of Commerce. He was selected as Barren County's outstanding young man and in 1956 as one of the outstanding young men in Kentucky by the Chamber of Commerce.

Nunn was elected Barren County judge in 1953, a Republican in a Democratic county. Known as a tough political organizer, he served as state campaign chairman for Sens. John Sherman Cooper and Thruston Morton and for President Eisenhower in 1956. In 1960 he managed the state campaigns of Senator Cooper and Richard M. Nixon, and in 1962 he managed Senator Morton's campaign for re-election.

Nunn first ran for statewide office in 1963 as the Republican candidate for governor against Democrat Edward T. Breathitt. Breathitt narrowly defeated Nunn by 12,603 votes (338,479 to 325,876), giving Nunn a strong showing for a Republican. He ran again in 1967 and won over Jefferson County Judge Marlow Cook in the primary. In the general election he defeated Democrat Henry Ward by 454,123 to 425,674. Nunn's campaign in 1967 took advantage of disarray in the Democratic party and turned on his criticism of the Democratic machine as inefficient and taxing. He said he would run government on a businesslike basis and that Henry Ward was a taxer. Nunn promised

175

not to raise taxes. He also closely allied himself to the national Republican party's campaign against Lyndon Johnson, and he brought several national Republican figures into the state to campaign for him. His victory made him the first Republican governor of Kentucky in twenty-one years.

As governor, Nunn faced a state administration and a General Assembly controlled by Democrats. Shortly after the fall election, the outgoing administration announced a projected revenue deficit of over $24 million. Nunn's first task, despite a campaign pledge not to raise taxes, was to balance the state budget. Nunn argued that the rules had changed; the previous administration had concealed the revenue shortfall, and now there was no alternative to new taxes. He immediately asked the General Assembly for an increase in the sales tax from $.03 to $.05 per dollar and for an increase in the motor vehicle license fee from $5.00 to $12.50. His total budget request called for an increase of $29 million.

In the ensuing fight Nunn exercised legislative leadership skills and control well beyond those shown by his Republican predecessors. His budget included substantial increases for mental health, for the aging Frankfort State Hospital and School, for education, including state colleges and universities, and for economic development programs. The budget was approved with bipartisan support and gave his administration the resources needed for major growth. His administration brought the University of Louisville into the state system and transformed a community college into Northern Kentucky State College. He added $82 million for teacher salaries and aid to secondary education, increased the higher education appropriation by 34 percent, and improved the state's mental hospitals. He put his weight behind the extensive Kentucky Educational Television system and expansion of the state parks.

In the 1970 General Assembly Nunn tried to repair his image as a tax governor. He proposed to eliminate the sales tax on prescription medicine and the use tax on automobiles transferred within a family; to reduce personal income tax on low-income families; and to increase tax credits for the blind and the elderly. The General Assembly supported his proposals on medicine and automobile transfers within families but not his other suggestions. The governor allowed the budget to become law without his signature.

The Nunn years coincided with national trauma. The Vietnam War and the bombing in Cambodia sparked protest on college campuses

across the nation; many American cities were embroiled in racial turmoil. Kentucky was not immune from these currents, and Governor
Nunn became aggressively involved.

Nunn saw himself as a strict enforcer of the law and allied himself
ideologically and politically with the Nixon administration. He had
supported Nixon early for the presidency in 1968, was active at the
1968 Republican National Convention, and was an important contributor at the state level to the political dialogue of the 1960s. Both within
Kentucky and as a spokesman for the national Republican party, he
spoke of his concern about the "radical" shift of the nation. He decried
the apathy of the "silent majority," that mass of middle-class Americans who, through their silence, allowed "radical elements" to control
events. Richard Nixon would later use the same concept but with
praise for the same "silent" group Nunn had chastised.

In 1968, riots broke out in Louisville following peaceful civil rights
marches. Nunn sent in the National Guard and for that action was
criticized by civil rights leaders across the state. Then in May 1970,
after the bombing of Cambodia, antiwar demonstrations at the University of Kentucky were followed by the burning of the old wooden
building that housed the Reserve Officers Training Corps. Nunn
called the Guard to Lexington and personally appeared on campus to
explain his actions and confront demonstrators.

Nunn had concentrated on mental health and hospitals, state parks
and resorts, child welfare, and education, including the universities
and the community college system. But his emphasis on social service
programs was partly obscured by the toughness of his political style
and the bluntness of his language. The *Louisville Courier-Journal*,
commenting on his administration, remarked, "On the whole, his
management of the state's finances has been sound. He may have left
the highway fund in a shaky state, as some have charged. But he took
a general fund facing a deficit, restored it to solvency, and kept it
healthy. No scandals have marred the Nunn record. He chose able
men to direct his revenue and finance departments, and their efficiency saved the state millions of dollars."

When he left office in 1971, Nunn entered private law practice in
Lexington. He ran for the United States Senate in 1974, losing to
Democrat Walter "Dee" Huddleston 528,550 to 494,337. He continued his work in Republican national politics and was an early backer
of Ronald Reagan in 1975. In 1979 he again ran for governor, this time
against Democrat John Y. Brown, Jr. Nunn emphasized excessive

spending, expanding state government, and increased state employment under the Democrats, in contrast to his own administration's
record in those areas. He also took aim at John Y. Brown's personal
behavior. Nunn hammered at Brown's playboy image, his failure to
release his tax returns, and his inexperience in and ignorance of government. Nevertheless, Brown won 558,088 to 381,278. Since then
Nunn has continued his legal practice.

SUGGESTED READINGS: Robert F. Sexton, ed., *The Public Papers of Governor
Louie B. Nunn* (1975); Louisville *Courier-Journal*, November 16, 17, 1967;
December 5, 7, 1971.

ROBERT F. SEXTON

## 1971-1974
# WENDELL HAMPTON FORD
1924-

Wendell Hampton Ford was born in Daviess County, the son of state
Sen. Ernest M. Ford and Irene Schenk Ford, on September 8, 1924.
He grew up on a farm near Thruston and often claimed during his
election campaigns to be "just a country boy from Yellow Creek." He
graduated from Daviess County High School and attended the University of Kentucky, but he left college for service in the United States
Army during World War II. In 1943 he married Jean Neel; they had
two children. After his discharge as a sergeant in 1946, Ford attended
the Maryland School of Insurance and upon graduation entered the
insurance business with his father. After being very active in civic organizations and politics, he was elected to the state Senate in 1965 and
two years later was elected lieutenant governor, serving with a Republican, Gov. Louie B. Nunn, after his Democratic running mate, Henry
Ward, lost to Nunn.

In 1971 Lieutenant Governor Ford challenged his former mentor,
ex-Gov. Bert T. Combs, whom Ford had served as chief administrative
assistant during Combs's tenure. Ford beat Combs in the primary and
went on to defeat his Republican opponent, Tom Emberton, by
442,736 to 381,479. A product of a politically active Democratic family, Wendell Ford is the first person to be elected successively lieutenant governor, governor, and senator from Kentucky. He has served
continuously in elective office since 1965.

Wendell Ford's political philosophy is more clear-cut than that of most political figures. The Jaycees' creed (Ford has served as national president of the Jaycees) permeates his political beliefs—a conservative, no-nonsense belief in free enterprise, hard work, and the "old ideals that made this country great." At the same time he has a strong populist streak, a high degree of confidence in government and its ability to work well when managed efficiently, and a belief that "service to humanity is the best work of life."

In the first session of the General Assembly from January 3 to March 3, 1972, Governor Ford proposed much legislation, implementing most of his campaign promises. Lt. Gov. Julian M. Carroll and Norbert Blume, the speaker of the house, worked effectively with the governor to bring about passage of most of Ford's legislative program and to block effectively what the governor opposed.

In his state of the commonwealth address Ford emphasized the need for reorganization and for more responsible and more representative government. In his budget message Ford asked for a severance tax on coal, a two-cent per gallon increase in the gasoline tax, a corporate tax increase, removal of the state sales tax on food, a major increase in expenditures for education, and revenue sharing of the gasoline tax with local governments. The severance tax drew expected fire from the coal industry, but others criticized the small amounts requested for mine law enforcement while applauding increased reclamation funding. Journalist Bill Billiter said, "Taken as a whole the tax and budget package lend credence to Ford's populist campaign theme of 'Fighter for the people.'" The governor requested significant new funding for the newest institutions in the system of higher education, the University of Louisville and Northern Kentucky State College, and he proposed strengthening the Council on Higher Education.

No bill that the governor supported failed to pass. Ford ran a tight ship with little opportunity for legislative independence or revolt. Sen. Edwin Freeman of Harrodsburg said that, "the Governor has had more control over this legislature than any I've ever attended." Ford vetoed several measures, most significantly the first collective bargaining bill for teachers, due to school boards' opposition.

At a special session of the General Assembly, called because of a bill "lost" during the regular session and a new United States Supreme Court decision on state residency requirements for voting, Ford proposed repassage of the lost bill establishing an environmental protection agency, appropriate changes in the residency requirements, and a refinement of the congressional districts in line with new census figures. He proposed returning some state coal-stripping fees to the counties where they were collected. Ford endorsed the General Assembly's approval of the proposed national Equal Rights Amendment, which had cleared Congress after the regular assembly session. All of his measures and endorsements passed.

Criticism of Governor Ford's administration centered for a time on the severance tax and fears that Kentucky coal sales would slump, but the energy shortages and the potential coal boom quieted those fears. Ford and his followers were criticized for purchasing insurance policies for state workers without competitive bidding in June 1972. These policies were purchased from backers of Ford's election campaign, but no law required competitive bids and earlier governors had followed similar practices.

Governor Ford had said in his first budget message, "Regulation of strip-mining will be an important function of the new environmental agency. We must save the mountains, the streams, the flatlands of the commonwealth from the onslaught of unlawful mining practices. The law is adequate. Enforcement is poor." Frequently the criticism of the Ford administration's enforcement centered on Thomas O. Harris, commissioner of natural resources, and his key role in the enforcement agencies. Harris impressed Ford with his accounts of what poor enforcement had done to encourage "the rape of the mountains." Ford had earlier assumed responsibility by stating in March 1972 that "I'm going to prove to you what can be done for our environment, rather than just offer rhetoric as has been others' experience in the past." Some critics charged that Ford and Harris did too little, others charged that they were too strict.

Throughout his administration, Governor Ford was both praised and criticized for his handling of the merit system. Ford was generally praised for being less ruthless in firing persons than his predecessor had been and for expanding the coverage of the merit system to previously excluded groups of workers. However, purists and opponents were still concerned with the firings that did take place, including the replacement of Nunn's holdover commissioner of personnel. They objected as well that political clearance was still required on those employees found qualified by merit examination.

In spite of major surgery for an aneurysm in June 1972, Ford led the Kentucky delegation at the Democratic convention in Miami

Beach. An early and avid Muskie supporter, he was disappointed in the McGovern nomination, but greeted the Democratic presidential candidate when he came to Kentucky. Ford took an active role in national party affairs. After only one full year in office, he was elected chairman of the Democratic caucus of the National Governors' Association.

During his term Ford made a significant impact on governmental organization. Where necessary he created new departments or consolidated existing duties; some departments became "super cabinets." Constitutional limits, including separately elected constitutional officers, sometimes prevented him from combining like functions. In November 1972 a new Department of Finance and Administration was created, combining the functions of the Kentucky Program Development Office and the existing Department of Finance. Six additional program cabinets would be announced and additional legislation sought in the 1974 session. The other cabinets created were development, transportation, education and the arts, human resources, consumer protection and regulation, and safety and justice. Environmental protection was authorized in the special session of 1972. The original claims of large savings were soon tempered or forgotten, but Ford was given credit for his attention to such a worthy but dry subject. Aided principally by the skilled and knowledgeable Jim Fleming, former director of the Legislative Research Commission, Ford made this government realignment a top priority.

The second session of the General Assembly in 1974 was influenced to an unusual degree by the oil embargo and petroleum shortages following the 1973 Israeli-Arab War. For some time Governor Ford had been discussing the states' role in the energy crisis and emphasizing Kentucky's role in coal technology and conversion. He served as vice chairman of the Natural Resources and Environmental Management Committee of the National Governors' Conference. He proposed that the assembly appropriate $14.7 million during the 1974-1976 biennium for a coal research program and a commitment of $57.7 million over the next six years for pilot projects in coal gasification and liquefaction.

In his budget message Governor Ford stressed the need to accommodate high inflation just to meet continuation budgets. Because of a budget surplus of $83.5 million from the concluding biennium and unallocated federal revenue sharing, prospects were less than bleak but uncertain. Because of reduced driving and lower gasoline tax income, the road fund would have to be supplemented with general revenue money. Ford advocated the use of federal revenue sharing only for nonrecurring expenses, primarily capital costs of construction. He proposed construction of a new teaching hospital at the University of Louisville, two new office buildings in Frankfort, and a new maximum security prison. General revenue expenditures were increased by $133 million for higher education and benefits for elementary and secondary teachers. Human resources expenditures were also increased with better benefits for dependent children, services for the aged, and increases in the food stamp program.

At the end of the legislative session on March 23, Ford formally announced that he was a candidate for the United States Senate. In the ensuing campaign against incumbent Republican Marlow Cook, the advantages of a current governor were apparent, particularly in allocating surplus funds. A major campaign issue arose over the proposed Red River Dam. Ford supported a dam at an alternative site, but Cook came out against any dam on the Red River. Wendell Ford won the election 399,406 to 328,982. On December 28, 1974, he resigned as governor to take advantage of Marlow Cook's generous early departure to give Ford seniority advantage over other members of his Senate class. Ford was to retain his Senate seat six years later by an even wider margin. In 1982 Ford was encouraged to run for governor again, but decided against it, believing that he could be of more service to Kentucky in the Senate.

National observers have credited Wendell Ford with being an important Senator. He has served on the commerce and energy committees, and during periods of heightened interest in seeking alternative energy sources he has effectively promoted government-sponsored research and development of coal. He worked closely with the late Sen. Henry Jackson, who chaired the Energy and Natural Resources Committee. Senator Ford has been extremely protective of tobacco interests along with his colleague and protégé, Senator Huddleston. For four years, Senator Ford served as chairman of the Senate Democratic Campaign Committee, appointed by the majority leader, and he has been credited with raising significant funds for his colleagues' races.

Wendell Ford's three years as governor coincided with a unique period of prosperity for Kentucky, when the state surpassed the national average on some positive economic measures. Those who worked with Governor Ford tell of the long hours and intense dedication that he gave to the governorship. A consummate politician, Governor Ford courted an urban base in seeking the gubernatorial nomination and did not forget urban needs when elected. He did not go out of his way to alienate coal interests and was careful not to harm them, but he imposed a severance tax over their opposition and sank large amounts of money into repairing earlier mining damage.

Ford raised revenues, significantly gasoline taxes, an act that he said did not violate his campaign promise not to raise general revenue taxes. As the energy picture darkened, Ford took a positive approach to the issues affecting Kentucky. He sought pilot research and pilot money for making coal a cleaner and more versatile fuel. He was a leader and a governor for his time and place in the best sense of representative government.

SUGGESTED READINGS: Landis Jones, ed., *The Public Papers of Governor Wendell H. Ford* (1978); Mike King, "Wendell Ford: A Tough Foe to Know," *Courier-Journal Magazine* (June 12, 1983), 6-12.

LANDIS JONES

1974-1979
# JULIAN MORTON CARROLL
1931-

Julian Carroll was born in McCracken County on April 16, 1931, the son of Elvie B. and Eva Heady Carroll. Elvie "Buster" Carroll was a tenant farmer, a tractor implements salesman, and a garage owner. After graduating from Heath High School where he served as student body president, Julian enrolled at Paducah Junior College. In 1951 he married Chariann Harting; they had four children. He received his associate of arts degree in 1952, and two years later obtained his bachelor of arts degree from the University of Kentucky as a political science major. In 1956 he obtained his law degree from the same institution. After serving as a military lawyer at Carswell Air Force Base in Texas, he joined the Paducah law firm of Reed, Scent, Reed, and Walton. Beginning in 1961, he ran successfully for the state legislature five times. From 1968 to 1970 Carroll was Speaker of the House. A religious man (a biography of him was subtitled *The Inside Story of a Christian in Public Life*), Julian Carroll became moderator of the Kentucky

Synod of the Cumberland Presbyterian Church in 1966-1967. While governor, Carroll took time out to deliver sermons at various churches both in and outside the state.

Carroll's big break occurred in 1971 when former governor Bert Combs of eastern Kentucky ran against Wendell H. Ford in the Democratic primary. Carroll was chosen for the second spot to provide a western Kentucky balance to the Combs ticket. Though Combs lost the primary, his eastern Kentucky votes enabled Carroll to win his nomination, and the Ford-Carroll ticket was victorious in the general election.

The one-consecutive-term rule for Kentucky governors led Wendell Ford to run for the United States Senate in 1974. Julian Carroll anticipated Ford's November 5 victory and for months studied the issues that would confront him as governor. Ford resigned on December 28, 1974. Carroll's months of preparation enabled him to come into office ready to move forward on the issues and programs he wished to pursue when the legislature again met in 1976.

Carroll proved to be a most energetic governor, hopping across the commonwealth, meeting with officials and groups. His day might begin with a breakfast meeting at Frankfort and end after he had delivered several speeches. He made himself available by tight scheduling, air travel, and long hours. He was committed to being out among the citizens of the commonwealth. His appearance as keynoter at numerous national conferences may have given Kentucky a competitive edge over other localities as a convention host. His presence throughout Kentucky helped make him a formidable candidate when he ran in 1975 for a full term. His 453,210 to 274,559 margin over Republican Robert E. Gable provided him with a mandate.

The governor was blessed with an improved economy. The unemployment rate was 4.1 percent against a national rate of 6.3 percent. Kentucky's coffers were filling. The Arab oil embargo had frightened many energy users into turning to coal, and Kentucky was realizing unprecedented revenues from her coal resources.

The centerpiece of Carroll's program was education. At the beginning of his term, teachers' salaries in Kentucky ranked forty-sixth among the states. Two years later the state ranked thirty-eighth and by the end of his term it was in the low thirties. Money was pumped into the Minimum Foundation Program; fees for required classes were eliminated and free textbooks instituted for grades K-12. During the

184

Carroll years a School Building Authority was established to help financially poor districts build new structures; pilot programs for gifted and talented youth were started; mandatory diagnostic testing to determine which students were weak in basic learning skills was begun; and vocational schooling and special education programs were expanded.

Higher education had a lower priority. In his 1976 budget message the governor stated that "we are no longer in the golden age of higher education growth" and cut the budget for colleges proposed by the Council on Higher Education by 40 percent. Because of the recent entry of what would become Northern Kentucky University and the University of Louisville into the state system and the political clout of the "golden triangle" (the area bounded by Covington, Louisville, and Lexington), the other regional schools fared poorly.

Energy independence was attractive to the governor of the nation's number one coal-producing state. In his 1978 state of the commonwealth address Carroll spoke about energy, declaring that "we have capitalized on the resurgence of coal utilization, and we have become a leader in energy research and development." He spoke of his "constant national involvement in the energy crisis." Such involvement included testifying before the Senate Government Operations Committee concerning the organization of a Department of Energy, testifying before the Senate Energy and National Resources Committee and the House Interstate and Foreign Commerce Committee regarding energy and power, attending meetings of the Appalachian Regional Commission's Energy Committee, and meeting with Pres. Jimmy Carter on a number of occasions. At the state level he keynoted the Governor's Energy Awareness Conference. Through the Resource Recovery Road Act he provided for "energy roads" to help in the hauling of coal. He created a cabinet-level Department of Energy and split the Public Service Commission into an Energy Regulation Commission that dealt with electric and gas companies and a Utility Regulatory Commission that handled telephone, water, and sewer companies.

Disasters dogged Kentucky during the Carroll years—floods in eastern Kentucky and Frankfort, the severe winters of 1977 and 1978, the Scotia mine disaster, the Beverly Hills Supper Club Fire. Kentucky's emergencies and disasters led to toughened enforcement of existing laws and to new regulations. A Department of Housing, Buildings, and Construction was formed, and the fire marshal's office was beefed up. All deep mines were presumed to be "gassy," and mine inspections were stepped up.

The governor attempted to strengthen the economic base of Kentucky by supporting downtown projects in the cities, expanding the state park system (including the development of the Kentucky State Horse Park), and creating the Kentucky Film Commission.

Carroll's activities took him out of Kentucky often. He was chairman of the National Governors' Association (he had chaired a similar association of lieutenant governors) and cochairman of the Appalachian Regional Commission. He testified before congressional committees on a number of occasions. Carroll may have been the first governor to support long-shot Jimmy Carter in his quest for the presidency.

On other state issues Carroll sided with the environmentalists against the promoters of a Red River Dam. He also favored a new car (lemon) law that failed to pass in the 1976 legislative session.

The last year of Carroll's administration was not a happy one. In the governor's absence, Lt. Gov. Thelma Stovall, as acting governor, called for a special session to cut taxes. Carroll warned legislators of the potential damage of such irresponsible behavior, but legislators, perhaps reacting against the tight reins with which the now lame-duck governor had held them in check, did not listen to him. Carroll's credibility was also badly shaken by allegations of personal favors for friends and relatives. Though Thelma Stovall's bid to become Kentucky's next governor failed, so too did the bid of Terry McBrayer, Julian Carroll's handpicked candidate.

The Louisville *Courier-Journal* summed up the Carroll years: "Kentucky is better for Julian Carroll's having been governor. Of that we feel confident."

In 1983 Carroll considered but decided against another run for the governorship. Gov. John Y. Brown appointed Carroll chairman of the nonprofit Kentucky War on Drugs in March 1983. A run for office in 1987 remains a distinct possibility.

SUGGESTED READINGS: Charles Paul Conn, *Julian Carroll of Kentucky: The Inside Story of a Christian in Public Life* (1977); "Biographical Sketch of Julian M. Carroll, Governor of Kentucky," *Register* 73 (October 1975), 335-336.

STUART SEELY SPRAGUE

# JOHN Y. BROWN, JR.
1933-

John Young Brown, Jr., flew into Louisville on March 27, 1979, and declared that he was a candidate for governor of the commonwealth. His announcement surprised many people, including the six other candidates for the Democratic nomination. The primary was only ten weeks away, and all six of them had been pursuing the nomination in conventional ways with varying amounts of money, energy, and political sophistication—some of them for years. Brown was not a conventional candidate, and his was not a conventional campaign. He took time out for a honeymoon with his new bride, a former Miss America named Phyllis George. He met with television producers, political advisors, and pollsters, and then plowed through the carefully planned campaigns of his competitors. His critics later charged that he spent as much as $2 million in what all agreed was a spectacular media blitz. With his glamorous wife at his side he appeared at hastily arranged gatherings all over the state. He made only two promises: He would run government like a business and be a salesman for Kentucky.

Brown had a number of assets in addition to the element of surprise and the interest that it generated. His name was familiar: his father, an attorney, had been a frequent although generally unsuccessfull contestant in Democratic politics for more than forty years. (John Y. Brown, Jr., once said that he was determined to win to vindicate the seven United States Senate races his father had lost.) The son was a somewhat mythical figure, a multimillionaire super-salesman who had promoted Kentucky Fried Chicken and Colonel Harland Sanders throughout the country and beyond the nation's borders.

Brown also had the proper Kentucky credentials. He was born in Lexington on December 28, 1933, the third of five children of Dorothy Inman Brown and John Young Brown. He earned his bachelor's and law degrees at the University of Kentucky. He demonstrated his interest in basketball by once owning the Kentucky Colonels professional team. And although he and his first wife, Eleanor Bennett Durall, divorced in 1977 after a seventeen-year marriage, he maintained a close relationship with their three children, John Y., III, Eleanor Faris, and Sandra Bennett.

Further, Brown looked the part he wanted to play. He was tall and well proportioned, with a shock of prematurely white hair: a figure who stood out in any crowd. A man of seemingly inexhaustible energy and boundless optimism, he also had considerable personal charm and impulsiveness, and he was an enthusiastic risk taker. He thus had many of the personal characteristics that captured the popular imagination. The message that he repeated throughout the primary was timely, as Ronald Reagan's election to the presidency the following year would confirm. We must do away with the old politics, Brown said, do away with the old politicians and the courthouse gangs, cut spending, cut waste, and make government more efficient.

Yet it was a hard-fought primary. Brown was a relative newcomer, and almost all of the other candidates had well-established political bases. Terry McBrayer of Greenup had the backing of the Carroll administration; Mayor Harvey Sloane of Louisville was popular in the commonwealth's largest urban area; Thelma Stovall, also from Louisville, had an organized labor background and, because she had vetoed the General Assembly's recission of the Equal Rights Amendment while lieutenant governor, was preferred by many activist women; Carroll Hubbard of Mayfield had strong support in western Kentucky; George Atkins of Hopkinsville appeared to some voters like a tall knight on a white horse; and Ralph Ed Graves of Bardwell sounded like an old-fashioned populist. Indeed, it initially seemed that Sloane had won, and he did not concede until two days after the May 29 primary election. When the results were finally tallied, Brown had won a plurality with 29.89 percent of the vote.

The gubernatorial campaign extended over five months and lacked the intensity of the primary. But it gave time for Brown's party to heal its wounds, and time for his message to become more familiar. It also gave him time to seek out people to join his new venture, should he be elected. Here, too, he broke the mold of his predecessors. It became known that although the ballast in his cabinet would be successful businessmen, he wanted to appoint at least one woman and at least one black person. Brown had a corner on excitement and newness, and his opponent, former governor Louis B. Nunn, who had held office from 1967 to 1971, was never able to generate the enthusiasm that marked the Brown campaign. In a state where registered Democrats outnumber registered Republicans 2½ to 1, a Republican is handicapped. The November results were foretold by people less accustomed to gambling than was the Democratic candidate. Brown won handily by 554,083 votes to Nunn's 376,809.

In his inaugural address Brown repeated his campaign promises to be the salesman for Kentucky in the marketplace and to manage state government in a businesslike and professional manner in the best interest of all taxpayers. (His specification of "taxpayers" rather than "citizens" reflected his business background, but he was not an elitist governor.) "We have a chance," he said, "to do it right." Perhaps the most surprising aspect of Brown's term—surprising to those who become skeptical of campaign promises—is that on balance, John Y. Brown, Jr., kept his. He increased the visibility in the marketplace of Kentucky products from coal to crafts, and he managed state government as he believed businesses should be managed. His slogan, sometimes softened by his explanation that government is a *service* business, was never abandoned. The imprint of his style could be seen immediately.

Instead of the usual party-connected, old-buddy appointments that frequently characterize a governor's staff, Brown assembled one that contained many new faces. Several were businessmen whom he persuaded to give a few years of service to the commonwealth: William T. Young, a Lexington Royal Crown Cola executive; William B. Sturgill, a former coal operator; George E. Fischer of International Business Machines; Ronald G. Geary, a Louisville certified public accountant and attorney; and Frank Metts, a Louisville real estate developer. There was a woman and a black: Jacqueline Swigart and William A. McAnulty. McAnulty resigned within a month, but the governor then appointed another black, George Wilson. The only familiar figures were two who had dropped out of the primary to support Brown, George Atkins and Ralph Ed Graves, and two who had served in the Carroll administration, Robert Warren and Roy Stevens. Some of Brown's appointees switched assignments and others returned to other pursuits, but at the end of the four years, Atkins, Fischer, Geary, Sturgill, Swigart, Warren, and Wilson were still in administrative positions.

This high degree of retention was principally due to Brown's willingness to delegate authority. He meddled little, if at all, in his appointees' work, yet he was entirely willing to share criticism of their unpopular decisions. Metts was the most controversial of his appointments because as secretary of transportation he attacked the political control

189

of road building. The Department of Transportation was the largest single employer in Kentucky, and its funds had usually been distributed with an eye to favoritism. Metts announced that contracts would be awarded strictly on the basis of bids and performance. He cut personnel and slashed entire departments, but he doubled the number of miles of roads that were resurfaced. Complaints did not faze Metts and Brown at all, and at the end of his term Brown considered the depoliticization of road building one of his greatest accomplishments.

The Brown administration spanned years of national economic stagnation and inflation. Kentucky was not immune to these national ills. The total decline in expected state revenue for fiscal years 1981 and 1982 was over $491 million. As President Reagan's policies went into effect, the commonwealth's share of federal revenues declined. Over a two-year period the shortfall of federal money was more than $900 million. Yet, without new taxes, Kentucky's books were balanced when Brown left office. Brown managed this in part by cutting the number of state employees from 37,241 to 30,783. (Most of this reduction was accomplished by attrition and transfer, thus minimizing the human cost.) At the same time, he instituted a merit pay policy. As a result, the salaries of those who remained rose an average of 34 percent by 1983.

The governor himself participated in these money-saving measures. He cut the executive office staff from ninety-seven to thirty, abolished the public information office, and sold seven of the eight state airplanes. (He bought a helicopter with some of the proceeds, which he once impetuously offered to put on the market to raise teachers' salaries—a gesture he later regretted when he decided to keep it.)

There were other successful examples of managing the commonwealth in what Brown thought was a businesslike way. He appointed a volunteer board of insurance experts who studied the state's exposures and policies, wrote specifications, put them out for bids, and recommended agents and companies. This procedure saved the commonwealth at least $2 million a year and brought better coverage. When he took office, the governor was astonished to discover that banks were not required to pay competitive interest rates on the state funds they held on deposit. Requiring bids and awarding deposits on the basis of the interest they would yield brought in an impressive $50 million to the general fund.

Sometimes Brown's style was less effective. He extended his "no meddling" policy to the General Assembly, a significant reversal of the practice of his predecessors. He said that he thought the governor already had enough power and that he wanted to widen the separation between the executive and legislative branches. Also unlike his predecessors, he did not participate in Democratic prelegislative caucuses to decide who would be Speaker of the House, president pro tem of the Senate, party majority leaders, and party whips.

The presentation of Brown's first budget was also unprecedented. Rather than sending it to the House early in the session so that there would be ample time for logrolling and other persuasive activities, Brown released it so late that there were few opportunities for negotiations of any kind. Most amazing of all, Brown went off to Florida for a vacation in the middle of the session.

Veteran lawmakers were initially disconcerted by the governor's hands-off attitude, but they soon learned to appreciate their new independence. However, one consequence of Brown's removal from their affairs was that programs that he favored, such as professional negotiations for teachers, multicounty banking, and a flat rate income tax, did not have legislative support and did not pass. Brown also failed to get public approval for a constitutional amendment that would permit a governor to hold successive terms. In this instance, his unwillingness to remove himself from the amendment's applicability was a significant factor.

Like his father, Brown was a political maverick, but unlike him, he did not seem spontaneously comfortable with lifelong Democrats. The years spent with Kentucky Fried Chicken, Inc., Lums, and Ollie's Trollies were years spent away from the commonwealth and far removed from Democratic party politics. The governor rarely supported or opposed local or statewide candidates, or played an active role in Kentucky political affairs. He did get involved in the primary campaign for his successor in 1983, but too late to accomplish the result he wanted. John Y. Brown, Jr., preferred the national scene. As he had done five times in the 1970s, he headed a national Democratic telethon during his last spring in office, but this time with disappointing results.

In only one way did Brown behave like a typical politician: He seemed to enjoy showing off his family and sharing his wife and children with the public. He even included Mrs. Brown in the spot reserved for the governor's picture on official state maps. For her part, she continued her career as a television sports commentator and at the same time made her own contributions to the Kentucky scene. She organized a thorough rehabilitation and refurbishing of the governor's mansion and enthusiastically publicized Kentucky crafts. Soon after Brown's term began, she bore him a son who was named Lincoln Tyler George, and at the end of his term, a daughter named Pamela Ashley. Phyllis George Brown's high visibility was unique among the wives of Kentucky governors, and she liked it as much as her husband did.

The governor's propensities for a jet-set life-style, late-night working sessions, intense telephone calls, and a few but hard-fought tennis games carried their own hazards. In the spring of 1982 he was hospitalized briefly for hypertension, and in the summer of 1983 he underwent a quadruple-bypass heart operation. During the immediate postoperative period he suffered a rare pulmonary disease that left him seriously ill for weeks. Brown emerged from his brush with death with his usual optimistic determination and—at least for a time—a new humility. He gave up smoking and took up jogging, but his term ended before the long-term consequences of his illness could be reflected in his administration.

A short-term evaluation of his governorship suggests that John Y. Brown, Jr., accomplished what he promised. He ran the state like a business, and he made Kentucky and its products more visible in the marketplace. The old politics and the old politicians found no haven in his administration. There were no scandals. Neither he nor any of his people was accused of corruption. He was a sound steward of the commonwealth's resources, but he was not a leader who proposed new programs in areas such as education or human services.

On March 15, 1984, hours before the filing deadline, Brown entered the Democratic primary for the United States Senate seat held by Walter "Dee" Huddleston. He withdrew from the race on April 27, saying "I'm simply not up to my best" because of his health problems of the past year. The future probably will bring further chapters to Brown's political career. It would not be businesslike to waste the experience that he had gained, or forego the pleasure that he had found in governing.

SUGGESTED READINGS: Brown's public papers are in the state archives. Professor Tachau is editing the volume of his papers for the *Public Papers of the Governors* series. In the absence of extensive studies of Governor Brown and his administration, the state's newspapers are the best source of information.

MARY K. BONSTEEL TACHAU

# MARTHA LAYNE COLLINS

Martha Layne Collins was born Martha Layne Hall on December 7, 1936, in the small Shelby County community of Bagdad, the only child of Everett and Mary Taylor Hall. Her father had been a school-teacher when he met Mary Taylor, one of ten children born to a Spencer County tenant farmer and his wife.

Everett Hall later went into the funeral home business and dabbled in local county politics; his daughter was drawn to Baptist Church activities, school work, and beauty contests. When she was in the sixth grade, the family moved to Shelbyville where they started the Hall-Taylor Funeral Home. Mary Hall, a strong force in her daughter's life, encouraged Martha in extracurricular events as well as in studies. Martha was selected as the Shelby County Tobacco Festival Queen in high school and became the Kentucky Derby Festival Queen in 1959. For a brief time she considered a modeling career.

After one year at Lindenwood College, a school for women near St. Louis, Missouri, Martha Hall enrolled at the University of Kentucky. She was elected president of her dormitory council at Keeneland Hall and was an active member of the Chi Omega social sorority. She graduated in 1959 with a degree in home economics.

Two years earlier at a Baptist summer camp in Shelby County she had met William Collins of Versailles, a student at Georgetown College. She and Collins were married shortly after she graduated from the University of Kentucky; she then taught at Fairdale and Seneca high schools while he worked toward his degree at the University of Louisville dental school. During this time the couple had their two children, Stephen and Maria Ann (known as Marla). In the mid-1960s the Collins family moved to Versailles where William started his dentistry practice and Martha taught at Woodford County Junior High School.

In Woodford County Martha Collins became interested in politics. She was recruited into a reform-minded local Democratic group headed by Anthony Wilhoit, later a Kentucky Court of Appeals judge, former state senator Tom Ward, and Vic Hellard, Jr., later a state representative and director of the Legislative Research Commission. Former governor Albert B. Chandler was titular head of the Democratic party in Woodford County at the time, although his local followers were challenged by the new group. Chandler ran in the 1967 Democratic gubernatorial primary and lost to state Highway Commissioner Henry Ward. In the general election, Chandler bucked the Democratic party and supported Republican candidate Louie B. Nunn, who was elected. The group that included Martha Collins maintained its loyalty to the Democratic party and worked diligently for Ward's candidacy.

Martha Collins's forte in politics from the beginning was hard work and the ability to organize on the precinct level. When J.R. Miller of Owensboro was putting together Lt. Gov. Wendell Ford's campaign for governor, he learned of Martha Collins's work in Woodford County. "She was kind of a typical Ford supporter, something of an outsider," recalled Lexington attorney Edward Prichard, who worked for former governor Bert T. Combs in the 1971 Democratic gubernatorial primary against Ford. "She grew up in an atmosphere of small-town politics and I think she just got caught up in it in Woodford County. She worked very hard and did a lot of detail work." Miller and Walter "Dee" Huddleston, Ford's campaign chairman in 1971, recruited Martha Collins and picked her to be the women's chairman for the Sixth Congressional District.

After Ford was elected governor, Martha Collins was chosen to be Kentucky's Democratic national committeewoman. She quit her teaching career, became a full-time worker at state Democratic party headquarters under Miller, worked in Huddleston's successful 1972 race for the United States Senate, and was a key person in building a stronger grassroots Democratic organization in Kentucky.

In 1975, after helping numerous candidates win elections, Martha Collins decided to run for the state office of clerk of the Court of Appeals, then the highest court in Kentucky. (The position has since become appointive). She had close ties to the Democratic party faction headed by Ford, who was elected to the United States Senate in 1974. Democratic Gov. Julian Carroll's faction supported L.E. (Gene) Cline of Olive Hill for the clerk's position. However, three other non-aligned Democrats entered the clerk's race, including Kelly Thompson, Jr., of Bowling Green, son of the well-known former president of Western Kentucky University.

Collins won the primary election, receiving 66,730 votes. Thompson was second with 48,624 votes, and Cline was third with 45,456 votes. In the general election, Martha Collins easily defeated Republican Joseph E. Lambert of Mt. Vernon by 382,528 to 233,442 votes. The major activity in the clerk's office during Martha Collins's term was the implementation of a newly voted constitutional change that restructured the Kentucky court system.

In 1979 Martha Collins entered the Democratic party primary for lieutenant governor along with five other major candidates. Although she raised only one-fifth as much campaign money as her main challenger, William M. Cox of Madisonville, she was again helped by the size of the candidate field. Cox, the best-organized candidate in the race and a former aide of Julian Carroll, was hurt in the final days when Jim Vernon, another candidate from Frankfort, alleged that Cox was the subject of a federal investigation.

Martha Collins and her all-volunteer campaign produced a paper-thin victory in the scramble. She received 109,031 votes (23 percent). Cox got 105,693, Todd Hollenbach of Louisville 96,019, and state Sen. Joe Prather of Vine Grove 91,583. Others in the race were Richard H. Lewis of Benton, who received 42,533 votes, and Vernon, who received 19,122. In the 1979 general election, Collins defeated Republican Harold Rogers of Somerset by a margin of 543,176 to 316,798 votes.

As lieutenant governor, Collins avoided taking a substantive role in Gov. John Y. Brown, Jr.'s, Democratic administration, which kept an arm's length away from the traditional party machinery that she knew. Instead she quietly traveled the state, making speeches and presiding at ribbon-cutting ceremonies that the governor did not relish. Four years later in her campaign for governor she frequently told of how she had visited all 120 counties in Kentucky, several of them many times.

On two occasions, however, as president of the state Senate Collins took controversial stands on legislation. In 1980 she voted against a professional negotiations bill for teachers, and in 1982 she voted against a bill that would allow multibank holding companies to buy banks across county lines. The Senate's 19-19 tie votes would automatically have defeated each of these measures, so Collins's votes did not affect the outcome, but she chose nevertheless to record them.

Collins's campaign for governor officially began a year and a half before the Democratic primary election in May 1983. What she had lacked in campaign funds when running for lieutenant governor was remedied four years later. A fund-raising team headed by her husband raised about $2.8 million for her primary race and a total of nearly $5 million for the primary and general election contests. With a smoothly run campaign and the backing of many Democratic regulars she again won a narrow primary victory in a three-candidate field. She defeated Louisville Mayor Harvey Sloane by 223,692 votes (33.97 percent) to 219,160 votes (33.28 percent). A third candidate, former Human Resources Secretary Grady Stumbo, helped by Governor Brown, finished strongly with 199,795 votes (30.34 percent).

The split party united behind Martha Layne Collins in the general election and helped her become the first woman governor in Kentucky's history. She also made history by receiving more votes, 561,674, than any previous gubernatorial candidate. Her margin was 107,024 votes over Republican state Sen. Jim Bunning of Fort Thomas, the former major league baseball pitching star, who received 454,650.

Collins emphasized in her campaign that she did not intend to raise taxes despite the revenue shortage facing the state, which lingered behind the rest of the nation in recovering from the deep 1982-1983 recession. As she prepared to face the 1984 legislature, she reiterated her no-tax pledge. A private committee, formed with her blessing, recommended before the General Assembly convened that major educational initiatives be postponed until a special legislative session in 1985.

In her state of the commonwealth speech to the 1984 General Assembly the new governor maintained her firm campaign stand that no new taxes were needed and that any education reforms would have to come from programs that did not cost "vast sums of money." But as the hue and cry for school improvements reached a crescendo and state revenue forecasts continued to be pessimistic, Governor Collins changed course and asked for tax increases to produce $324 million in additional funds. Most of the new revenue was earmarked for an array of educational advancements in the state's elementary and secondary schools. Debate over which taxes would be increased delayed action on the governor's omnibus education/taxation bill, and it soon became apparent that she did not have the votes in the House of Representatives to approve her legislative proposals. All but a handful of the one hundred house members faced reelection in 1984 and were reluctant to consider any tax increases.

The governor conceded defeat two weeks before the end of the session and withdrew her tax package to settle for a "bare-bones" continuation budget. She blamed the legislature for not having the political courage to raise taxes and improve the state's low-ranked educational system. Many legislators argued that the new governor failed to provide the necessary leadership to increase taxes.

In a session noted for its lack of action the General Assembly satisfied the public's demand for a stiff drunk driving law. It also approved a controversial multibank holding company measure that allowed Kentucky banking companies to purchase other banks in the state. The measure passed without the signature of the governor, who had opposed it as lieutenant governor in the 1982 legislature. At the same time, the General Assembly ignored efforts to reform the state's archaic constitution. Some of the fund transfers used to balance the 1984-86 general fund budget were challenged in court by Attorney General David Armstrong on constitutional grounds. Gov. Collins attracted national attention during the summer of 1984 when she chaired the Democratic National Convention and was one of the potential vice-presidential candidates interviewed by Walter F. Mondale.

SUGGESTED READINGS: The best sources of information now available on Governor Collins are the state newspapers.

ED RYAN

# Contributors

Note: The institution granting the contributor's highest degree is named in parentheses following the contributor's name.

Thomas H. Appleton, Jr. (Kentucky) is managing editor of the Kentucky Historical Society. Contributed: Augustus Everett Willson; Augustus Owsley Stanley.

Nancy Disher Baird (Western Kentucky) is associate professor of library special collections at Western Kentucky University. Her books include *David Wendel Yandell: Physician of Old Louisville* (1978); *Luke Blackburn: Physician, Governor, Reformer* (1979); *Tradition and Progress: A History of Hummel Industries, Incorporated* (1981); *Bowling Green, A Pictorial History* (1983), coauthor. Contributed: Luke Pryor Blackburn.

Paul W. Beasley (Kentucky) is vice-president for academic affairs and dean of Winthrop College, North Carolina. His dissertation was written on "The Life and Times of Isaac Shelby, 1750-1826." Contributed: Isaac Shelby.

Nicholas C. Burckel (Wisconsin) is associate director of the Library/Learning Center, University of Wisconsin-Parkside. He edited *Racine: Growth and Change in a Wisconsin County* (1977) and coedited *Immigration and Ethnicity* (1977), *Progressive Reform* (1980), *Kenosha Retrospective* (1981), and *Wisconsin Yesterday and Today* (1984). Contributed: James B. McCreary; J.C.W. Beckham.

Charles J. Bussey (Kentucky) is associate professor of history at Western Kentucky University. He is coeditor and contributor to *America's Heritage in the Twentieth Century* (1978) and a contributor to John Carroll, ed., *European Traditions in the Twentieth Century* (1979) and James Klotter and Peter J. Sehlinger, eds., *Kentucky Profiles: Biographical Essays in Honor of Holman Hamilton* (1982). Contributed: John Adair; Joseph Desha.

Thomas D. Clark (Duke) is professor emeritus at the University of Kentucky. Among his numerous works are *A History of Kentucky* (1937, 1960), *The Kentucky* (1942), *Frontier America* (1959), *The Emerging South* (1961), and *Agrarian Kentucky* (1977). Contributed: "The Kentucky Governorship: An Overview."

Helen Bartter Crocker (Western Kentucky) is associate professor of history at Western Kentucky University. She is the author of *The*

*Green River of Kentucky* (1976). Contributed: Charles Anderson Wickliffe.

William E. Ellis (Kentucky) is professor of history at Eastern Kentucky University. His articles have appeared in a number of journals. Contributed: William Jason Fields; Ruby Laffoon.

H. E. Everman (Louisiana State) is professor of social sciences at Eastern Kentucky University. His books include *The History of Bourbon County, 1785-1865* (1977), *A Survey of Man, Culture, Society* (1980), and *Governor James Garrard* (1981). Contributed: James Garrard.

Kenneth E. Harrell (Louisiana State) is professor of history and dean of the College of Humanistic Studies, Murray State University. He edited *The Public Papers of Governor Edward T. Breathitt* (1983). Contributed: Edward Thompson Breathitt, Jr.

Lowell H. Harrison (New York) is professor of history at Western Kentucky University. His books include *John Breckinridge, Jeffersonian Republican* (1969); *The Civil War in Kentucky* (1975); *George Rogers Clark and the War in the West* (1976); and *The Antislavery Movement in Kentucky* (1978). Contributed: Beriah Magoffin; George W. Johnson; Richard Hawes; Simon Bolivar Buckner.

Melba Porter Hay (Kentucky) is associate editor of *The Papers of Henry Clay* at the University of Kentucky. Contributed: James Dixon Black; Edwin Perch Morrow.

Frank H. Heck (Minnesota) was professor emeritus of history at Centre College of Kentucky when he died in March 1983 soon after completing his manuscript. Among his works were *The Civil War Veteran in Minnesota Life and Politics* (1941); *Proud Kentuckian: John C. Breckinridge, 1821-1875* (1976); and *A Century and a Half on Main Street: Trinity Episcopal Church, 1829-1979* (1979). Contributed: Robert Perkins Letcher.

James F. Hopkins (Duke) is professor emeritus of history, University of Kentucky. He is the author of *A History of the Hemp Industry in Kentucky* (1951) and *The University of Kentucky: Origins and Early Years* (1951). He was coeditor of the first six volumes of *The Papers of Henry Clay* (1959-1981). Contributed: Christopher Greenup; George Madison; Gabriel Slaughter.

Victor B. Howard (Ohio State) is professor of history at Morehead State University. He is the author of *Black Liberation in Kentucky: Emancipation and Freedom, 1862-1884* (1983). Contributed: James Clark; John Jordan Crittenden.

Robert M. Ireland (Nebraska) is professor of history, University of

Kentucky. He has written *The County Courts in Antebellum Kentucky* (1972), *The County in Kentucky History* (1976), and *Little Kingdoms: The Counties of Kentucky, 1850-1891* (1977). Contributed: J. Proctor Knott; John Young Brown.

Landis Jones (Emory) is professor of political science and director of liberal studies, University of Louisville. He edited *The Public Papers of Governor Wendell H. Ford, 1971-1974* (1978). Contributed: Wendell Hampton Ford.

John E. Kleber (Kentucky) is professor of history and director of the academic honors program at Morehead State University. He edited *The Public Papers of Governor Lawrence W. Wetherby* (1983). Contributed: Lawrence W. Wetherby.

James C. Klotter (Kentucky) is general editor of the Kentucky Historical Society. He is the author of *William Goebel: The Politics of Wrath* (1977), coauthor with Hambleton Tapp of *Kentucky: Decades of Discard, 1865-1900* (1977), coeditor with Tapp of *The Union, the Civil War and John W. Tuttle* (1980), and coeditor of and contributor to *Kentucky Profiles: Biographical Essays in Honor of Holman Hamilton* (1982). Contributed: William O'Connell Bradley; William Sylvester Taylor; William Goebel; Simeon Willis.

Frank F. Mathias (Kentucky) is professor of history at the University of Dayton. He is the author of *Albert D. Kirwan* (1975) and *GI Jive: An Army Bandsman in World War II* (1983) and the editor of *Incidents and Experiences in the Life of Thomas W. Parsons* (1975). Contributed: Thomas Metcalfe; John Breathitt; James Turner Morehead.

Frederic D. Ogden (Johns Hopkins) is professor emeritus of political science at Eastern Kentucky University. His books include *The Poll Tax in the South* (1958) and *The Public Papers of Governor Keen Johnson* (1982), editor. Contributed: Keen Johnson.

Thomas L. Owen (Kentucky) is associate archivist of the University of Louisville Archives and Research Center. He teaches courses in local history and writes for Louisville area newspapers and magazines. Contributed: John Larue Helm; John White Stevenson.

James A. Ramage (Kentucky) is professor of history at Northern Kentucky University. He is the author of *John Wesley Hunt: Pioneer Merchant, Manufacturer and Financier* (1974); "Holman Hamilton: A Biographical Sketch" and "Civil War Romance: The Influence of Wartime Marriage on the Life and Career of John Hunt Morgan," in James C. Klotter and Peter J. Sehlinger, eds., *Kentucky Profiles: Bio-*

*graphical Essays in Honor of Holman Hamilton* (1982). Contributed: Lazarus Whitehead Powell; Charles Slaughter Morehead.

George W. Robinson (Wisconsin) is professor of history at Eastern Kentucky University. In addition to editing *The Public Papers of Governor Bert T. Combs* (1979), he is director of the Bert T. Combs Oral History Project. Contributed: Bert T. Combs.

Charles P. Roland (Louisiana State) is professor of history at the University of Kentucky. His works include *The Confederacy* (1960), *Albert Sidney Johnston, Soldier of Three Republics* (1964), and *The Improbable Era: The South since World War II* (1975). Contributed: Albert Benjamin Chandler.

Ed Ryan (Kentucky Wesleyan) reported on Kentucky politics from the Frankfort office of the Louisville *Courier-Journal* before his death in 1984. Contributed: Martha Layne Collins.

Robert F. Sexton (Washington) is executive director of the Prichard Committee for Academic Excellence at Lexington. He edited *The Public Papers of Governor Louie B. Nunn* (1975) and is general editor of *The Public Papers of the Governors of Kentucky*. Contributed: Flem D. Sampson; Louie B. Nunn.

John David Smith (Kentucky) is assistant professor of history at North Carolina State University at Raleigh. He coedited (with William Cooper, Jr.) *Window on the War: Frances Dallam Peter's Lexington Civil War Diary* (1976), compiled *Black Slavery in the Americas: An Interdisciplinary Bibliography, 1865-1980* (1982), 2 vols., and wrote *An Old Creed for the New South: Proslavery Ideology and Historiography, 1865–1918* (1985). Contributed: James F. Robinson.

Stuart Seely Sprague (New York) is professor of history at Morehead State University. He is author of *Kentuckians in Missouri* (1983); *Introducing Genealogy: A Workbook Approach* (1983); editor of *Essays in Eastern Kentucky History* (1983); and coauthor of *Frankfort: A Pictorial History* (1980). Contributed: William Owsley; Julian Morton Carroll.

Thomas H. Syvertsen (Kentucky) is lecturer in history at Indiana University Southeast and the University of Louisville. His dissertation was "Earle Chester Clements and the Democratic Party, 1920-1950." Contributed: Earle Chester Clements.

Mary K. Bonsteel Tachau (Kentucky) is professor of history at the University of Louisville. The author of *Federal Courts in the Early Republic: Kentucky 1789-1816* (1978), she is editing *The Public Papers of Governor John Y. Brown*. Contributed: John Y. Brown, Jr.

Harry M. Ward (Columbia) is professor of history at the University of Richmond. His books include *Department of War, 1781-1795* (1962); *"Unite or Die:" Intercolony Relations, 1690-1763* (1971); *Richmond During the Revolution* (1977), coauthor; and *Duty, Honor, or Country: General George Weedon and the American Revolution* (1979). Contributed: Charles Scott.

Ross A. Webb (Pittsburgh) is professor of history at Winthrop College. His books include *Benjamin Helm Bristow, Border State Politician* (1969) and *Kentucky in the Reconstruction Era* (1979). Conbributed: Thomas Elliot Bramlette; Preston Hopkins Leslie.

# Index